A COMMENTARY ON *LAUDATO SI'*

A COMMENTARY

ON

Laudato Si'

*Examining the Background,
Contributions, Implementation,
and Future of Pope Francis's
Encyclical*

KEVIN W. IRWIN

Paulist Press
New York / Mahwah, NJ

Cover image © by RoyStudio/depositphotos.com
Cover design by Tamian Wood
Book design by Lynn Else

Library of Congress Control Number: 2016949694

ISBN 978-0-8091-5319-0 (paperback)
ISBN 978-1-58768-661-0 (e-book)

Published by Paulist Press
997 Macarthur Boulevard
Mahwah, New Jersey 07430

www.paulistpress.com

Printed and bound in the
United States of America

Contents

Preface

It all began at lunch at a restaurant in downtown Washington, DC, in 1991. My friend Patricia Bauman and I were talking about issues of ecology and the environment. Her comment about the existing literature on ecology and Catholicism was, in her judgment, "broad but not deep." She asked me if I wanted to think about pursuing this as part of my research. And so it began.

It involved dialogue with and learning from colleagues from the theological community. Then came an invitation-only conference at Georgetown University in 1993, sponsored by her family foundation, and the publication of *Preserving the Creation*, with articles from the conference papers by Richard Clifford, Gabriel Daly, Daniel Cowdin, and me.

It also included participation in conferences on environmental justice sponsored by the USCCB in the late 1990s and subsequent international conferences in Leuven and Rome. Among those dialogue partners were Patrick Allitt, Deborah Blake, Anne Clifford, Drew Christiansen, SJ, Carol Stockhausen, Carol Dempsey, OP, Hugh Feiss, OSB, Dan Finn, Walt Grazer, Dennis Hamm, SJ, Zachary Hayes, OFM, John Haught, Kenneth Himes, OFM, Christene Frier-Hinze, John McCarthy, Donna Orsuto, and David Toolan, SJ.

More recent consultations sponsored by the USCCB and my academic home, The Catholic University of America, included dialogue with Mary Ashley, Michael Baur, John T. Brinkman, David Cloutier, Anselma Dolcich-Ashley, Elizabeth Groppe, Scott G. Hefelfinger, Donald Kettler, Christiana Z. Peppard, Jame Schaefer, Bernard Unabali, Jeremiah Vallery, Keith Douglass Warner, Matthew Philipp Whelan, and Tobias Winright.

My single involvement with a Muslim-Catholic dialogue on the environment was the 1996 conference held in Rome, cosponsored by the Pontifical Council for Interreligious Dialogue and the Royal Academy for Islamic Civilization Research. Among the invited participants was Sister Marjorie Keenan of the Pontifical Council for Justice and Peace, whose guidance over these years has been invaluable. My single involvement ecumenically was as part of the U.S. Roman Catholic-United Methodist dialogue for three years on the Eucharist and Ecology, whose membership included Drew Christiansen, SJ, Angela Christman, Edgardo Colon-Emeric, Connie Lasher, James Massa, Edward Phillips, Kendal Soulen, Karen Westerfield Tucker, and Sondra Wheeler.

One of my major interests and hopefully lasting contributions to this field is reviving, rearticulating, and emphasizing that *sacramentality* is the underlying substratum always at work in the celebration of liturgy and the sacraments. Liturgy is ecology in practice, and ecology is celebrated in and through the liturgy. This has led to reflection on distinguishing things from nature that are raised up and used in sacraments—light, darkness, earth, fire, water—from things which are the result of human ingenuity and work, oil, bread, and wine. Among other things, natural symbols require that we revere the earth and its resources and do not presume to overuse or abuse them in any way. Manufactured symbols mean valuing, relying on, and revering human imagination, artistry, and human work. Issues of a just wage and humane living conditions are interconnected with the use of "the work of human hands" and the sweat of the human brow.

The fact that we use creation in worship raises issues that can no longer be taken for granted, such as access to clean water and the fruit of the earth for all who dwell on this good earth to harvest and to eat. The use of baked bread and fermented wine at the Eucharist makes us aware of those who do not have enough bread to eat and drink to preserve life.

In my book *Models of the Eucharist,* I argued that the Eucharist was integral to and integrative of the Christian life. The first chapter of that book is titled "Cosmic Mass," which argues that the principle of sacramentality grounds the liturgy and theology of the Eucharist. Little did I know that I would be "on the same page" as Pope Francis, who argues for *an integral ecology* in *On Care for Our*

Preface

Common Home and specifies that the Eucharist "joins heaven and earth" and is an act of "cosmic love" (n. 286).

I owe James Starke, my research assistant at CUA, an enormous debt of gratitude for his ever efficient and meticulous assistance in the writing of this book.

I want to thank Patricia Bauman and her husband, John Landrum Bryant, for their insight, initial challenge, and ongoing support for this research, which hopefully will become a modest contribution to the craft of contemporary Catholic Theology.

Ash Wednesday of 2016

Introduction:
Why This Book Now?

Pope Francis is a man on a mission. Like the Jesus of the Gospels, this first Jesuit pope is nothing less than a *living parable*. He talks the talk, but he also walks the walk. He does both in *On Care for Our Common Home*.

Through this encyclical he invites us to listen to his words on a number of interrelated topics focused on a decidedly Catholic theology of creation and of the environment. Through this encyclical he invites us to see parts of the world through a lens that is decidedly Catholic, that is, global and universal. This pope is particularly attentive to those on the margins, on the periphery. In Francis's papacy, what seemed like the center is now the periphery and what seemed like the neglected periphery is now center stage.

One clear example of where this pope's heart lies is in the way he has arranged his trips outside of the Vatican and the speeches he gives while traveling. Pope Francis certainly hit a homerun when he came to these United States in the fall of 2015, but his first trip outside mainland Italy was to the island of Lampedusa (July of 2013) to preach and welcome immigrants to the shores of Italy who were suffering economic hardship and trying to escape civil wars not of their making. He then went to Brazil (2013), Israel, South Korea, Albania, Turkey (2014), Sri Lanka, the Philippines, Bosnia-Herzegovina, Bolivia, Ecuador, Paraguay, Cuba, and then the United States. After visiting Mexico in February of 2016, he has plane reservations for eleven international trips through 2018 and fourteen other trips he has agreed to but are still unscheduled. None so far is a return trip to the United States.

The periphery has become the center and the center has become the periphery.

Not only do these destinations matter, but the timing matters as well. He deliberately went to the Philippines in January of 2015 to console the victims of the typhoon Yolanda and to visit places destroyed by it. That visit "set up" the publication of *On Care for Our Common Home.* The publication in mid-June of 2015 showed a man on a mission to influence the Paris talks on climate change the following November.

Like his predecessors in the papacy (some who like himself have traveled the world stage and others who did not), Pope Francis teaches by preaching and through the writing of encyclicals. From the beginning of his papacy, it was clear that the pope wanted to address what he judges to be a worldwide crisis about the environment. It was equally clear, however, that he wanted to address this issue in the context of a document that lays out a very Catholic theology of creation, Catholic practices about education and formation, lifestyle issues, especially as ecology impacts on the poor, and many traditions that comprise Catholic spirituality.

As we have come to expect in *On Care for Our Common Home,* the pope does not hesitate to challenge as well as to comfort, to critique as well as to inform. This book is meant to be a complement to the encyclical and to indicate its timeliness and the way it reflects Pope Francis's vision for the world and how he understands his teaching role in a truly global church in a multicultural world. The goal of this commentary is to place *On Care for Our Common Home* in the context of previous church teachings and to set the stage for further developments in thought and action to confront the ecological crisis today for the world of tomorrow.

This book is divided into four unequal chapters:

Chapter 1, "Background," offers a review and summary of several sets of documents published before *On Care for Our Common Home* on issues related to ecology and the environment, addressed in five major sections: (1) The first is background on the official

Roman Catholic magisterium. (2) The second is the contribution of the Second Vatican Council. (3) The third concerns papal teachings from John XXIII to Francis. (4) The fourth considers Episcopal Conference teachings, with special attention to the CELAM document from Aparecida (2007), whose drafting committee was headed by Archbishop Bergoglio (who later became Pope Francis). It also includes documents published by the (American) USCCB and regional documents from American bishops. (5) The fifth summarizes key insights and practices from ecumenical perspectives, with emphasis on Patriarch Bartholomew and the Orthodox church, as well as a (national) bilateral dialogue statement on the Eucharist and ecology.

Chapter 2, "Contributions," offers a summary of what Pope Francis adds to our understanding of the environment from the perspective of Catholic (magisterial) teaching, theology, spirituality, liturgy, and practice. The term "contributions" is designed to be inclusive of the way the pope integrates now familiar themes from the prior magisterium in a new context, with added emphasis or explanation (for example, "dominion" and "stewardship," among many others) and new ideas he himself sets forth. That this is a *theological* commentary should be borne in mind in order to respect others who will comment on the other fields that the pope judges are to be included in the encyclical. Among them are science, economics, politics, and business ethics.

Chapter 3, "Implementation," delineates and expands on a number of issues that Pope Francis raises for reflection and action. Fidelity to the "see, judge, act [and celebrate]" methodology is the requirement that what we now "see" in a new light through papal teaching requires that we make judgments based on that teaching, which together lead to new or changing patterns of "action" and "celebration" communally, collegially, and personally. Some issues are joined together because the pope himself argues repeatedly about "interconnectedness," and in my opinion, these seem to be both interconnected and intertwined. Others topics (for example, liturgical practice) are intrinsically linked together by the pope and in this chapter. It is foreseen that these others will lead to additions being made to this chapter since the implementation of the encyclical will be ongoing.

Chapter 4, "Beyond," asks the questions "Where do we go from here?" and "How do we move forward?" While these are perennial questions asked after the publication of a church document (from conciliar texts to a pope's daily homily), this is particularly true for an encyclical of this size, scope, breadth, and challenge. The ideas raised here are meant to be discussion starters for conversations about the nature and scope of papal authority and papal teachings today, and more specifically where we might go and how we might move forward in light of *On Care for Our Common Home*. They involve "talking the talk" and "walking the walk" in the footsteps of Pope Francis, a man on a mission.

CHAPTER ONE

Background

This chapter offers a review and summary of several sets of documents published before *On Care for Our Common Home* on issues related to ecology and the environment, addressed in five major sections:[1] (1) The first is background on the official Roman Catholic magisterium. (2) The second is the contribution of the Second Vatican Council. (3) The third concerns papal teachings from John XXIII to Francis. (4) The fourth considers Episcopal Conference teachings, with special attention to the CELAM (Latin American Bishops' Conference) document from Aparecida (2007), whose drafting committee was headed by Archbishop Bergoglio (who later became Pope Francis). It also includes documents published by the (American) USCCB and regional documents from American bishops. (5) The fifth summarizes key insights and practices from ecumenical perspectives, with emphasis on Patriarch Bartholomew and the Orthodox church, as well as a (national) bilateral dialogue statement on the Eucharist and ecology.[2]

I. ROMAN CATHOLIC MAGISTERIUM

By way of introduction, it is important to recall the distinctions that can and should be made to distinguish the kinds of documents issued from the Catholic magisterium.

CHURCH COUNCILS

It is commonly held that among the documents from the Holy See as published in the Vatican's official organ, *Acta Apostolicae*

Sedis (published in Latin starting in 1909), the highest authoritative rank is ascribed to the "acts of the Second Vatican Council." This accords with the church's traditional understanding that ecumenical councils are the highest authoritative sources that express orthodox belief.

Here, a distinction needs to be made about the "hierarchy" of the "acts" of Vatican II because the Council fathers issued three kinds of documents: constitutions, decrees, and declarations. This is to say that here in chapter 1, I will cite *Gaudium et Spes,* the Pastoral Constitution on the Church in the Modern World, which is one of the four constitutions from Vatican II. (The others are *Sacrosanctum Concilium,* the Constitution on the Sacred Liturgy; *Lumen Gentium,* the Constitution on the Church; and *Dei Verbum,* the Constitution on Divine Revelation.) In terms of "rank," a constitution is the highest, then follow decrees, and finally declarations.

At the same time, just because a conciliar decree or declaration is not a constitution does not mean that it does not carry significant weight. For example, *Nostra Aetate,* the "Declaration of the Relationship of the Church to Non-Christian Religions" (promulgated in 1965), has come to be among the most important of the council's texts for the ongoing commitment to the Roman Catholic Church's relations with Jews and Muslims, largely under the influence of postconciliar papal leadership (for example, Pope John Paul II). This is to say that sometimes the intrinsic merit of a teaching shines through and is compelling based on the teaching itself. For example, while not the teaching of a council, Pope Paul VI's encyclical *Evangelii Nuntiandi* is said to be Pope Francis's "favorite church document."[3]

One possible immediate consequence for appreciating *On Care for Our Common Home* is that its quick and broad ecumenical reception and appreciation,[4] as well as the appreciation of many in the scientific community,[5] may mean that the topic is seen to be timely, and that preserving the environment is a moral and spiritual imperative.

PAPAL DOCUMENTS

The same *Acta Apostolicae Sedis* publishes papal documents and pronouncements. After it cites texts from an ecumenical council as having the highest authority, it then includes such documents as "decretals," "encyclical letters," "apostolic exhortations," addresses to consistories, apostolic constitutions, *motu proprio(s)*, and other papal pronouncements.[6] These latter include postsynodal exhortations, annual "Messages" for the World Day for Peace (January 1), to the Diplomatic Corps, to the Roman Rota, and so on. There are also occasional messages to Vatican congregations (for example, on Catholic education) or, among others, to the Pontifical Academy of Sciences on the occasion of special meetings. Then there are messages to other organizations, for example, the United Nation's Food and Agriculture Organization. In addition, the pope gives an address when he accepts the credentials and welcomes new ambassadors to the Vatican from countries throughout the world, or when he addresses the leadership of countries, as when Pope Francis addressed the European Parliament (November 24, 2014), the U.S. Congress (September 24, 2015) and the United Nations (September 27, 2015). Papal teachings also come in the form of instruction or catechesis that the pope delivers each week at a general papal audience (on Wednesdays). For example, Pope John Paul II often gave a series of such teachings at papal audiences, such as his commentary on the Book of Genesis, which became the basis for his "theology of the body."

An encyclical is an authoritative teaching document from the pope. It is part of the ordinary magisterium and requires "religious assent" from the faithful to whom such a document is normally addressed. This is to say that a papal encyclical is written by and published on the authority of the pope, is part of what is called "the ordinary magisterium" and is to be welcomed, studied, and followed. While dissenting from an encyclical is possible, nonetheless one should not dissent (that is, disagree by choosing to think or act contrary to papal teaching) without a good and defensible reason. At the same time, it is important to acknowledge, for example, that surveys show that a majority of American Catholics do not agree with the prohibition on using artificial birth control asserted in Pope Paul VI's *Humanae Vitae*.[7] Nevertheless, noncompliance does not mean that a teaching is wrong. In addition, the study of the "reception" of church teaching, such as that of Vatican II, has ushered in a fruitful avenue of study and debate, a task well beyond this book. The presumption in what follows is that what the pope teaches in *On Care for Our Common Home* is true theologically and is the authentic teaching of the church (see further).

Less easy to characterize are the postsynodal apostolic exhortations published under the authority of the pope. These are documents issued with the pope's signature after a worldwide Synod of Bishops has been held at the Vatican to discuss a particular topic, for example, justice in the world, priestly formation, religious life, the Word of God in the Life and Mission of the Church, and the new evangelization. In 2013, Pope Francis issued *Evangelii Gaudium* ("The Joy of the Gospel"), subtitled "On the Proclamation of the Gospel in the Modern World." Where postsynodal documents "rank" in the hierarchy of Vatican documents has not been settled. While this document bears the name of the pope, its contents reflect weeks of meetings attended by bishops and advisors from the entire world. In the case of *Evangelii Gaudium*, the synod was held October 7–28, 2012. As is customary, the synod ended with the presentation of a "final list of propositions" from the participants for the pope's consideration as to whether they should be in the postsynodal exhortation. This is why some theologians would argue that a postsynodal exhortation is the result of a collegial process and therefore would "rank" somewhere below a statement from an ecumenical council and above an encyclical, the latter whose authorship is the pope's alone. In 1998, Pope John Paul II distinguished "collegiality" strictly speaking (for example, in debates and the drafting of the documents of Vatican II) from a "collegial spirit" (see below).[8] A postsynodal exhortation seems certainly to be the product of a "collegial spirit," even if it is not the result of "collegiality" strictly speaking. On the other hand, other theologians would argue that it is a document from the pope himself since he decides what is to be included and in effect does not necessarily accept in its entirety the "final list of propositions" offered to him by the synod fathers. In what follows, the contents of *Evangelii Gaudium* will be summarized as part of Pope Francis's teaching, appreciating that it comes from a synodal process, which is the process Pope Francis regards as very important in the church today (see further).

The key phrase for the following summary of previous magisterial teachings on ecology and the environment is *continuity and development*. Much of what Pope Francis says in *On Care for Our*

Common Home is not totally new. He cites his predecessors generously: Paul VI, John Paul II, and Benedict XVI. What he does do
is raise this teaching to the level of an encyclical and make it a
part of the church's magisterium of social justice teachings (*On
Care for our Common Home*, n. 15).[9] A rule of thumb when reading Vatican documents on a particular topic, for example, ecology
and environment, is to compare a document with what Vatican
documents before it and after it have said on the same subject,
hence the phrase "continuity and development." In *On Care for
Our Common Home*, Pope Francis repeatedly indicates his reliance
on the work of his immediate predecessors in the papacy. They
are "building blocks" in the crafting of a papal magisterium on
the environment. What I regard as "development" is contained in
chapters 2 and 3, summarizing Pope Francis's particular (primarily
theological) contributions in the encyclical.

EPISCOPAL CONFERENCE DOCUMENTS

In the Roman Catholic Church, an Episcopal Conference, Conference of Bishops, or National Conference of Bishops is an official assembly of all the Catholic bishops of a given country or
territory. Many episcopal conferences had long existed as informal entities before the Second Vatican Council. But at the Second Vatican Council, the bishops voted to establish permanent
episcopal conferences throughout the world by the Decree on the
Pastoral Office of Bishops (*Christus Dominus*) in 1965 (n. 38), subsequently implemented by Pope Paul VI's 1966 *motu proprio* titled
Ecclesiae Sanctae.[10] In the United States, for example, the National
Catholic Welfare Conference was established in 1919 (and located
in Washington, DC) to serve the Roman Catholic Church in the
United States. This was superseded by the establishment of the
United States Conference of Catholic Bishops (USCCB) in 1966.[11]

Episcopal conferences are generally defined by geographic bor-
ders, with all the bishops in a given country belonging to the same
conference, which might also include neighboring countries. This
is the case with CELAM (the episcopal conference for Latin and
South America), to which Pope Francis belonged as archbishop
of Buenos Aires (more on CELAM below, section 4, subsection 1).
Certain tasks and authority are assigned to episcopal conferences,

for example, with regard to some liturgical norms (understanding also that some liturgical norms are decided by the diocesan bishop). Episcopal conferences receive their authority under universal law or particular mandates. In certain circumstances, as defined by canon law, the decisions of an episcopal conference are subject to ratification from the Holy See. Individual bishops do not relinquish their authority to the conference, however, and remain responsible for the governance of their respective dioceses.

In 1998 (as cited above), through his *motu proprio Apostolos Suos*, John Paul II clarified that the declarations and statements of such conferences "constitute authentic magisterium" when approved unanimously by the conference. If such declarations and statements were not approved unanimously, however, then the conference would need to have recourse to the Holy See who would decide whether a decree approved by a two-thirds majority of the conference would receive a *recognitio* (that is, "recognition of approval"). This process of receiving a *recognitio* at present also governs how vernacular liturgical texts are now approved, namely, that the local members of a conference vote to approve them, after which the texts are sent to the Congregation for Divine Worship for its *recognitio*.[12] In an ambiguous phrase, the pope went on to assert that the *recognitio* of the Holy See would not be granted if the bishops' conference vote "is not substantial."[13] At this juncture the distinction (noted previously) that Pope John Paul II made between "collegiality" and a "collegial spirit" deserves a bit more exploration.

This issue goes at least as far back, for the current context of episcopal conferences, to the Vatican discussion around the question of whether or not episcopal conferences have teaching authority at all, an issue brought to light by the (U.S.) National Conference of Catholic Bishops' (now the USCCB) document "The Challenge of Peace" (1983), and later the document "Economic Justice for All" (1986).[14] Joined by several other national episcopal conferences, the (U.S.) NCCB engaged in an informal dialogue with the prefect for the Congregation for the Doctrine of Faith, Cardinal Joseph Ratzinger (later Pope Benedict XVI) on this issue. In this discussion, Ratzinger claimed that "a bishops' conference as such does not have a *mandatum docendi* [teaching mandate]."[15] The ensuing debates engaged this question under, among other aspects, the

concept of "collegiality" and whether or not the teaching authority of Episcopal Conferences could be rooted in an exercise of
collegiality. One heavily criticized response was given by the International Theological Commission, presided over at that time by
Cardinal Ratzinger, which stated that the application of "collegiality" to episcopal conferences was only by analogy, and improper.[16]
Shortly thereafter, the 1985 Extraordinary Synod took up the issue
and called for greater study into the theological and juridical
nature of episcopal conferences, which call led to a working draft
document from the Vatican that was made available for response
by Episcopal Conferences, theologians, and canonists. After heavy
criticisms of the working draft, a new draft was formulated and
later promulgated, *motu proprio*, by John Paul II as *Apostolos Suos*.
In *Apostolos Suos*, John Paul II distinguishes between exercises of
"collegiality" and exercises of "collegial spirit." He makes clear that
the work of Episcopal Conferences "never takes on the collegial
nature proper to the actions of the order of Bishops as such" and
so is never an act of episcopal collegiality in the strict and proper
sense.[17] Nevertheless, John Paul II indicates that the joint exercise
of pastoral functions within an episcopal conference is "a concrete
application of collegial spirit (*affectus collegialis*),"[18] although no
clear indication is given of what this term means theologically.
Nevertheless, while *Apostolos Suos* does not settle the question of
"collegial spirit," it does answer affirmatively to the Episcopal Conferences' ability to make doctrinal statements (that is, that Episcopal Conferences have teaching authority), although with very clear
conditions that must be met. The implication of these conditions
and their precise impact on the teaching authority of episcopal
conferences is still an ongoing question.[19]

The fact that Pope Francis quotes so generously in *On Care for
Our Common Home* from documents of episcopal conferences is
at least notable on the merits of the topics chosen and the assertions made. It is also most notable for the fact that such texts
from local bishops' conferences are cited in a papal document. In
effect, this is one way that this pope shows respect for his brother
bishops—all of whom are ordained to "the order of bishops."
In the encyclical, Pope Francis refers twenty-one times to documents of episcopal conferences that deal with the environment.
This is significant for (at least) two reasons. First, it is an exercise

in effective collegiality and effective synodality. This is to say that the pope relies on the insights of his brother bishops and raises up the wisdom that comes from all parts of the world.[20] Second, it is an exercise in how the church's teaching develops, specifically on the environment. As will be noted in the summary of these texts (below), documents from episcopal conferences about the environment stretch back to 1981 when the German bishops wrote a pastoral letter on creation and the future of humanity. The evolution of the thought contained in these documents is notable and has clearly influenced the thinking of Pope Francis.

RELATIVE AUTHORITATIVE WEIGHT

Some indication has already been made as to how these various documents relate to one another, for example, that the *Acta Apostolicae Sedes* indicates that texts from an ecumenical council have the highest authority, followed by papal documents. However, as can be observed from the above discussion, the status of episcopal conference documents is not entirely clear and is an area that needs more attention from specialists in such fields as ecclesiology and canon law. However, some relevant points of contact are laid out here to provide a general framework for understanding the place of episcopal conference documents as well as documents from individual bishops:[21]

- Documents of ecumenical councils are of the highest weight, followed by papal documents such as "decretals," "encyclical letters," "apostolic exhortations," and so on.
- Episcopal Conference documents will always be of lesser weight than documents of the universal magisterium (for example, ecumenical councils and certain papal documents) addressed to the universal community of the faithful.
- For any document, factors such as audience (specific group vs. universal audience) and reception are important in considering the weight of all document types, for example, documents addressed to a universal audience (such as Francis's encyclical) are generally given greater weight than documents addressed to a particular group (such as Francis's addresses to the FAO); more well received documents are

generally given greater weight than less well received documents (recall the examples of *Humanae Vitae* and *Nostra Aetate* above; recall that less reception does not mean that the teaching is false).

- "Collegial spirit," "consensus," and work/preparation are factors in considering the weight of, especially, Episcopal Conference documents (in addition to the factors of audience and reception): the greater these factors, the greater the potential weight of the document. This includes not only "collegial spirit," "consensus," and work/preparation *within* one Episcopal Conference, but would also apply when several Episcopal Conferences address the same issue or teaching.
- General principle observes that when "a higher authority" (for example, the pope) affirms a *teaching* already taught by "a lower authority" (for example, an episcopal body), additional weight is granted to the *teaching* (noting the identification of the specific *teaching*, which is not necessarily the *document* as a whole).
- Furthermore, general principle holds that more weight is granted to a *document* of "a lower authority" (for example, an episcopal body) cited in "a higher authority" (for example, the pope) insofar as the lower-authority document's arguments and contents support the *teaching* as interpreted and used by the higher authority, necessarily taking into account the intention of the higher authority in citing the lower-authority document.

From these points of contact, some general observations for Pope Francis's encyclical follow:[22]

- The points above suggest that a particular *teaching* in Pope Francis's encyclical (that is, "a higher authority") is given a greater significance when it relies on the same *teaching* as found in several Episcopal Conferences (that is, "lower authorities"). But, it should be clearly maintained that the pope's use of several Episcopal Conference documents is not an exercise of the "collegiality" of the College of Bishops, properly and strictly speaking. Nevertheless, this may suggest that the exercise of "collegial spirit" grows in strength toward "collegiality" to the degree that the "consensus" moves toward "unanimity" (of all bishops worldwide).

- Francis's encyclical (that is, "a higher authority")—because it contains a *teaching* taught by several Episcopal Conferences (that is, "lower authorities," for example, the Episcopal Conferences of CELAM, of the Philippines, of Japan, of the United States, and so on)—can be given more weight as a *document* insofar as the arguments and contents of the encyclical are necessary for and support the common *teaching*.

- An Episcopal Conference *document* (that is, "lower authority," for example, the CELAM *Aparecida Document*)—when it contains a *teaching* taught by several Episcopal Conferences (that is, "lower authorities," for example, the Episcopal Conferences of the Philippines, Japan, the United States, and so on) and subsequently taught in Pope Francis's encyclical (that is, the "higher authority")—can be given more weight insofar as the arguments and contents of the Episcopal Conference document (for example, *Aparecida*) are necessary for and support the common *teaching* as interpreted and used by Francis's encyclical.

II. VATICAN II ON THE ENVIRONMENT

For the sake of inclusion and because is ranks higher than the ordinary papal magisterium, the first text of note is from the 1965 Pastoral Constitution on the Church in the Modern World, *Gaudium et Spes*, from the Second Vatican Council.[23] As an entrée to the church's published teaching on the environment, this text is actually more notable for what it does not say, or for what it says cryptically, about creation and the environment generally or for what it says about resources specifically.[24] Where it notes these issues it speaks about them from anthropological and ethical perspectives, naming human beings as the center of creation (n. 12) responsible for respecting creation's autonomy and for insuring equitable distribution of its goods (nn. 36, 39). In spelling out principles for a just economy, the document identifies human beings as responsible for consolidating control over creation in order to insure an economic order that respects the dignity of all human persons (nn. 9, 33), which theme recurs when the text discusses the relationship between nature and culture (n. 33). In light of this teaching, we can say that human beings have a fundamental responsibility to insure the preservation of the earth and its resources.

III. RECENT PAPAL TEACHING ON THE ENVIRONMENT

INTRODUCTION: POPES AS PEOPLE

I think it appropriate to begin this section on the papal magisterium by quoting the Latin American proverb, "We drink from our own wells." Popes are individuals with personality differences, different ethnic backgrounds, and their own life experiences all of which (and more) they bring to the papacy. Popes drink from their own wells as they lead the church in their particular and unique ways. At the risk of enormous oversimplification, I think it important to note the following.

John XXIII had been a Vatican diplomat assigned to several places which left indelible impressions on him. Among his international postings were in Bulgaria, Greece, Turkey, and Paris. It is argued that his life and work in Paris put him in regular contact with scripture scholars and theologians whose influence on him bore fruit in the calling and in conducting the Second Vatican Council. His firsthand experience in countries with small Roman Catholic populations had an influence on him in terms of ecumenism and the need for inter religious dialogue.

Paul VI spent over thirty years in the Service of the Vatican's Secretariat of State, after which he was named archbishop of Milan. As a true Vatican diplomat, Paul had honed skills dealing with those countries with which the Vatican had diplomatic relations as well as experience with the worldwide church through diplomats and the international Catholic episcopacy. As the first modern pope to travel outside Italy, he exemplified his deep interest in ecclesiology and his respect for local (diocesan) churches as well as the variety (and complexity) of leading a universal church comprised of the union of local churches. His diplomatic skills helped him in continuing John's dream of completing Vatican II.

John Paul II was the philosopher pope, by training through teaching at university and writing and then in leading the church. He was the pope to oversee the consolidation of the teachings and practices of and from Vatican II in promulgating the revised *Code of Canon Law* in 1983, calling the Extraordinary Synod in 1985, promulgating the *Catechism of the Catholic Church* in 1992, and calling for and observing carefully the drafting of the *Compendium of the Social Doctrine of the Catholic Church* in 2005.[25]

Benedict XVI was the professor pope theologian. As a trained theologian, whose signature book, *Introduction to Christianity*, is still a best seller, he assisted John Paul II by serving as the cardinal prefect of the Congregation for the Doctrine of the Faith for twenty-two years before being elected pope. Among other things, he took steps to clarify what the Roman Catholic Church taught and teaches in ecumenical circles and in dealing with specific theologians whom Ratzinger judged had veered from authentic doctrine.

Francis is the first Latin American pope, the first Jesuit pope, and a decidedly pastoral pope, especially compared with his immediate predecessors. Yet prior to being named an auxiliary bishop in Argentina, Jorge Bergoglio had served in several roles as a Jesuit superior, including being a provincial. In the numerous biographies about him, it is stressed that he dealt each day with immediate pastoral issues such as irregular marriages, ecological devastation, unemployment, and so on.

If I were to suggest a triptych to illustrate the gifts of the three most recent popes, I would suggest that John Paul taught us *what* we believe, Benedict XVI taught us *why* we believe it, and Francis teaches us *how* to live what we believe.

1. JOHN XXIII

At the very beginning of *On Care for Our Common Home*, Pope Francis writes about Pope John XXIII's *Pacem in Terris*:

> More than fifty years ago, with the world teetering on the brink of nuclear crisis, Pope Saint John XXIII wrote an Encyclical which not only rejected war but offered a proposal for peace. He addressed his message *Pacem in Terris* to the entire "Catholic world" and indeed "to all men and women of good will." Now, faced as we are with global environmental deterioration, I wish to address every person living on this planet. In my Apostolic Exhortation *Evangelii Gaudium*, I wrote to all the members of the Church with the aim of encouraging ongoing missionary renewal. In this Encyclical, I would like to enter into dialogue with all people about our common home.[26]

There are two important points to note. First, both John XIII's *Pacem in Terris* and Francis's *On Care for Our Common Home* are not addressed to the usual people inside the church, but they include the broad expanse envisioned by John XXIII, that is, people of goodwill. Second, Pope Francis's citing of John XXIII writing at the brink of a nuclear disaster could well indicate that for Francis the state of the (neglected) environment is cause for similar urgent worldwide concern.[27]

In addition, it is important to note Pope Francis's reliance on the "see, judge, act" method adopted by John XXIII in *Mater et Magistra* (n. 236). The then Archbishop Bergolio used this explicitly in his editorial work on the CELAM document from Aparecida in 2007 (see below). In point of fact John adopted this from Pius XII who relied on the work of Cardinal Joseph Cardijn (1882–1967) of Belgium, who worked with the poor and adopted this triad as his approach to implementing the church's social justice teaching.

2. PAUL VI

The same anthropologically based themes of human responsibility and the dignity of human work for the common good in *Gaudium et Spes* are found in Pope Paul VI's 1967 encyclical *Populorum Progressio* (nn. 22–28).[28] Four years later in *Octogesima Adveniens* (1971), Pope Paul speaks of the "environment" and directly chastised human beings who have forsaken their responsibility and, "by an ill-considered exploitation of nature," risk "destroying it and becoming in…turn the victim of this degradation," such degradation as "pollution and refuse, new illness and absolute destructive capacity," resulting in intolerable living conditions for posterity (n. 21).[29] In connection with the United Nations–sponsored Conference on the Environment at Stockholm in 1972, Pope Paul VI reiterates previously stated concerns, he but also makes significant additions. He explicates that "the environment essentially conditions man's life and development, while man, in his turn, perfects and ennobles his environment through his presence, work and contemplation."[30] He urges people to use their native capacity for good, specifically their intelligence, to renew nature that is ravaged and exploited, the pollution of which includes water, air, and space affecting human, animal, and vegetable creation.[31] He articulates the theme of interdependence (of all things on the earth), noting a corresponding solidarity among them.[32] Five years later (occasioned by the fifth worldwide day of environment), he returns again to the theme of responsibility to hand over a healthy environment to future generations and notes that human beings have the choice whether to construct and ennoble the world about them, or to destroy it and squander its goods.[33] It is in this text for the first time that the pope refers to human beings in the key, biblically inspired phrase "custodians of creation." He concludes with a forceful appeal, based on interdependence, of a "fraternal sharing and protection of a good environment."[34]

3. JOHN PAUL II

Our treatment of the writings of John Paul II is proportionately longer than those of other popes. This is because we are drawing on five encyclicals (whose relative theological weight is described above) and because of the development in his thought toward the inclusion of various fields and concerns related to ecology (a key "building block" toward Pope Francis's encyclical) and because of the length of his pontificate.[35]

John Paul II's first encyclical, *Redemptor Hominis* (1979), was the first time he touched on a number of themes he later revisited more fully.[36] The environment is a case in point. In two paragraphs, the pope notes that the destruction of creation is one of the things of which human beings today are afraid (n. 15) and that we have to make choices, before approaching the third millennium, about progress or threats to its very existence (n. 16).[37] Central to the pope's unsurprising anthropocentric focus here is the dignity of human persons, the responsibility that human beings bear for equitable sharing of the earth's resources, for the wise use of their talents to work and produce goods and for how issues of the environment are linked to the world economy. To the assertions of Paul VI about the earth's goodness, John Paul II juxtaposes the sin of Adam with the redemption of Christ, the second Adam (n. 8). Yet he articulates a less than happy picture of creation today by stating that it may well be subject to futility (citing Rom 8) and that human beings' responsibility in dominion has led to the pollution of the natural environment and to armed conflicts (n. 8). Human beings have a dignity beyond compare in creation; therefore, humanity also has deep responsibility for it as its "intelligent and noble 'master' and 'guardian', and not as a heedless 'exploiter' and 'destroyer'" (n. 15).[38] Many of our fears, the pope writes, come from what human beings produce, or how they use their creative capacities, or how they have neglected to insure that "progress" and "development" "make human life on earth 'more human' in every aspect of that life" (n. 15). Because of human capacity for thought and moral action, the pope insists on the priority of "ethics over technology, in the primacy of the person over things, and in the superiority of spirit over matter" (n. 16). It is significant that the pope speaks about support for the world economy and the principle of solidarity to lead to "a wider and more immediate redistribution of riches and of control over them" (n. 16). Because human beings have capacities which other orders of creation do not, they bear responsibility to preserve creation.

In an address while visiting the United States in 1979, John Paul II speaks again about how human beings bear distinct responsibility for the land. Addressing farmers directly, he speaks of their genius, skillfulness, sweat, and toil, which cooperate with God the Creator in producing goods that sustain the lives of millions.[39] In articulating three attitudes which farmers should have, the pope identifies gratitude, conservation, and generosity: for our purposes the second is of chief importance. He challenges the farmers to "conserve the land well, so that your children's children and generations after them will inherit an even richer land than was entrusted to you." "In farming, you cooperate with the Creator in the very sustenance of life on the earth."[40] Protecting the earth's resources is the duty of farmers for the sake of later generations. According to the pope, this can and should be accomplished through the capacity and generosity of human persons.

In a 1980 message to the United Nations conference on new developments and strategies, and again when addressing the Pontifical Academy of Sciences, the pope urges all nations to end all waste—especially energy—"so that the most effective and appropriate energy resources are made available without unnecessary waste and exploitation of materials."[41] He calls for the preserving and sharing of the world's energy resources for all the world's inhabitants.[42]

In his encyclical *Laborem Exercens* (1981), the pope reiterates his thought that by divine intention human beings reflect "the very action of the Creator of the universe" when they "subdue" and "dominate the earth" (n. 4; reiterated and explicated more fully in n. 25).[43] He then asserts that "the earth" is "that fragment of the universe" that human beings inhabit, as well as "the whole of the visible world insofar as it comes within range of the influence of human beings and of their striving to satisfy their needs." The earth refers to "all the resources that the earth (and indirectly the visible world) contains and which, through the activity of persons, can be discovered and used for their ends" (n. 4).[44] It is through work that human beings become more and more the masters of the earth, exercising this task in accord with and "within the Creator's original ordering" (n. 4).[45] Human beings thus have responsibility to preserve and share resources of the whole earth with all that dwell in it.

In his 1984 address to the Pontifical Academy of Sciences, the pope again calls for adequate programs for helping the world's inhabitants overcome the imbalance of agricultural practices, the advance of deserts, ecological disasters caused by human rapacity against the earth, water, and atmosphere, the ever more alarming destruction of animal and plant life, and grave and mortal illnesses affecting human life itself. Order and justice must be reestablished, he states, and harmony between man and nature must be restored. He also writes that human beings must strive for a technology that will free the poor peoples, relieve oppressed nature, and promote projects and agreements. Space technology, he observes, can make a highly effective contribution to this cause.[46]

In a catechesis leading up to the 1986 World Environment Day, the pope forthrightly asserts that the protection of the environment is fundamentally an ethical question and one that demands that human beings today provide for those who come after us on earth.[47] This theme recurs in the pope's address to the Pontifical Academy of Sciences in 1987 where he speaks about the ethical and moral principles that must govern science and technology. Regarding the environment, the pope specifically notes that the rational use of resources must include a harmonization between nature and human settlements in order to overcome the destruction of the earth's natural resources and that the findings of science "must be put to use in order to ensure a high productivity of land in such a way that the local population can secure food and sustenance without destroying nature."[48]

During the first part of 1986, John Paul II devoted a number of general audience talks to a commentary on the Book of Genesis. Two of these pertain to the environment. On April 2, the pope refers to the proper autonomy of creation and to the problem often termed today as that of "*ecology*, that is the concern to protect and preserve the natural environment."[49] On April 23, he notes the relationship of human beings with each other (male-female) and with all of creation, and he specifies that it is the free will of human beings that enables them to choose good or evil,[50] which, by extension and in context, supports the pope's overriding concern that human beings care for each other and for all creation.

In *Sollicitudo Rei Socialis* (1987), John Paul II reiterates the above themes but also advances his thought and specifies his concern about development and preserving resources specifically. For the first time he notes today's *ecological concern* about "the limits of available resources, and of the need to respect the integrity and the cycles of nature and to take them into account when planning for development, rather than sacrificing them to certain demagogic ideas about [development]" (n. 26).[51] He urges a "rigorous respect for *justice*" aimed at "a fair distribution of the results of true development" (n. 26). In exercising dominion over creation, the pope reminds us that we, as human beings, "have a certain affinity with other creatures" (n. 26),[52] that Genesis teaches us our "duty of cultivating and watching over [the garden]," but that this dominion "imposes limits upon the use and dominion over things" (n. 29).[53] These limits include avoiding "*indiscriminate* possession of created things and the products of human industry" (n. 29).[54] Because of the limited amount of natural resources, the pope warns us—lest we use these limited resources "as if they were inexhaustible, with absolute dominion"—that natural resources are not only here for the use of this generation, but "above all for generations to come" (n. 34).[55] He states that the *dominion* granted to human beings by God is not an absolute power, nor can one speak of a freedom to "use and misuse" or to dispose of things as one pleases. The limitation imposed from the beginning by the Creator himself and expressed symbolically by the prohibition not to "eat of the fruit of the tree" (see Gen 2:16–17) shows clearly enough that, when it comes to the natural world, we are subject not only to biological laws, but also to moral ones, laws which cannot be violated with impunity (n. 34). Furthermore, he states that the damage wrought by pollution of the environment diminishes the quality of life in industrialized zones (n. 34). He reiterates the theme that human beings have the responsibility to share the good things God has given to all (n. 35).

The document *Peace with God the Creator, Peace with all Creation* (World Day of Peace Message, January 1, 1990) is John Paul II's most focused, single-topic treatment of the environment as a moral crisis (nn. 5, 6, 15) and of his thought about the "new ecological awareness" (n. 1).[56] He reiterates previous papal teachings on the goodness of creation (nn. 3–5), that the earth's resources are for the common good and use of all (n. 8) and that human beings have the responsibility to insure more equitable distribution of the world's goods through a "new solidarity" (n. 10), especially among developing and highly industrialized nations. The urgency expressed here comes from a number of tragic causes, including poverty, war, and the lifestyle of modern society, all of which lay bare the depth of what he terms today's ecological "moral crisis" (nn. 11–13). He calls on men and women to adopt habits of "simplicity, moderation, discipline…[and] a spirit of self-sacrifice" (n. 13) to deal with the ecological crisis. Characteristically, the pope encourages a true international approach to solving it (n. 9). Significantly, he warns of interference "in one area of the ecosystem without paying due attention both to the consequences of such interference in other areas and to the well-being of future generations" (n. 6). "The earth," he continues, "is ultimately a common heritage, the fruits of which are for the benefit of all" (n. 8).

Two additional aspects of this message are particularly notable. First, the pope speaks of the "aesthetic value of creation" calling on human beings to contemplate not only nature but also "the works of human ingenuity" (n. 14). Methodologically, this assertion offers one very fruitful way forward toward developing even more substantial Catholic approaches to the ecological crisis.[57] Second, toward the end of the statement John Paul II invites "ecumenical and interreligious cooperation" on the environment. Specifically, he states the following:

> All the more should men and women who believe in God the Creator, and who are thus convinced that there is a well-defined unity and order in the world, feel called to address the problem. Christians, in particular, realize that their responsibility within creation and their duty toward nature and the Creator are an essential part of their faith. As a result, they are conscious of a vast field of ecumenical and interreligious cooperation opening up before them. At the conclusion of this message, I should like to address directly my brothers and sisters in the Catholic Church, in order to remind them of their serious obligation to care for all of creation. (nn. 15–16)[58]

He closes by reiterating his 1979 proclamation of St. Francis of Assisi as "the heavenly patron of those who promote ecology" (n. 16).[59]

In a 1990 address to the Pontifical Academy of the Sciences' study week participants, John Paul II reiterates his interest in the "aesthetic appreciation" of creation (n. 2) and repeats his challenge that human beings accept responsibility for other creatures (n. 4).[60] He specifies that stewardship implies moral obligations and that "ecological commitment is not only a question of concern for natural beings and the atmosphere around them [but] it is a question of morality, and therefore of man's responsibilities within God's designs. In this context, man's ultimate well-being may be summed up as 'peace with God the Creator, peace with all of creation.'"[61] Of particular note in this statement, however, is the context of what might best be termed as the *interdependence* of all creation. At the beginning of the address the pope states (n. 1), "the depletion of the earth's tropical biodiversity is indeed a very serious problem: it threatens countless other forms of life. Even the quality of human life, because of its dependence on the dynamic interaction of other species, is being impoverished."[62]

This sense of interdependence is also reflected in his 1991 address to the Pontifical Academy of Sciences and Pontifical Council for Culture when he states that our contemporaries are turning to scientists for an

> increased protection of the human person and nature…[and that because of] accidents and mistakes in judgment which assume the dimension of ecological catastrophes, they are more aware of the dangers resulting from the irrational use of nature, which has been put at their disposal by the Creator. They see that the exploitation of the earth's resources has consequences for culture and human beings. (n. 7)[63]

He calls for "decent planning in the use of the planet's resources [that] will greatly contribute to preserving nature, the human person and his culture."[64]

In November of 1991, the pope addressed the Pontifical Academy of Sciences on the topic of population. Here, he notes (n. 1) the "accelerated increase in world population and the availability of natural resources…[and] the present imbalances in demographic distribution, in movements of migrants [and] in the allocation and consumption of resources."[65] Characteristically he lays some of the blame for environmental damage and the increasing "scarcity of natural resources" on human errors, noting that the "availability of resources is obstructed by various social, economic and political factors" and that "the conservation of resources presupposes peaceful coexistence."[66] He concludes by noting that "the dynamics of population growth, the complexity of uncovering and distributing resources, and their mutual connections and consequences for the environment constitute a long-term and demanding challenge." He calls for "a new and more austere manner of living."[67]

In the fall of 1993, John Paul II once more spoke to the Pontifical Academy of Sciences in an address titled "Nations Need an Environmental Ethic."[68] In it he notes the "ever expanding danger from pollution and other side effects of the production and use of chemicals" and judges that the deliberations from that meeting of the pontifical academy will have "great relevance to the growing public concern about the environment" (n. 1). He argues that "development, which insures the conditions required for the exercise of fundamental rights, belongs to the domain of universal human rights. It is a direct consequence of the universal destination of the goods of creation" (n. 2). He bases his call for "respect for the natural environment and the correct and moderated use of the resources of creation" on the human person's "spiritual nature" and "transcendent vocation" (n. 3). He concludes by saying that "we must all learn to approach the environmental question with solid ethical convictions involving responsibility, self-control, justice and fraternal love" (n. 5).

In the encyclical letter *Centesimus Annus* (1991, to coincide with the one hundredth anniversary of the publication of the landmark *Rerum Novarum* by Leo XIII), John Paul II returns to the familiar anthropological foundation for his teaching on equitable distribution of the earth's resources.[69] It is an "anthropological error," he asserts, that human beings forget that the earth's goods come from "God's prior and original gift of the things that are" (n. 37). In n. 38, the pope makes the following statement contextualizing and asserting the importance of "human ecology":

In addition to the irrational destruction of the natural environment, we must also mention the more serious destruction of the *human environment*, something which is by no means receiving the attention it deserves. Although people are rightly worried—though much less than they should be—about preserving the natural habitats of the various animal species threatened with extinction, because they realize that each of these species makes its particular contribution to the balance of nature in general, too little effort is made to *safeguard the moral conditions for an authentic "human ecology."* Not only has God given the earth to man, who must use it with respect for the original good purpose for which it was given to him, but man too is God's gift to man. He must therefore respect the natural and moral structure with which he has been endowed. In this context, mention should be made of the serious problems of modern urbanization, of the need for urban planning which is concerned with how people are to live, and of the attention which should be given to a "social ecology" of work.

Human beings err, he argues, when they think they can make "arbitrary use of the earth" without reference to "a prior God-given purpose." In addition, he reasserts his notion of *dominion* whereby human beings dominate the earth by "making it a fitting home" (n. 53). A new reason why human beings regrettably seek to "possess things rather than relate them to the truth" is because they lack "that disinterested, unselfish and aesthetic attitude that is born of wonder in the presence of being and of the beauty which enables one to see in visible things the message of the invisible God who created them" (n. 37). This text is significant more for what it underscores about how Christians view creation, earth and its resources—namely, a sacramental vision of reality—than for what it says specifically about preserving resources. In effect, however, the fact that less is specified here than could have been may be an appropriate lasting legacy for ongoing theological thought on this issue in line with the thought of John Paul II himself.

In his 1995 encyclical *Evangelium Vitae,* John Paul II's initial consideration of the dignity of the human person is stated negatively: when the sense of God is lost, then human beings do not consider themselves as "mysteriously different" from other orders of creation and should not regard themselves as "merely one more living being" (n. 22).[70] Without the sense of God, "nature itself, from being *'mater'* (mother) is now reduced to being 'matter', and is subject to every kind of manipulation." More positively, he asserts that "there is a truth of creation that must be acknowledged, or a plan of God for life which must be respected." In noting positive signs about life in our day he lists "growing attention being paid to the *quality of life* and to *ecology*, especially in more developed societies, where people's expectations are no longer concentrated so much on problems of survival as on the search for an overall improvement of living conditions" (n. 27). The pope's anthropocentric axis about creation and the dominion that human beings are to exercise are reiterated here as well (n. 34). Of all God's creatures it is the human person that is made in the divine image, "after [the divine] likeness" (Gen. 1:26), and human beings alone are capable of knowing their creator. The pope applies the Genesis text about tilling and looking after the garden (Gen 2:15) to the responsibility human beings have

> towards *the environment in which he lives*, towards the creation which God has put at the service of his personal dignity, of his life, not only for the present, but also for future generations. It is the *ecological question*—ranging from the preservation of the natural habitats of the different species of animals and of other forms of life to "human ecology" properly speaking— which finds in the Bible clear and strong ethical direction, leading to a solution which respects the great good of life, of every life. (n. 42)

In his Lenten messages in 1992, 1993, and 1996, John Paul II articulates his concern about preserving and sharing creation. In 1992, he states that because "creation belongs to everyone" therefore "a generous and bold reform of economic structures and agrarian policies needs to be fostered, so as to ensure well-being and the conditions required for the rightful exercise of their human rights."[71] "The goods of creation," he continues, "are meant for us all…[and] a clear awareness that it is the Creator's will to place the goods of creation at the service of everyone should inspire work for the genuine and complete development of the person and of all people."

In 1993, he specifies the vital need for water.[72] He charges that human beings themselves have been "the cause of the barrenness of lands which have become desert, just as he has caused the pollution of formerly clean waters. When people do not respect the goods of the earth, when they abuse them, they act unjustly, even criminally, because for many of their brothers and sisters their actions result in poverty and death." He asserts that on a global scale "uncontrolled industrial development and the use of technologies which disrupt the balance of nature have caused serious damage to the environment and caused grave disasters." In 1996, the pope returned to the related issue of food distribution.[73] He asserts that "the earth has the resources necessary to feed all humanity," and that "we need to learn to use them intelligently, respecting the environment and the rhythms of nature."

In his apostolic letter *Orientale Lumen* (1995, the centenary of Leo XIII's *Orientalium Dignitas*), John Paul II called for continued efforts at "catholicity to be restored" for the East and West.[74] Under the sections of the document focused on monasticism, the issues of creation, the cosmos, and the human person come to the fore. Praising the monastic life, John Paul II writes that "the monastery is the prophetic place where creation becomes praise of God and the precept of concretely lived charity becomes the ideal of human coexistence" (n. 9); here, in the monastery, "the Eucharist is the culmination of this prayer experience" (n. 10); and finally, "in the liturgical experience, Christ the Lord is the light which illumines the way and reveals the transparency of the cosmos, precisely as in Scripture" (n. 11) and in the sacraments "creation communicates to each individual the power conferred on it by Christ" (n. 11). This final section, on "liturgy for the whole man and the whole cosmos" (n. 11), focuses on the "totality" of the person and creation, emphasizing that in liturgy nature is revealed as "a gift offered by the Creator to humanity" (n. 11) and which itself "is summoned to give thanks" (n. 11), thus concluding, "to those who seek a truly meaningful relationship with themselves and with the cosmos, so often disfigured by selfishness and greed, the liturgy reveals the way to the harmony of the new man, and invites him to respect the Eucharistic potential of the created world" (n. 11). Furthermore, the remaining subsections return to the theme of creation as centered on Christ, for example, "contemplating Christ in the hidden recesses of creation and in the history of mankind" (n. 12); the prayer of the church (especially in the monastery) is "not only for the human person but for every creature…that all may be converted to the saving stream of Christ's love" (n. 14).

In his 1998 apostolic letter *Dies Domini* ("on the day of the Lord"), John Paul articulates the way the Sabbath is a celebration of the Creator's work (nn. 8–30), then as the day of "the new creation" (nn. 24–25) and as "the eighth day, image of eternity" (n. 26).[75] These rich theological themes are introduced (n. 4) by the pope's frank admission that the custom of the "weekend" has become more widespread during which "free time" participation in cultural, political, and sporting activities occur, as opposed to a day for rest and celebration (at home and in church). These themes recur in the writings of Jorge Bergolio as archbishop and in the writings of Pope Francis. For John Paul, the theology of creation is always Christological ("through whom all things were made"), paschal (fully revealed in Christ as "the first fruits of those who had fallen asleep," 1 Cor 15:20), and he offers a positive assessment of God's work in creation and the work of human beings in our daily lives (nn. 8–10). The theology of *Shabbat* is both about creation (for example, the Genesis accounts) and salvation (that is, the liberation from the slavery of Egypt in Deuteronomy.) He argues that Sabbath as a day of "rest" and "remembering" (nn. 15–16) should be carried over into our understanding of Sunday. He points (in n. 27, fn. 32) to the example of the hymns that are assigned to Evening Prayer in the Liturgy of the Hours in the Catholic breviary tradition as one example of the way that the liturgy itself offers a theology of creation and redemption.[76]

In his catechesis of January 26, 2000, John Paul II explicates the creative activity of God ascribed to the Trinity, a theme which becomes central to Pope Francis's thought.[77] He speaks about the Father to whom "the creative act is appropriated in the first place," the Son—Word and Wisdom—through whom God created the world, and the Spirit who moved over the waters (Gen 1:1) and renews the face of the earth (Ps 104). "So, in beholding the glory of the Trinity in creation, man must contemplate, sing, and rediscover wonder." In doing so, man is therefore called to "rediscover our kinship with the earth, to which we have been linked since our own creation (see Gen 2:7)."

This trinitarian emphasis is deepened on August 2, 2000, when, in another catechesis, John Paul II states, "many voices have recognized in creation the presence of its Author and Lord," such as the Egyptian kings and poets, the Greek philosophers, Muslims (Koran II, 21–23), and Jews (M. Buber).[78] The "Christian gaze" (n. 3) contemplates the whole Trinity: both "in Sacred Scripture there is a divine manifestation" and in "nature, too, in a certain sense, is 'the book of God'" (n. 3). When the Christian contemplates creation in its "grandeur and beauty" (n. 4), he says, s/he turns to the "Father from whom everything flows," the Son—Word and Wisdom—who "is present at the moment of creation," and the Spirit who "nourishes from within" (nn. 4–5). Thus, John Paul II remarks, "the biblical concept of creation 'includes not only the call to existence of the very being of the cosmos, that is to say *the giving of existence*, but also the presence of the Spirit of God in creation, that is to say the beginning of God's salvific self-communication to the things he creates" (n. 5).

The following year (in his catechesis of January 17, 2001), John Paul II refers both to the responsibility of "stewardship" and the need for "an ecological conversion."[79] He refers to Psalm 148 (vv. 1–5), which "summons all creatures" and "brings us into a sort of cosmic church, whose apse is the heavens and whose aisles are the regions of the world, in which the choir of God's creatures sings his praise" (n. 1). Yet he notes, the plan of God for man—in man's relationship with God, fellow men, and even nature—indicated at creation (Genesis) and anticipated at the end of this world (Isaiah and Revelation), is in "conflictual tension" with the alternative plan man pursues from his own prerogatives and in sin (n. 1). While man's mission, given by God who created man in his image, is to be a steward of God's creation, "humanity has disappointed God's expectations" (n. 3). "Man, especially in our time," he continues, "has without hesitation devastated wooded plains and valleys, polluted waters, disfigured the earth's habitat, made the air unbreathable, disturbed the hydrogeological and atmospheric systems, turned luxuriant areas into deserts and undertaken forms of unrestrained industrialization, degrading that 'flowerbed'…which is the earth, our dwelling-place" (n. 3). Because of this, the pope calls for support of ecological conversion and encourages "not only a 'physical' ecology…but also a 'human' ecology" in order to prepare "for future generations an environment more in confor-mity with the Creator's plan" (n. 4).

In his 2003 encyclical *Ecclesia de Eucharistia*[80] (n. 8), John Paul II writes poignantly in a personal way and then makes two notable assertions about the Eucharist. He asserts that it is a "cosmic sacra-ment" celebrated "on the altar of the world." (Pope Francis refers to this phrase in his encyclical, n. 236.) John Paul II writes the following:

> When I think of the Eucharist, and look at my life as a priest, as a Bishop and as the Successor of Peter, I naturally recall the many times and places in which I was able to celebrate it. I remember the parish church of Niegowić, where I had my first pastoral assignment, the collegiate church of Saint Florian in Kraków, Wawel Cathedral, Saint Peter's Basilica and so many basilicas and churches in Rome and throughout the world. I have been able to celebrate Holy Mass in chapels built along mountain paths, on lakeshores and seacoasts; I have celebrated it on altars built in stadiums and in city squares....This varied scenario of celebrations of the Eucharist has given me a power-ful experience of its universal and, so to speak, cosmic character. Yes, cosmic! Because even when it is celebrated on the hum-ble altar of a country church, the Eucharist is always in some way celebrated on the altar of the world. It unites heaven and earth. It embraces and permeates all creation. The Son of God became man in order to restore all creation, in one supreme act of praise, to the One who made it from nothing. He, the Eternal High Priest who by the blood of his Cross entered the eternal sanctuary, thus gives back to the Creator and Father all creation redeemed. He does so through the priestly ministry of the Church, to the glory of the Most Holy Trinity. Truly this is the *mysterium fidei* which is accomplished in the Eucharist: the world which came forth from the hands of God the Creator now returns to him redeemed by Christ.[81]

4. BENEDICT XVI

Often called "the green pope," Benedict XVI is known both for what he did in the Vatican to preserve energy (by installing solar panels, and so on) and by his frequent writings on the environment. These began within a year of the inauguration of his pontificate when in a November 2005 catechesis he refers to the praise of God in the psalms in the covenant and in creation.[82] In this same catechesis he notes, in particular, how the word "mercy," taken from the Hebrew *hesed*, rings out. *Hesed*, he observes, was "used in the Bible to express the Covenant that exists between the Lord and his People," to express "faithfulness, loyalty, love, and of course, God's mercy." According to the psalmist, "The first visible sign of this divine love…is to be sought in creation," in which there is a cosmic revelation: "thus, a divine message exists, secretly engraved in creation and a sign of the *hesed*, the loving fidelity of God who gives his creatures being and life, water and food, light and time." "Consequently," he concludes "we rise from the works of creation to the greatness of God and to his loving mercy."

In his homily for the Mass of Corpus Christi in 2006, Benedict gives voice to the assertion of John Paul II about the relationship of the Eucharist to the cosmos.[83] It is certainly the most explicit and fulsome description of this relationship in the papal magisterium to date. He speaks directly of the symbol of bread and wine as the fruit of the earth and the work of human hands: "Bread is not purely and simply what we produce, something made by us; it is fruit of the earth and therefore is also gift." There is a "synergy of the forces of earth and the gifts from above," he asserts, and moreover "creation, with all of its gifts, aspires above and beyond itself to something even greater…we detect in the piece of bread, creation is projected towards divinization, toward the holy wedding feast, toward unification with the Creator himself." At the same time, he reminds us that some gifts from creation, like water, have been misused, leading to desertification and people dying of thirst. Yet in the eucharistic wine we find the "exquisiteness of creation" and the "feast of joy."

In an address to the Diplomatic Corps Accredited to the Holy See in 2007, he speaks about the international situation and focuses on the challenges that need to be addressed by the whole international community.[84] Among the key issues are lack of food, water, and shelter, issues he sees as particularly troubling in today's world, "which has the resources, the knowledge, and the means available to bring it to an end." Indeed, he asserts, the wealthiest, developed nations have a responsibility to poorer nations, not only on the issues of food, water and shelter, but also on the issues of disarmament, humanitarian crises, and "attacks on life from conception to natural death." Nevertheless, Benedict identifies positive elements as well, which include intercultural and interreligious dialogue, international support of human rights and other international aid. While poverty is explicitly noted but the environment, per se, is not a major factor here, these are brought together by Pope Francis.

The following summer (2008), in a give-and-take with the Clergy of the Diocese of Bolzano-Bressanone, Benedict responds to a variety of questions, such as that of Father Golser who observes that the church seems to have "retired to the sacristy."[85] This problem, notes Golser, has implications in the political realm, especially in the area of environmental concerns that come to be debated in the secular sphere not on the basis of the value of creation, but on scientific concerns for glaciers, landslides, energy cost, traffic, and pollution. In his response, Benedict points out that, although recent theology has given less attention to the doctrine of creation, creation and redemption form an "indissoluble bond." God is the *Creator Spiritus*, the Reason that exists in the beginning...who did and can enter into history." And yet the pope recognizes, Christians in particular have been accused of being responsible for the destruction of the environment because of the abuse of Genesis's call to "subdue the earth." Without denying Christian involvement, Benedict moves forward with a corrective view, teaching that the task to subdue the earth "was never intended as an order to enslave it but rather as the task of being guardians of creation and developing its gifts; of actively collaborating in God's work ourselves, in the evolution that he ordered in the world so that the gifts of Creation might be appreciated rather than trampled upon and destroyed." As part of this corrective, human beings must turn from viewing matter as only material and ourselves as the ultimate demand with no need "superior to our own." We must stop the attempts to "possess all that is possible to possess," and we must turn instead to "treat it [creation] according to God's perspective, to recall [that] creation begins with God and life has greater dimensions." Ultimately, Benedict concludes, the "two dimensions—Creation and redemption, earthly life and eternal life, responsibility for the Creation and responsibility for others and for the future—should be juxtaposed."

Recalling what was said above about the relative theological weight to be given to papal documents, it is notable that Benedict addresses the environment in his encyclical letter *Caritas in Veritate* (2009): *"The way humanity treats the environment influences the way it treats itself, and vice versa"* (n. 51, emphasis original).[86] Today, he argues, there is a need for *new lifestyles* (n. 52). For Benedict, nature and society/culture are integrated such that the decline and desertification of one leads to the impoverishment of the other, and yet the peace of one leads to protection of the other; war and resource hoarding (especially water) lead to the destruction of peoples, while incentives for economic and cultural development lead to greater protection of nature. Additionally, he continues, the church "must above all protect mankind from self-destruction" by promoting a "human ecology" that she must proclaim in the public sphere (n. 51). Next, Benedict teaches that the problematic moral tenor of society, which lacks respect for human life, is contradictory to the desire for future generations to respect the natural environment, which it does not respect: indeed, "the book of nature is one and indivisible: it takes in not only the environment but also life, sexuality, marriage, the family, social relations: in a word, integral human development" (n. 51). Finally, Benedict reemphasizes that the ultimate source of truth and love "cannot be mankind, but only God, who is himself Truth and Love," and so, true development toward the protection of the environment and the betterment of society "is not based simply on human choice, but is an intrinsic part of a plan that is prior to us and constitutes for all of us a duty to be freely accepted" (n. 52).

In his 2010 World Day of Peace Message, *If You Want to Cultivate Peace, Protect Creation* (ten years after Pope John Paul II's World Day of Peace Message on the environment), Benedict reiterates a number of themes already seen in papal teachings and gives them added force by addressing a worldwide audience.[87] "If you want to cultivate peace," he begins, "protect creation." According to Benedict, respect for creation is significant because first, according to the *Catechism*, "creation is the beginning and the foundation of all God's works" (CCC, 198),[88] and second, "its preservation has now become essential for the pacific coexistence of mankind." In today's world, threats to peace and human development—threats brought about by war, terrorism, and so on—are tied to man's relationship with the natural environment, especially man's responsibility as steward of creation with special concern for the poor and future generations. Benedict observes that his predecessors—John XIII, Paul VI, and John Paul II—have consistently called for care of creation amid a growing ecological crisis caused by, among other things, conflict over resources, which in turn causes increased conflict with sociological, economic, political, cultural, and moral consequences. Indeed, the ecological crisis is a "cultural and moral crisis" of humanity that requires a "profound cultural renewal" and a renewed "lifestyle marked by sobriety and solidarity."

He continues this important message by reminding us that "Biblical Revelation made us see that nature is a gift of the Creator," and within creation human beings have "a duty to exercise responsible stewardship over creation, to care for it and to cultivate it." Unfortunately, he confesses, human beings have neglected their duty in practical matters through a "lack of far-sighted official policies or the pursuit of myopic economic interests." Therefore, from both an economic and juridical standpoint, he calls for "a greater sense of intergenerational solidarity…which embraces time and space," prudent use of natural resources as a common good, and a lessening of self-interest in policy making and aid distribution. Benedict encourages that this intergenerational solidarity must lead to new lifestyles and look toward the potential of solar energy, water distribution, rural development and small farmers, the link between climate change and poverty, technology use, and models of consumption and production.

Finally, this new orientation toward solidarity is anchored in a "human ecology" because, as Benedict asserts, "the book of nature is one and indivisible; it includes not only the environment but also individual, family, and social ethics." As such, human ecology calls for affirmation of the inviolability of human life, the family, and respect for nature. However, he warns that respect for nature ought not lead to a "new pantheism tinged with neo-paganism, which would see the source of man's salvation in nature alone, understood in purely naturalistic terms": it cannot "absolutize technology and human power." Rather, contemplation of the cosmos should lead us to marvel at "the creative work of the Father and the redemptive work of Christ."

The final document for consideration is Benedict's address to the German Bundestag in 2011, in which he speaks about the cooperation of nations along with the Holy See in addressing the world's problems.[89] Among his concerns is the ecological movement that has been spurred on by young people who have "come to realize that something is wrong in our relationship with nature… that the earth has a dignity of its own." Recognizing its positive aspects, Benedict also calls for growth in the ecological movement, especially in its need to attend to the "ecology of man," man who "has a nature that he must respect and that he cannot manipulate at will." Such conceptions, which recognize a "creative reason, a *Creator Spiritus*," underlie the cultural heritage of human rights, equality, human dignity, and responsibility.

5. FRANCIS

On March 19, 2013, Pope Francis preached to the world for the first time as pope.[90] The feast was the Solemnity of St. Joseph. The occasion was the Mass to inaugurate his pontificate. In that homily he referred to Joseph as the *custos*, "protector" (no fewer than three times), of Jesus, Mary, and the church. He then invited all his hearers to be "protectors" of creation. The die was cast.

Francis continues the same homily by applying Joseph's role and example to us, which themes would be reiterated and expanded in *On Care for Our Common Home.* He speaks about how protecting creation is everyone's responsibility, not just Christians, that this responsibility extends from "the beauty of the created world" (citing the Book of Genesis and St. Francis of Assisi), to "respecting the environment in which we live" to "protecting people" to "showing loving concern for each and every person." He addresses "all those who have positions of responsibility in economic, political and social life, and all men and women of goodwill: let us be 'protectors' of creation, protectors of God's plan inscribed in nature, protectors of one another and of the environment." While admitting that this will take effort and hard work, he also emphasizes that tenderness is a virtue of the strong, not the weak. When referring to his Petrine ministry, he sets in motion his concern for the poor by challenging himself to "open his arms to protect all of God's people and embrace with tender affection the whole of humanity, especially the poorest, the weakest, the least important, those whom Matthew lists in the final judgment on love: the hungry, the thirsty, the stranger, the naked, the sick and those in prison (see Matt 25:31–46). Only those who serve with love are able to protect!"

Not two months later (June 2013), Francis returns to what will become familiar themes for him, at this point offered in a condensed way in a catechesis, especially when compared with the encyclical.[91] Cultivating, preserving, and caring for creation is, Francis writes, "an instruction of God which he gave not only at the beginning of history, but has also given to each one of us," a call "to grasp the pace and the logic of creation" (see Benedict XVI). Rather than taking pride in man's ability to dominate, possess, manipulate, and exploit the earth, Francis calls for a recovery of an "attitude of wonder, of contemplation, of listening to creation." This requires what the popes have called a "human ecology," which is closely connected to "environmental ecology." Thus, the problem becomes more than mere economics and takes on an ethical and anthropological character. Francis reminds us "that whenever food is thrown out it is as if it were stolen from the table of the poor, from the hungry!" Moreover, as Christ taught in his actions in feeding the multitude, where all were satisfied and the remnants were gathered and not thrown out, food must be shared fairly, "with solidarity," so that no one is deprived of what they need. In this way, "human and environmental ecology go hand in hand."

By his own admission, Francis's first encyclical, "On the Light of Faith" (*Lumen Fidei*, June 29, 2013), was largely authored by Benedict XVI. Its sections on faith and reason, however, are quoted fulsomely in *On Care for Our Common Home* in its section on faith and science (n. 141, which quotes *Lumen Fidei* n. 34: "The gaze of science thus benefits from faith: faith encourages the scientist to remain constantly open to reality in all its inexhaustible richness. Faith awakens the critical sense by preventing research from being satisfied with its own formulae and helps it to realize that nature is always greater. By stimulating wonder before the profound mystery of creation, faith broadens the horizons of reason to shed greater light on the world which discloses itself to scientific investigation").[92]

Other notable sections in *Lumen Fidei*, which come to bear in *On Care for Our Common Home*, are on faith and the common good, on faith and the family, on a light for life in society, and on consolation and strength amid suffering (see *Lumen Fidei*, nn. 51, 52, 54–55, 56, and 57).

One month later Francis took his first trip outside of Rome to the island of Lampedusa (July 8, 2013) where thousands of migrants have sought refuge and where countless have died in the attempt. That migration is one of Francis's major concerns is seen in his repeated references to the scandal of not opening one's home countries to them and by incorporating it into *On Care for Our Common Home*. In the homily at Lampedusa, he recalls the words of the Lord to Cain:[93] "Where is your brother? His blood cries out to me." Francis then directs this question at himself, and at all of us. In the world today, however, he remarks with concern that "the other" is no longer our "brother and sister to be loved, but simply someone who disturbs my life and my comfort." The world has lost its bearing, and so no longer cares for what God created, for the poor or for creation. So often those in need, Francis observes, "fail to find understanding, fail to find acceptance, fail to find solidarity," and yet their "cry rises up to God!" His call for a response to this issue is poignant: we should now weep over our indifference and ask for forgiveness for our complacency that has created tragedy throughout the world.

Later that same year, in his postsynodal exhortation *Evangelii Gaudium* (November 24, 2013), he stated that the Synod of Bishops, "attentive to the promptings of the Holy Spirit who helps us together to read the signs of the times," gathered in the XIII Ordinary General Assembly from October 7–28, 2012 to discuss the theme *The New Evangelization for the Transmission of the Christian Faith*.[94] The main conclusion of the synod fathers was in reaffirming that the new evangelization summons all, and it is carried out in three principal settings: first, in ordinary pastoral ministry; second, among the baptized who have no meaningful relationship to the church; and third, those who either do not know Jesus or who have rejected him (n. 15). However, that care for creation and the environment is an undercurrent in the new evangelization is clear in Francis's postsynodal exhortation *Evangelii Gaudium*. That care for creation is an undercurrent in this exhortation is clear in the following selected texts from it that are then cited in *On Care for Our Common Home*: n. 56 of *Evangelii Gaudium* is cited in n. 56 of *On Care for Our Common Home*, 215 is cited in 89, 231 in 110, 237 in 141, 210 in 152, 222 in 178, 209 in 196, 256 in 199, 261 in 216, and 71 in 225.[95] Furthermore, what Pope Francis argues as an *integral ecology* in *On Care for Our Common Home* has its precedents in the following assertions (among others) from *Evangelii Gaudium* nn. 56, 181, 215, and 257.[96]

A year later on a visit to the Food and Agricultural Organization of the United Nations (located in Rome) for the second International Conference on Nutrition (November 20, 2014), the pope lamented that, although the fate of all nations is interconnected, this connection is often obscured by conflict, the notion of the absolute sovereignty of each state, and the interest of "small power groups."[97] Amid this conflict, he observed, the basic needs of many go unmet, such as the need for proper nutrition, which has been made into a commodity to "market priorities" and the "primacy of profit," and which creates what John Paul II had called already (at the first International Conference on Nutrition) a "paradox of abundance," where there is food for everyone but not everyone can eat.[98] Francis responds to this paradox, arguing that "interest in the production, availability and accessibility of foodstuffs, in climate change and in agricultural trade should certainly inspire rules and technical measures, but the first concern must be the individual person, who lacks daily nourishment... and instead fights only for survival." Thus, Francis calls governments and international organizations to a "spirit of dialogue and mutual listening" in order to develop equitable international systems guided by ethical criteria (truth, freedom, justice, and solidarity) and legal criteria (the right to nutrition, life, dignified existence, and to be protected by the law).

A few months later (February 2015), Francis recalls his message to the FAO in a video message to the participants of the 2015 "Expo of Ideas" in Milan.[99] Here, he strongly reiterates the problem of the "paradox of abundance" and offers three concrete practices for overcoming this issue: move from urgencies to priorities, be witnesses of charity, and be guardians, not masters of the earth.

Finally, that what John Paul II called "human ecology" is not forgotten in the writings of Pope Francis is seen in his April 2015 catechesis where he states: "A human being needs the reciprocity of man and woman."[100] Francis draws on the teaching that God created man and woman—"as a couple"—in his image, explaining that they stand, not in opposition or in subordination, "but for the sake of communion and generation, always in the image and likeness of God." Against the efforts of today's society "to cancel out sexual difference," Francis points out that "God entrusted the earth to the alliance between man and woman," and moreover, its [the alliance's] failure deprives the earth of warmth and darkens the sky of hope." Even so, Francis recognizes that this is a work in progress, for example, in recognizing that there is far more needed to advance women.

"THE SIGNS OF THE TIMES"

Toward the end of his poignant and pertinent encyclical *Pacem in Terris* (1961), John XXIII uses the phrase coined by Pius XII—"the signs of the times"—which phrase has been associated with Pope John's approach to the way the church should relate to the world, not least by his calling the Second Vatican Council. Our review of official church teaching on the environment has revealed both *continuity and development*. The sheer volume of such teaching, from tentative first steps to (now) a papal encyclical indicates the attentiveness and concern church leaders place on matters of ecology. Even more important is the fact that this teaching has decidedly evolved, largely based on the fundamental principle of the common good. Paul VI spoke of human beings as "custodians of creation" and of the need for an "integral development" across the globe. John Paul II spoke to the broader issue of energy and the need not to exploit materials destined for the common good. His notion of *justice* includes "a fair distribution of the results of true development." He furthered the work of his predecessors by asserting that human beings have a certain affinity with other creatures and that there is an "interdependence of all creation." His coining of the phrase "human ecology" was a decided amplification and complement to the then commonly understood "natural ecology," which often distinguished between human beings and the rest of all that dwell on earth. His deep and abiding concern for human life is reflected throughout the documents of his papacy, but to this he added the import of the quality of life and ecology. His dramatic call for "a global ecological conversion" led the way for Benedict XVI to link "human ecology" with "environmental ecology" in an inseparable way.

That recent church teaching regards ecology as one of the "signs of the times" to which we must respond and that the world in which we live requires our respect and attention is clear. Repeatedly throughout *On Care for Our Common Home*, Pope Francis cites and relies on these and other similar teachings from the recent magisterium (not only popes, but also from episcopal conferences and ecumenical leaders, as argued below) to launch a new phase in reading "the signs of the times" for the twenty-first century.[101]

IV. RECENT EPISCOPAL CONFERENCE TEACHING ON THE ENVIRONMENT

CELAM *APARECIDA DOCUMENT* (2007): FIFTH GENERAL CONFERENCE OF BISHOPS OF LATIN AMERICA AND THE CARIBBEAN

The key phrase methodologically in this discussion and the next is *episcopal collegiality*.[102] That Pope Francis cites already existing documents in *On Care for Our Common Home* from a number of episcopal conferences worldwide (including the United States) indicates respect for and a reliance on the wisdom of his brother bishops.[103]

In my opinion, the most important footnote in *On Care for Our Common Home* is fn. 24 to the 2007 *Aparecida Document* of the Bishops Conference of Latin America and the Caribbean (technically called CELAM, from Consejo Episcopal Latinoamericano). The *Aparecida Document* is a fulsome text that places the environment in the context of evangelization as the overarching theme of the Fifth General Conference of CELAM, with additional themes that are carried over into Francis's papacy, especially in *Evangelii Gaudium* (see above) and *On Care for Our Common Home*.

With regard to the environment, the pope's personal experience in Latin America involved deforestation, air and water pollution, and intrusion of nonnative businesses using Argentina's resources (among other things). His collaboration with Latin American and Caribbean bishops at meetings of their conference confirmed these experiences. In 2007, CELAM met for their Fifth General Conference in Aparecida, Brazil, to reflect on a number of issues. Their very inclusive "Concluding Document" addresses "the evangelizing action of the Church" (n. 1).[104] Most notably the then archbishop of Buenos Aires, Jorge Bergoglio, was its final editor. The document skillfully and thoroughly combines evangelization with a number of related issues—catechesis, education, liturgy, and sacraments—in the context of decreased participation in church life and liturgy.

What may come as a surprise is the frequency with which and the manner in which the *Aparecida Document* deals with ecology and the environment. Not surprisingly, many of the themes seen here are fleshed out more fully and added to *On Care for Our Common Home*. In effect, this is *the key document* which leads to the pope's encyclical. Among the themes enunciated in the *Aparecida Document* are the following:

- the "see, judge, act" method (n. 19) (often used in social justice methodologies as noted when discussing Pope John's use in *Mater et Magistra* above, sometimes expanded to include "celebrate")
- stewardship (24)
- Eucharist (25, 251)
- Creation is good but its beauty is blemished (27)
- natural resources and biofuels, global warming (66)
- the unsustainable habits of some industrialized countries (66)
- biodiversity (83)
- the Amazon (85)
- the Antarctic (87)
- good news of human dignity (104 ff.)
- good news of life (106 ff.)
- nature under threat (113, referring to Luke 12:12 and Gen 1:29, 2:15)

- trinitarian communion (109)
- good news of the family (114 ff.)
- good news of human activity and work (120 ff.)
- science and technology (123–24)
- good news of the universal destiny of goods and ecology (125–26)
- creation as from God's provident love (125)
- quotes St. Francis of Assisi "our sister, mother earth" (125)
- the notion of "human ecology" and transcendence (126)
- episcopal conferences and communion among the churches (181)
- Liturgy, Eucharist and Sunday (250–52)
- Danger of individualist consumerism (397)
- care for the environment (471 ff.)
- an analysis of the prevailing current economic model (473)
- things to do for and about the environment (474)
- uses of and cautions about the Internet (486–88)

Ecology and Environment in Context. What this list reveals and what even a cursory reading of the document itself reveals is that issues of ecology and the environment are treated in a document that integrates them into the larger framework of issues about evangelization at the beginning of the third millennium. The CELAM bishops view reality through a wide-angle lens so that ecology and evangelization, the environment and poverty, the teachings of the Catholic church and deforestation, for example, are all of a piece. This document provides some of the background to what the pope will call "integral ecology" in the encyclical. Notably, this document speaks of "holiness" directly and asserts the following:

n. 148: In sharing this mission the disciples journey toward holiness. Living it in mission leads them into the heart of the world. Hence, holiness is not a flight toward self-absorption or toward religious individualism, nor does it mean abandoning the urgent reality of the enormous economic, social, and political problems of Latin America and the world, let alone a flight from reality toward an exclusively spiritual world.

EPISCOPAL CONFERENCE DOCUMENTS QUOTED IN *ON CARE FOR OUR COMMON HOME*

The following are episcopal conference documents cited by Pope Francis in *On Care for Our Common Home* (again recall that there are countless others) and an indication of the insight(s) he drew from them:

- Southern African Catholic Bishops' Conference. *Pastoral Statement on the Environmental Crisis* (September 5, 1999)[105]

Coming in a key section of the encyclical (his "urgent appeal" in n. 14), the quotation of the Southern African Catholic Bishops serves as a support of Francis's exhortation for a **new and universal solidarity.**" Indeed, the quotation from the SACBC is a parallel exhortation to Francis's own, and Francis's use of it gives voice to a more universal concern that is manifested in a local/regional setting. In this way, one could suggest that his use of the quotation is not simply a reference on a point of coincidence, but even a symbolic taking up of a local voice in the name of other such voices.

- CELAM, *Aparecida Concluding Document* (May 2007).[106]

Francis's use of the *Aparecida Document* in n. 38 should be taken alongside general, undocumented references he makes to the Congo as well as specific, documented references to other Catholic Bishops' Conferences such as, in this case, the Philippines (see below). These references, taken together, provide data points on the **problem of the ecological crisis** (here, specifically, it is the issue of the **loss of biodiversity**) that Francis is laying out, which data points serve to bolster a convincing argument of the problem's pervasiveness and importance.

- Catholic Bishops' Conference of the Philippines. Pastoral letter *What Is Happening to Our Beautiful Land?* (January 29, 1988).[107]

Like the above citation of the *Aparecida Document*, Francis's use of the Catholic Bishops' Conference of the Philippines in n. 41 should be taken alongside general, undocumented references he makes to the Congo and specific, documented references to other Catholic Bishops' Conferences. As indicated above, these references, taken together, provide data points on the **problem of the ecological crisis**. Additional force can be attributed to this particular quotation from the Filipino bishops for its vivid imagery and expressive language, which asks, "Who turned the wonderworld of the seas into underwater cemeteries bereft of colour and life?"

- Bolivian Bishops' Conference. Pastoral letter on the Environment and Human Development in Bolivia *El universo don de Dios para la vida* (March 23, 2012).[108]

Francis's use of the Bolivian Bishops' Conference in n. 48 serves as support to his teaching on **integral ecology** (proposed in n. 48 in an inchoate way). Of particular note is the way in which Francis leans on the **"everyday experience and scientific research"** indicated in the quotation. This quotation could symbolically stand in for the work/preparation performed by numerous other Bishops' Conferences (not only the Bolivian bishops) with the understanding that the experience of numerous bishops' conferences and their own study and inclusion of scientific research likewise supports the positions taken in *On Care for Our Common Home*.

- German Bishops' Conference. Commission for Social Issues, *Der Klimawandel: Brennpunkt globaler, intergenerationeller und ökologischer Gerechtigkeit* (September 2006).[109]

Francis's comparative reference to the German Bishops Conference in n. 48 is within the context of his listing of *some* **examples of the ecological problems**, especially those that most impact the poor, that are not adequately represented on the global agenda. The German document itself provides numerous examples, within and beyond Europe, of such problems. The three sections of the German document specifically referenced by Francis cover threats to food security (*Gefahren für die Ernährungssicherheit*), spread of diseases (*Ausbreitung von Krankheiten*), and increase of war and flight, that is, refugees from either war or extreme poverty (*Zunahme von Krieg und Flucht*).

- Bishops of the Patagonia-Comahue Region (Argentina). *Christmas Message* (December 2009).[110]

The quotation of the Bishops of the Patagonia-Comahue Region in n. 51 serves a similar function as the quotation from the Bolivian bishops, though here with specificity on "experience." The quotation itself is given in support of Francis's argument that **inequality is international** in scale and requires **differentiated responsibilities**. Specifically, the quotation demonstrates how the actions of a developed nation can have negative impacts on developing nations. As with other references, there is no reason to believe that the use of this quotation is completely localized (that is, restricted to Argentina), but rather is one symbolic local expression of a universal concern.

- United States Conference of Catholic Bishops. *Global Climate Change: A Plea for Dialogue, Prudence and the Common Good* (June 15, 2001).[111]

Coming toward the end of chapter 1 of the encyclical (n. 52)—a chapter that has relied largely on Bishops' Conferences in developing regions (directly quoting only these, with one comparative reference to a German document)—that this quotation comes from the U.S. bishops seems less than arbitrary. On the topic of **differentiated responsibility**, Francis considers the responsibility of developed countries toward the poor. In using the quotation of the U.S. bishops, Francis parallels his own call for developed countries to take responsibility for the poor by citing a developed country *in the action of* a call for care of the poor, thus implicitly noting the dynamic required of differentiated responsibility and explicitly emphasizing the raison d'être of the call. It should also not go without note that this quotation also synthesizes differentiated responsibility with what one might call **overplayed economics**, a concern throughout the first chapter.

- CELAM, "Aparecida Concluding Document" (May 2007).[112]

Francis's use of the *Aparecida Document* in n. 54 verges on making the (exact) exhortation of *Aparecida* his own. In his argument against the **overplaying of economics**, Francis moves from his own implicit exhortation for "legal framework which can...ensure the protection of ecosystems" (calling this framework "indispensible," n. 53) to a specification of his more implicit exhortation (n. 54): that is, he will move in n. 54 to explicitly specify that economic interests should not prevail, economics should not be overplayed. Significantly this specified exhortation is not his own, but that of the *Aparecida Document*. Francis remarks, "the *Aparecida Document* urges that *'the interests of economic groups...should not prevail'*" (the italicized words being those of the *Aparecida Document*).

- German Bishops' Conference. *Zukunft der Schöpfung – Zukunft der Menschheit. Einklärung der Deutschen Bishofskonferenz zu Fragen der Umwelt und der Energieversorgung* (1980).[113]

The German Bishops' Conference quotation given in n. 69, alongside a quote from the *Catechism* (CCC, 339), provides current-day support of Francis's teaching on the **goodness inherent in creatures** against **"tyrannical anthropocentrism,"** a teaching Francis arrives at through scripture. After his scriptural argument (nn. 65–68), Francis appeals to the teaching of the church "in our time," where he then makes reference first to the German bishops and then to the *Catechism*. Such an approach places the weight of the quotation on its demonstration of the relevancy, and new articulation, of a teaching held from scripture. The quote from the German bishops, in particular, highlights the contemporary philosophical issues tied up with, for example, utilitarianism.[114]

- Canadian Conference of Catholic Bishops, Social Affairs Commission. Pastoral letter *You Love All that Exists...All Things Are Yours, God, Lover of Life* (October 4, 2003).[115]

In support of his claim that we "should not...overlook the fact that **each creature has its own purpose**," Francis cites John Paul II (*Catechesis*, January 30, 2002), the Canadian Conference of Bishops, the Catholic Bishops of Japan, John Paul II twice more (*Catechesis*, January 26, 2000; *Catechesis*, August 2, 2000), and finally Paul Ricoeur (*Philosophie de la Volunte*), all in rapid succession. The force of these six citations appears largely rhetorical—occurring without great explanation either before, after, or between; that is, they provide succinct, insightful, poignant, and rhetorically powerful expressions of Francis's original claim that each creature has its own purpose. This suggestion of citation for rhetorical force can be supported from Francis's own affirming language in the *brief* introductions to each of the quotes and in the rhetorically eloquent quotes themselves. For example, Francis states, "The Canadian bishops rightly pointed out that no creature is excluded from this manifestation of God: 'From panoramic vistas to the tiniest living form, nature is a constant source of wonder and awe. It is also a continuing revelation of the divine.'"

- Catholic Bishops' Conference of Japan. *Reverence for Life: A Message for the Twenty-First Century* (January 1, 2000).[116]

As noted above, Francis's citation of the Japanese bishops is largely for rhetorical force, with the various quotations providing succinct, insightful, and poignant expressions of Francis's claim that each creature has its own purpose. In quoting the Japanese bishops, Francis says, "The bishops of Japan, for their part, made a thought-provoking observation: 'To sense each creature singing the hymn of its existence is to live joyfully in God's love and hope.'"

- National Conference of the Bishops of Brazil. *A Igreja e a Questão Ecológica* (1992).[117]

In n. 88, Francis first references (by comparison) and then directly quotes the bishops of Brazil as a significant expansion of his argument that "**each creature has its purpose**." In the relevant line of argumentation, Francis first specifies this claim by identifying the purpose of each creature, which is to show forth God (n. 86); he then offers St. Francis's *Canticle* as an indication of our response: praise. Next, Francis references the Brazilian bishops in order to *expand* on the idea that creatures show forth God, saying, "The bishops of Brazil have pointed out that nature as a whole *not only manifests* God but is also *a locus of his presence*" (n. 88, emphasis added). Significantly, nowhere previously (for this same argument on the "harmony of creatures" and the "manifestation" of God in creation) does Francis explicitly teach that nature is a "locus" of God's presence; only here is it specified, and with strong reliance on an Episcopal Conference.[118]

- Conference of Dominican Bishops. Pastoral letter *Sobre la relación del hombre con la naturaleza* (January 21, 1987).[119]

Simply put, Francis's use of the Dominican bishops in n. 92 is as a supplementary, explanatory note on **integral ecology** as tied to **universal communion**. Francis explains his main claim here— "Everything is connected. Concern for the environment thus needs to be joined to a *sincere love* for our fellow human beings and an unwavering commitment to resolving the problems of society"— with his own reflection on "sincere love": "We can hardly consider ourselves to be *fully loving* if we disregard any *aspect of reality*." Joined to this clause by a colon, the quotation from the Dominican bishops then further unfolds "aspect of reality," identifying "peace" and "justice" as two of these "aspects" (indeed, essential ones).

- Paraguayan Bishops' Conference. Pastoral letter *El campesino paraguayo y la tierra* (June 12, 1983).[120]

Francis makes clear the standing of his quotation of the Paraguayan bishops in n. 94: it is an example of a practical consequence of his claim in this section (that **the rich and poor have equal dignity**). He simply states, "This [claim] has practical consequences, such as those pointed out by the bishops of Paraguay." Francis's use of this quote as an example does not as strongly suggest the same sort of symbolic application as other quotations already observed, at least in terms of the specific examples indicated by the Paraguayan bishops.

- New Zealand Catholic Bishops Conference. *Statement on Environmental Issues* (September 1, 2006).[121]

Francis's quotation of the New Zealand bishops in n. 95 serves as a striking rhetorical device to drive home the **implications of his claim that "the natural environment is a collective good."** After the more positive conclusion that "if we make something our own, it is only to administer it for the good of all," Francis then makes the negative conclusion: "If we do not [administer it for the good of all], we burden our consciences with the weight of having denied the existence of others." On this second (negative) point, Francis draws on the New Zealand bishops for a striking, and largely rhetorical, example that provides a jolting comparison of what some (perhaps many?) may perceive as, at worst, indifference with killing: Francis puts forth, "That is why the New Zealand bishops asked what the commandment 'Thou shalt not kill' means when 'twenty percent of the world's population consumes resources at a rate that robs the poor nations and future generations of what they need to survive.'"

- *Love for Creation: An Asian Response to the Ecological Crisis*, Declaration of the Colloquium, sponsored by the Federation of Asian Bishops' Conferences (Tagaytay, January 31–February 5, 1993).[122]

Francis's reference (by comparison) to the Federation of Asian bishops in n. 116 is a parallel exhortation to his own for the need to reinterpret man's relation to the universe, especially in light of more recent perspectives that see man (and science) as interpreting "dominion" with an unhealthy view of "mastery." Francis's words clearly draw strongly on the exhortation given by the Asian bishops, though it is significant that Francis does not make these words his own (as he does, for example, with the *Aparecida Document*). Nevertheless, an examination of the two quotes reveals their strong affinity (especially in the italicized phrases):

Francis himself states: "Often, what was handed on [in modernity] was a Promethean vision of mastery over the world, which gave the impression that the protection of nature was something that only the faint-hearted cared about. Instead, our "dominion" over the universe *should be understood more properly in the sense of responsible stewardship*" (after which he references, by comparison, the Asian Bishops).

The Asian bishops, in *Love for Creation*, 3.3.1–2, state: "While we appreciate the great contributions that science is making in

understanding and handling ecological problems, we emphasize the faith dimensions, acknowledging God as Creator,
trusting his active presence and contemplating the beauty of
his creation. Therefore, the concept of man as master of the
universe *should be replaced by the concept of stewardship with
responsibility* for the well-being of this world."

- Episcopal Commission for the Pastoral Concerns in Argentina. *Una tierra para todos* (June 2005).[123]

Francis's quotation of the Argentinian Episcopal Commission
in n. 134 is couched within a large section on some specific areas
of concern for the ecological crisis, especially those **concerns moti-
vated by anthropocentrism**; of more direct concern for n. 134 is
the use of **genetically modified cereals**. Francis's general thrust
is to demonstrate that a wider view of the effects of such technologies must be considered, that, for example, while GM cereals
are not conclusively harmful to human health, their overproduction can lead to harm to the person as a whole. One example of
such an often unperceived harm is in the effects on local farmers,
whose plight is represented by the Argentinian bishops. It is significant that Francis connects this specific Argentinian concern to
a more universal problem. Thus, like in several examples above,
the concrete, local concern of the Argentinian bishops symbolically speaks for specific issue that, while local to Argentina, also
impacts a wider global community. The difference here, as compared to other cases of such symbolic representation, is that what
is addressed seems to be a specific issue (overproduction of GM
cereals has negative impacts on the human person), impacting the
global community, rather than a *general principle*.

- Portuguese Bishops' Conference. Pastoral letter *Responsabilidade Solidária pelo Bem Comum* (September 15, 2003).[124]

Francis's quotation of the Portuguese Bishops' Conference in
n. 159, which regards **solidarity as a basic question of justice,**
blurs the line between the quotation as support (for example, Paraguayan bishops in n. 94) and the actual taking on of it as his own
(for example, the *Aparecida* quotation in n. 54). The words of the

Bishops are not themselves exhortatory, but Francis's introduction to them gives such quality. He remarks, "The Portuguese bishops *have called upon us* to acknowledge this obligation of justice." This is, arguably, the clearest articulation of Francis's encyclical as (partially) a response to the concerns of Bishops' Conferences, which until now has been largely implicit (with exceptions).[125]

- Bolivian Bishops' Conference. Pastoral letter on the Environment and Human Development in Bolivia *El universo don de Dios para la vida* (March 23, 2012).[126]

Francis's use of the Bolivian bishops in n. 170 comes in a specific critique of the need to reduce **emission pollution**, and the basic argument is for differentiated responsibility, already developed earlier in the encyclical. The benefit of the quotation from the Bolivian bishops is its application of the general principle—differentiated responsibility—to the specific problem under consideration, emission pollution.

- Mexican Bishops' Conference, Episcopal Commission for Pastoral and Social Concerns. *Jesucristo, vida y esperanza de los indígenas e campesinos* (January 14, 2008).[127]

Francis's reference (by comparison) to the Mexican bishops' document (the reference is to the document *as a whole*, rather than a specific passage) in n. 189 is as a specific example of Francis's concern that **overproduction** negatively impacts regional economies. The Mexican bishops' document is concerned with the international trade relation of Mexico, especially with the United States and Canada, observing that new (less restricting) tariff laws should open up Mexico to trade with, especially, these two countries. However, this cannot be done without care and discretion, for (and this is Francis's main takeaway from the document) "when market forces are imposed on the rights of individuals and peoples, profit becomes a supreme value and major interest groups, which exclude the poor, create an unjust global economic system and conform inhumane."

- Australian Catholic Bishops' Conference. *A New Earth: The Environmental Challenge* (2002).[128]

Francis's quotation of the Australian bishops in n. 218 is in support of a teaching on **conversion as necessary for reconciliation with creation** that he derives primarily from St. Francis. The appeal to the Australian bishops complements, and is a contemporary expression of, what Pope Francis more primarily derives from St. Francis of Assisi. Indeed, after indicating St. Francis's view, Pope Francis says, "The Australian bishops spoke of the importance of *such* conversion for achieving reconciliation" (emphasis added).

Variety and Insight. Among other things, this listing of insights gleaned from episcopal conference documents indicates a broad variety of ideas from nothing less than the expanse of the church worldwide. Reading between the lines of the encyclical is the pope's concern that the church as universal be represented and the experience of the developing world ("the periphery") be brought to the table.

UNITED STATES CONFERENCE OF CATHOLIC BISHOPS (USCCB)

There are three major texts to discuss from the United States Conference of Catholic Bishops. The first text, "Renewing the Earth" (1991), is broad and far reaching compared to the second, "Global Climate Change: A Plea for Dialogue, Prudence and the Common Good" (2001, cited by Pope Francis in *On Care for Our Common Home*). The third, "Global Climate Change" (2010), like the second text, addresses climate change.

"Renewing the Earth" (1991).[129] In response to Pope John Paul II's World Day of Peace Message in 1990, "Peace with God the Creator, Peace with All Creation," the U.S. bishops drafted their own document the following year. It begins by boldly asserting that the environmental crisis is a moral challenge involving the closely intertwined issues of environment, energy, economics, equity, and

ethics (n. 1, under the title "Signs of the Times"). The bishops set for themselves six goals for the statement (n. 1):

1. to highlight the ethical dimensions of the environmental crisis;
2. to link questions of ecology and poverty, environment and development;
3. to stand with working men and women and poor and disadvantaged persons, whose lives are often impacted by ecological abuse and tradeoffs between environment and development;
4. to promote a vision of a just and sustainable world community;
5. to invite the Catholic community and men and women of goodwill to reflect more deeply on the religious dimensions of this topic; and
6. to begin a broader conversation on the potential contribution of the church to environmental questions.

The bishops then assert prophetically (given the text of *On Care for Our Common Home*) (n. 1):

Above all, we seek to explore the links between concern for the person and for the earth, between natural ecology and social ecology. The web of life is one. Our mistreatment of the natural world diminishes our own dignity and sacredness, not only because we are destroying resources that future generations of humans need, but because we are engaging in actions that contradict what it means to be human. Our tradition calls us to protect the life and dignity of the human person, and it is increasingly clear that this task cannot be separated from the care and defense of all of creation.

After citing initiatives from bishops in various parts of the United States and other countries to these pastoral realities and challenges, the document sets forth the biblical data and principles of Catholic social teaching on the issue (nn. 2–3). In summary fashion the bishops assert (n. 3):

Background

We believe that the following themes drawn from this tradition are integral dimensions of ecological responsibility:

- a *God-centered and sacramental view of the universe*, which grounds human accountability for the fate of the earth;
- a consistent *respect for human life*, which extends to respect for all creation;
- a worldview affirming the ethical significance of *global interdependence and the common good*;
- *an ethics of solidarity* promoting cooperation and a just structure of sharing in the world community;
- an understanding of *the universal purpose of created things*, which requires equitable use of the earth's resources;
- *an option for the poor*, which gives passion to the quest for an equitable and sustainable world;
- a conception of *authentic development*, which offers a direction for progress that respects human dignity and the limits of material growth.[130]

A particular characteristic feature of this document is the way the bishops respect and invite the participation of all sectors of society to dialogue and act (n. 5, which assertions again are prophetic of what Pope Francis has taught in *On Care for Our Common Home*). The bishops write the following:

- We ask *scientists, environmentalists, economists, and other experts* to continue to help us understand the challenges we face and the steps we need to take. Faith is not a substitute for facts; the more we know about the problems we face, the better we can respond.
- We invite *teachers and educators* to emphasize, in their classrooms and curricula, a love for God's creation, a respect for nature, and a commitment to practices and behavior that bring these attitudes into the daily lives of their students and themselves.
- We remind *parents* that they are the first and principal teachers of children. It is from parents that children will learn love of the earth and delight in nature. It is at home that they develop the habits of self-control,

concern, and care that lie at the heart of environmental morality.

- We call on *theologians, scripture scholars, and ethicists* to help explore, deepen, and advance the insights of our Catholic tradition and its relation to the environment and other religious perspectives on these matters. We especially call upon Catholic scholars to explore the relationship between this tradition's emphasis upon the dignity of the human person and our responsibility to care for all of God's creation.

- We ask *business leaders and representatives of workers* to make the protection of our common environment a central concern in their activities and to collaborate for the common good and the protection of the earth. We especially encourage pastors and parish leaders to give greater attention to the extent and urgency of the environmental crisis in preaching, teaching, pastoral outreach, and action, at the parish level and through ecumenical cooperation in the local community.

- We ask the *members of our Church* to examine our life-styles, behaviors, and policies—individually and insti-tutionally—to see how we contribute to the destruction or neglect of the environment and how we might assist in its protection and restoration. We also urge *celebrants and liturgy committees* to incorporate themes into prayer and worship that emphasize our responsibility to pro-tect all of God's creation and to organize prayerful cel-ebrations of creation on feast days honoring St. Francis and St. Isidore.

- We ask *environmental advocates* to join us in building bridges between the quest for justice and the pursuit of peace and concern for the earth. We ask that the poor and vulnerable at home and abroad be accorded a spe-cial and urgent priority in all efforts to care for our envi-ronment.

- We urge *policy makers and public officials* to focus more directly on the ethical dimensions of environmen-tal policy and on its relation to development, to seek the common good, and to resist short-term pressures in order to meet our long-term responsibility to future generations. At the very minimum, we need food and energy policies that are socially just, environmentally benign, and economically efficient.

- As *citizens*, each of us needs to participate in this debate over how our nation best protects our ecological heritage, limits pollution, allocates environmental costs, and plans for the future. We need to use our voices and votes to shape a nation more committed to the universal common good and an ethic of environmental solidarity.[131]

The document ends with a call to conversion and a word of hope. Implicit here is that the environment needs careful study and tending involving all sectors of society for whom this may well represent real challenges.

"Global Climate Change: A Plea for Dialogue, Prudence and the Common Good" (2001).[132] In June of 2001, the U.S. bishops approved a document about global climate change specifically that was largely influenced by the teachings of John Paul II. The subtitle sets up the core of what the bishops want to address: "A Plea for Dialogue, Prudence and the Common Good." The bishops assert the following in the introduction:

The continuing debate about how the United States is responding to questions and challenges surrounding global climate change is a test and an opportunity for our nation and the entire Catholic community. As bishops, we are not scientists or public policymakers. We enter this debate not to embrace a particular treaty, nor to urge particular technical solutions, but to call for a different kind of national discussion. Much of the debate on global climate change seems polarized and partisan. Science is too often used as a weapon, not as a source of wisdom. Various interests use the airwaves and political process to minimize or exaggerate the challenges we face. The search for the common good and the voices of poor people and poor countries sometimes are neglected.

53

At its core, global climate change is not about economic theory or political platforms, nor about partisan advantage or interest group pressures. It is about the future of God's creation and the one human family. It is about protecting both "the human environment" and the natural environment. It is about our human stewardship of God's creation and our responsibility to those who come after us. With these reflections, we seek to offer a word of caution and a plea for genuine dialogue as the United States and other nations face decisions about how best to respond to the challenges of global climate change.

When referring specifically to this document and the American audience to which it is addressed, the bishops state the following:

Therefore, we especially want to focus on the needs of the poor, the weak, and the vulnerable in a debate often dominated by more powerful interests. Inaction and inadequate or misguided responses to climate change will likely place even greater burdens on already desperately poor peoples. Action to mitigate global climate change must be built upon a foundation of social and economic justice that does not put the poor at greater risk or place disproportionate and unfair burdens on developing nations.

The message reiterates the following five principles of Catholic social teaching on which to base arguments about global climate change (and ecology more generally):

- The universal common good
- Stewardship of God's Creation and the Right to Economic Initiative and Private Property
- Population and Authentic Development

[Given that this is not regularly or fulsomely addressed, it is important to indicate the bishops' line of reasoning here:

Population and climate change should be addressed from the broader perspective of a concern for protecting human life, caring for the environment, and respecting cultural norms and the religious faith and moral values of peoples. Population is not simply about statistics. Behind every demographic number is a precious and irreplaceable human life whose human dignity must be respected.

The global climate change debate cannot become just another opportunity for some groups—usually affluent advocates from the developed nations—to blame the problem on population growth in poor countries. Historically, the industrialized countries have emitted more greenhouse gases that warm the climate than have the developing countries. Affluent nations such as our own have to acknowledge the impact of voracious consumerism instead of simply calling for population and emissions controls from people in poorer nations.]

- Caring for the Poor and Issues of Equity
- The Public Policy Debate and Future Directions

Not surprisingly the bishops offer an international, interdependent view when they assert:

Catholic social teaching calls for bold and generous action on behalf of the common good. 'Interdependence,' as Pope John Paul II has written, 'must be transformed into *solidarity*.... Surmounting every type of *imperialism* and determination to preserve their *own hegemony*, the stronger and richer nations must have a sense of moral *responsibility* for the other nations, so that a *real international system* may be established which will rest on the foundation of the *equality* of all peoples and on the necessary respect for their legitimate differences.'

"Global Climate Change" (2010).[133] A decade later and in response to a bill then before Congress about climate change titled *The American Clean Energy and Security Act of 2009*, the bishops and other leaders of the National Religious Partnership for the Environment outlined in a letter to Congress with broad agreement on four key principles:

- The principle of prudence requires us to act to protect the common good by addressing climate change.
- The consequences of climate change will be borne by the world's most vulnerable people and inaction will only worsen their suffering.
- Policies addressing global climate change should enhance rather than diminish the economic situation of people in poverty.
- Policies should help vulnerable populations here and abroad adapt to climate impacts and actively participate in these efforts.[134]

They concluded with an appeal that American Catholics contact their congressional representatives to support the bill.

REGIONAL UNITED STATES BISHOPS' DOCUMENTS

In addition to teaching documents from all the members of an episcopal conference are the documents issued by the bishops from part of the conference. With regard to the environment, what are likely the best known and the most influential are two from the U.S. bishops in Appalacia titled "This Land is Home to Me: Pastoral Letter on Powerlessness in Appalachia" (1975) and "At Home in the Web of Life" (1995)[135] and one from the U.S. and Canadian bishops of the Northwest titled "The Columbia River Watershed: Caring for Creation and the Common Good: An International Pastoral Letter by the Catholic Bishops of the Watershed Region" (2001).[136] Such texts are normally focused on regional issues and contain both teaching and suggested practices.

Catholic Bishops of Appalachia. This Land is Home to Me: A Pastoral Letter on Powerlessness in Appalachia by the Catholic Bishops of the Region (1975, 1980, 1985, 2000).[137] The signatories of this document were diocesan (arch)bishops from the twenty-five (arch) dioceses that encompass Appalachia. The subtitle "on Powerlessness" indicates the breadth of the document where issues of environment and ecology are framed within the wider context of a host of issues: natural resources, changing employment patterns, economy, family life, and so on. The style of the letter stands in contrast with almost all of the other documents reviewed above. Its poetic and inspirational language reflects both a mastery of the issues at hand and yet a pastoral heart that invites reflection and action. One of the major themes in the document is the way that the phrase "coal is king" is changing. This includes the decline in coal use (inter)nationally with the resulting need to find other sources of employment. The decreased influence of labor unions is decried as one example of the changes that are reoccurring. In the context of unemployment, the bishops challenge the construction of additional prisons in the area with their attendant drain on society and systemic culture of violence. In the second part, they call for reflection on the sources of the Catholic tradition to deal with such issues and end, in part three, with a call for hope. The interrelationship of environmental concerns within a large context is seen in the final paragraph which notes (among other things) energy consumption patterns and lifestyle, strip mining and deep mining, land acquisition, retribution and redistribution, exploitation of cheap labor, union reform and extension, public voice in local, state, and national politics, cooperatives, education, health systems, family life, the elderly, and the music and poetry that have characterized this area.

At Home in the Web of Life: A Pastoral Message on Sustainable Communities in Appalachia (1995, 2000).[138] Marking the twentieth anniversary of the first edition of *This Land Is Home to Me*, the bishops of Appalachia again wrote about the particular challenges of their area, again emphasizing issues of ecology and the environment in relation to a number of other issues, all placed within the notion of "sustainable communities" (as seen in the subtitle). The poetic introductory paragraphs deal with creation as God's word with the revelation specifically of mountains and forests. The document offers a brief history of those who settled here, from the "native peoples" to those who now live here with their attendant challenges—pollution, garbage, construction of prisons—and opportunities such as how to move from a "coal" economy to choices that lead to a sustainable economy for all. Once again, in part 2 the bishops reflect on biblical and church teaching to raise up the interrelated principles of human dignity, community, economics, subsidiarity, ownership, ecology, sustainability, government, and "facing the future." These lead, in part 3, to the call for sustainable communities, sustainable development, sustainable agriculture, sustainable forestry, sustainable ownership, sustainable technologies, sustainable cultures, sustainable families (noting the contribution of women in particular), and sustainable churches.

Like the previous document, parallel columns of text contain quotations from the bible, church leaders, and contemporary authors (including, for example, Francis of Assisi, Hildegard of Bingen, and John Paul II).

It is also notable that as official church documents begin to use "human ecology" in relation to "natural ecology" (see John Paul II, *Centesimus Annus*, n. 38, 1991), this document speaks of "social ecology." In either case, contextualizing concern for natural resources within a number of interrelated issues and including human beings as integral members of the ecological landscape are among the developing themes in official church teaching at this stage which will be more fully developed in the years to come.

The Columbia River Watershed: Caring for Creation and the Common Good: International Pastoral Letter by the Catholic Bishops of the Watershed Region [the Pacific Northwest] (2001).[139] While more modest in length than the Appalachian bishops' efforts, this text from the American and Canadian bishops of the region (the Columbia River Watershed) is a thorough, compelling, and invitational document dealing with their treasured resource, the Columbia River Basin. Signed by eleven (arch)bishops, the document was the result of a process of distilling Catholic (especially social) teaching, dialogue among the local populations' nine "listening sessions" during 1999, and twenty-one "resource consultants." However brief, the summary of Catholic teaching forms an integrated framework for understanding the many facets of the ecological issues local people now deal with regarding the Columbia River. That the region faces a "moral" and "spiritual" crisis regarding the river is made clear.

The last section on "considerations for community caretaking" offers both a summary of the bishops' teaching and the applications they foresee regarding the river basin:

- consider the common good
- conserve the watershed as common good
- conserve and protect species of wildlife
- respect the dignity and traditions of the region's indigenous peoples
- promote justice for the poor, linking economic justice and environmental justice
- promote community resolution of economic and ecological issues
- promote social and ecological responsibility among reductive and reproductive industries

[Here, they explain "reductive industries extract from the earth goods that are not renewable, such as metals and petroleum. Reproductive industries harvest from earth's bounty renewable goods such as timber and agricultural products."]

- conserve energy and establish environmentally integrated alternative energy sources
- respect ethnic and racial cultures, citizens and communities.[140]

While these principles and action items reflect the particularity of the Pacific Northwest, it is also clear they are applicable (sadly) to many other instances of ecological abuse and violence done to this good earth.

V. ECUMENICAL PERSPECTIVES

INITIATIVES FROM AND WITH THE ORTHODOX CHURCH

Modern popes from Paul VI on have implemented the desires of the bishops at Vatican II, whose Decree on Ecumenism, *Unitatis Redintegratio*, called for dialogue among churches with the goal of reunion.[141]

That Pope Francis singled out the contributions of Patriarch Bartholomew and the Orthodox church on the environment in

On Care for Our Common Home (nn. 7–9) is very significant for at least three reasons. First, this citing expresses ecumenism in action and the pope's desire to foster reunion with the Orthodox as he has stated and demonstrated again and again during his pontificate.[142] Second, the ongoing debate about the relationship of religion and science is raised up as something that is not particular to the Roman Catholic Church. Third, the urgency with which Pope Francis has approached this issue has been more than matched by the efforts by the Orthodox dating back to 1987.[143]

There are a host of other ecumenical voices and texts about ecology and the environment.[144] What will follow is a representative sample in order to indicate the growing religious consensus about the environment and the necessity that religious leaders and church members address it.

The key phrase here is *ecumenical collegiality* in the way the pope gives pride of place in the encyclical (nn. 7–9) to the statements from Patriarch Bartholomew and to the initiatives he has spearheaded on the environment by the Eastern Orthodox church.[145] Among other prominent voices are those from the Muslim community in, for example, the declaration from the International Islamic Climate Change Symposium (August 17–18, 2015).[146]

The use of the word "initiatives" in this subtitle is deliberate because there is an intrinsic (not to say unique) relationship among the initiatives undertaken by the Orthodox: the conduct of prayer services for creation, the issuance of statements (encyclicals and common declarations) about the environment, and the holding of seminars about the environment. These are followed by summaries of common declarations between Roman Catholic and Orthodox leadership.

World Day of Prayer for Creation. In 1989, Patriarch Dimitrios (with the approval of the Holy Synod) declared that from then on the Orthodox churches would celebrate a World Day of Prayer for the Protection of the Environment on September 1, the first day of their liturgical year. This means that the liturgy of the day was adjusted to reflect and underscore praise and thanks as well as intercession for creation.[147]

Background

On August 10, 2015, Pope Francis decreed that Roman Catholics would join the Orthodox in observing the world day of prayer for creation on the same day.[148] The pope himself presided at the Evening Prayer, Liturgy of the Word on September 1 at St. Peter's, after which he greeted over a dozen ecumenical representatives who were present for the service.

Annual Encyclicals. It was customary for Patriarch Dimitrios (d. 1991) and is now for Patriarch Bartholomew to issue a statement on September 1 (almost) annually. It is titled an "encyclical" (a very brief letter, quite unlike the Catholic papal encyclicals).[149] From among the many statements on the environment by the patriarchs, it is argued that these encyclicals contain the seeds of the fundamental theological and spiritual principles that guide their ecological vision.[150] Particular Orthodox contributions to the theology of environment include the way liturgy serves as an integrating element of Orthodox belief and prayer. For Bartholomew, liturgy is closely linked to the reality of *communion*, especially as reflected in the interrelatedness of all creatures on the earth. The patriarch's repeated reminder that the human person is central to creation leads him to distinguish between *anthropomorphism* as the problem, not *anthropocentrism*. (Recall that Francis uses the phrase "tyrannical anthropocentrism" in his encyclical, nn. 68, 115–22, 137.)

Especially because icons hold a central place in Orthodox theology and practice, it is not surprising that Bartholomew argues that creation is linked to an icon in the same way as the human person, too, is created "in the image [or icon] and likeness of God" (Gen 1:26). He invites the Orthodox to contemplate the Creator God through the icon of the created world.[151] That we are all *priests* of creation, offering back to God that which God gave and gives to us in creation and redemption is a recurring and foundational theme in the patriarch's statements. Not surprisingly *eschatology* also figures prominently in his writings, especially as an eschatological vision requires action now for this generation and generations to come.

The following brief review of the contents of these encyclicals indicates the ways in which the Orthodox approach to the environment (largely based on scriptural, patristic, theological, and liturgical evidence) stands alongside the way Catholics respond to the same challenges by way of our social justice teachings (as articulated above).[152]

1989 – (Dimitrios) "The Church Cannot Remain Idle"
- Dimitrios refers to the patristic tradition to ground our collective response. His critique of consumption among many is placed within his treatment of "communion."

1990 – (Dimitrios) "Stewards, Not Proprietors"
- The patriarch urges acquiring an "ascetic ethos" regarding the use of the natural environment.

1992 – (Bartholomew) "Matter and Spirit"
[Because Dimitrios died in 1991, there was no encyclical that year.]
- The human person "stands at the border" between material and spiritual creation, and therefore bears significant responsibility for it.

1993 – "Creation *Ex Nihilo*"
- Through a "eucharistic use of the world," human beings are partakers of the world and are not consumers.

1994 – "All of Creation Groans"
- Bartholomew argues that a critique of individualism leads to collective responsibility, and a sacramental lens on creation leads to revering creation in a sacramental way. An ecological ethos includes a theology of the Eucharist and of all liturgy.

1995 – "King, Priest and Prophet"
- The ultimate destiny of all of humanity is to be priest, prophet, and king in the eternal kingdom and therefore to act here and now in a way that shows responsibility for the environment.

1996 – "A Spiritual, Not Scientific Problem"
- The patriarch addresses reconciliation as a way to combine a true and stable relationship between humankind and the physical world.

1997 – "Creation and Fall"
- Adam and Eve were given the command to labor and to exercise dominion to keep and preserve what was given them. He quotes the church fathers that a "merciful heart" will seek not only the heavenly kingdom, but also not tolerate any harm to animals and plants.

1998 – "Creation and Idol"
- Bartholomew recounts how "humanity" loved creation more than the Creator, made it an idol, and was/is not a "grateful consumer of creation." He applies this to the present, when humanity fashioned from the latest scientific discoveries "weapons of mass murder and a system of human annihilation."

1999 – "Creation and Creator"
- Bartholomew emphasizes the need to help all humanity to realize the "ethical and theological dimension" of the environmental crisis. He then outlines initiatives that the patriarchate is undertaking to this end.

2001 – "Harmony Between Matter and Spirit."
- The patriarch challenges human beings who are indifferent to maintaining the integrity and natural balance of the created order. He links the "overthrow" of this intended harmony (Gen 2:15) to disruptions in nature causing natural disasters and physical suffering.

2002 – "Unpaid Debt to Nature"
- In very direct language, the patriarch links "recent floods in Europe, India and Russia" that were "caused by global warming." He then challenges "the excessive waste of energy by isolated individuals."

2003 – "Extreme Weather and Extreme Behavior"
• Bartholomew addresses humanity's responsibility for rising temperatures, which have led to a number of extreme manifestations including extensive forest fires. He urges prayer for the protection of the environment and "for the repentance of man," whose thoughtless and arrogant actions "provokes most, not to say all, natural catastrophes."

2004 – "What Have We Achieved?"
• The patriarch looks back on the initiative the patriarchate has undertaken from the perspective of the church fathers who "have always insisted on the critical importance of self-examination as a pre-condition for spiritual growth." He credits the patriarchate for linking environmental issues with education, ethics, communication, justice, and poverty. He then asks how many Orthodox clergy and laity are willing to accept these teachings and implement them in their own practice.

2005 – "Doing, Not Just Saying"
• This follow-up to the previous encyclical applies its teachings to "vast expanses around polluting factories and industrial zones that emit toxic waste" and the sad fact that "the number of such dead expanses is constantly growing."

2006 – "Catastrophic Arrogance"
• Bartholomew critiques humanity's egocentrism in terms of the manner of overconsumption, the burden "on the natural environment by such pollution that the earth's temperature is rising and many of nature's balancing acts are now unstable, with all that this implies."

2007 – "Creation Continues to Groan"
• Relying on "environmental scientists" the document addresses the potential devastation caused by climate change for "the entire ecosystem," which is "interdependent upon one another like a chain." He laments that while awareness is increasing, action is decreasing. What is needed is "an environmental ethic" that is "Eucharistic,

accompanied by doxology toward God." The patriarch does not shrink from using the word "sin" when asserting, "the abuse of the world and participation therein without reference to God is sinful both before the Creator and before humanity as creation."

2009 – "The Global Market and the Natural Environment"
- In the context of the United Nations Climate Change Conference in Copenhagen (December of 2009) the patriarch asserts, "human progress is not just the accumulation of wealth and the thoughtless consumption of the earth's resources." He challenges (perhaps excoriates) those who find vast sums of money to support "the financial system that betrayed them" but are unwilling to allot even the least portion of money to remedy "the piteous state that creation has been reduced to because of these very values." He specifies food for the hungry and safe drinking water.

2010 – "The Financial Crisis and the Ecological Crisis"
- Citing the initiatives of Patriarch Dimitrios in the late 1980s, Patriarch Bartholomew addresses the present grave financial crisis and argues that any solution must be marked by a shift to environmentally viable development whose priority will be the environment.

2011 (Untitled)
- Bartholomew recognizes the important measures being taken to protect land, water, and air, but points to the need to also recognize the importance of "fauna and flora." He points in a particular way to humanity's special relationship with animals throughout the history of the world and their importance for a balanced ecosystem. Indeed, humanity's relationship with animals develops parallel to relationship with God, as the many examples of the saints and their nearness with God's creatures demonstrates.

2012 (Untitled)
- The patriarch asserts that the changes to the environment— observed by scientists and religious leaders alike—and the

excessive abuses taking place "are not inspired by God but initiated by humans." Then he appeals to prayer for the environment (begun in an official way by his predecessor, Dimitrios), which implores God to change the mindset of the world and speaks to each individual in a call for personal conversion and reconciliation with the environment.

2013 (Untitled)
- While approving of scientific research, the patriarch critiques those "activities invisible to the naked eye" that potentially bring imbalance and destruction to the environment, primarily the changes made to genetics and the manipulation of atomic phenomena that unleash vast power and have the potential to "obliterate all traces of life and civilization." The patriarch questions the arrogance behind such projects, which seek to oppose God's wisdom and improve his work, relying on human ingenuity rather than God's graciousness. A long period of discernment is necessary to understand such changes and manipulations to nature.

2014 (Untitled)
- Bartholomew applauds the efforts to improve the environmental situation advanced by various institutions and programs, but he observes that this, in itself, is insufficient. He calls for a renewal of the human family, an invitation for the indwelling of the Spirit in each person, and a change in mindset that respects "the contribution of every living being and vegetable in the universal liturgy of life."

2015 (Untitled)
- Additionally, later in the same year of the publication of Francis's *On Care for Our Common Home*, Bartholomew looks to the church fathers and the contemporary application of their mindset in the requirement for Christians to "restrict and reduce their needs as far as possible." Against consumerist habits of waste, vain desires of prosperity, and greed, the patriarch proposes an ethos of asceticism.

Quoting Francis's *On Care for Our Common Home*, he notes that the earth being "an immense pile of filth" not only describes the material, but also the spiritual. Christians are therefore called not only to material asceticism, but also to the proclamation of the joy and peace of the Gospel.

Summer Seminars on Ecology. Beginning in 1987, the leaders of Eastern Orthodoxy met to discuss issues related to ecology and the environment. From the early 1990s to the present, the Ecumenical Patriarchate in Istanbul has hosted regularly scheduled meetings on the environment with international and ecumenical participants. These meeting took two forms. One was held at the seminary on the island of Halki, whose topics included "Living in the Creation of the Lord" (1991), "Environment and Religious Education" (1994), "Environment and Ethics" (1995), "Environment and Communications" (1996), "Environment and Justice" (1997), and "Environment and Poverty" (1998). In addition, the Religious and Scientific Committee of the Orthodox church has held eight international, interdisciplinary, and interreligious symposia to study the fate of the rivers and seas, which cover two-thirds of the world's surface. The coincidence of the topics of these meetings on water and Pope Francis's reminder in the (early paragraphs of the) encyclical that access to clean water is a right (see nn. 27–31) should not be overlooked. The topics studied by this Orthodox committee are the following:[153]

- Revelation and the Environment (1995), held on a ship traveling through the Aegean and Eastern Mediterranean.
- The Back Sea in Crisis (1997), on the Black Sea.
- River of Life: Down the Danube to the Black Sea (1999).
- The Adriatic Sea: A Sea at Risk, a Unity of Purpose (2002).
    - This was particularly notable because of the document of the so-called Venice Declaration on environmental ethics cosigned by Pope John Paul II and Patriarch Bartholomew, emphasizing the moral and spiritual duty of all people.[154]
- The Baltic Sea: A Common Heritage, a Shared Responsibility (2003).

- The Amazon: Source of Life (2006), cosponsored by the patriarch and the Secretary-General of the United Nations, Kofi Annan.
- The Arctic: Mirror of Life (2007).
- Restoring Balance: The Great Mississippi River (2009).

Patriarch Bartholomew's Statements Quoted in On Care for Our Common Home. Given this admittedly brief review of statements from the Ecumenical Patriarchate, as well as the common declarations from the patriarch and the popes, it is not surprising that early on in *On Care for Our Common Home* Pope Francis pays the patriarch the enormous compliment of quoting him extensively in the first paragraphs. Those citations are the following:

- In n. 8 of *On Care for Our Common Home*, Francis quotes Bartholomew's *Message for the Day of Prayer for the Protection of Creation* (September 1, 2012).[155] Francis says, "Patriarch Bartholomew has spoken in particular of the need for each of us to repent of the ways we have harmed the planet, for 'inasmuch as we all generate small ecological damage,' we are called to acknowledge 'our contribution, smaller or greater, to the disfigurement and destruction of creation.'" That the same statement includes an admission of "sinfulness" and the need for "repentance" is particularly noteworthy.
- Again in n. 8 of *On Care for Our Common Home*, Francis quotes Patriarch Bartholomew's *Address in Santa Barbara, California* (November 8, 1997),[156] referencing in particular the "sins" against creation as articulated by the patriarch. The patriarch's own words articulate the problem: "for human beings...to destroy the biological diversity of God's creation; for human beings to degrade the integrity of the earth by causing changes in its climate, by stripping the earth of its natural forests or destroying its wetlands; for human beings to contaminate the earth's waters, its land, its air, and its life—these are sins." This quote is all the more notable because Pope Francis himself uses the word "sin" only four times in the rest of the encyclical, once in relation to sin in Genesis (n. 66) and when citing

the harmony St. Francis envisioned (nn. 66 and 218) and St. Bonaventure (n. 239) in the rest of the encyclical. The most direct assertion is in n. 66 where he states, "This is a far cry from our situation today, where sin is manifest in all its destructive power in wars, the various forms of violence and abuse, the abandonment of the most vulnerable, and attacks on nature."

- In n. 9 of *On Care for Our Common Home*, Francis quotes from the Bartholomew's *Lecture at the Monastery of Utstein, Norway* (June 23, 2003),[157] in which the patriarch argues—in the context of the importance of fasting in the Christian life—that a new asceticism "entails learning to give, and not simply to give up. It is a way of loving, of moving gradually away from what I want to what God's world needs. It is a liberation from fear, greed and compulsion."
- Again in n. 9 of *On Care for Our Common Home*, Francis quotes from Bartholomew's "Global Responsibility and Ecological Sustainability," Closing Remarks, Halki Summit I, Istanbul (June 20, 2012), in which the patriarch articulates in a capsule form a number of themes he regularly articulates. The patriarch asserts that Christians are called "to accept the world as a sacrament of communion, as a way of sharing with God and our neighbors on a global scale. It is our humble conviction that the divine and the human meet in the slightest detail in the seamless garment of God's creation, in the last speck of dust of our planet."[158]

Common Declarations between Roman Catholic and Orthodox Leadership. As noted above, one of the unique features of the 2002 Fourth Ecological Symposium on the Adriatic Sea was the issuing of the Common Declaration of Patriarch Bartholomew and John Paul II (the Venice Statement).[159] In it, both church leaders call for

an act of repentance on our part and a renewed attempt to view ourselves, one another, and the world around us within the perspective of the divine design for creation. The problem is not simply economic and technological; it is moral and spiritual. A solution at the economic and technological level can be found only if we undergo, in the most radical way, an inner change of heart, which can lead to a change in lifestyle and of unsustainable patterns of consumption and production. A genuine conversion in Christ will enable us to change the way we think and act.[160]

Then, after admitting humanity's faults and past actions to deal with environmental issues, they call for a new approach in thought, action, and prayer that addresses these environmental goals:

1. To think of the world's children when we reflect on and evaluate our options for action.

2. To be open to study the true values based on the natural law that sustain every human culture.

3. To use science and technology in a full and constructive way, while recognizing that the findings of science must always be evaluated in the light of the centrality of the human person, of the common good, and of the inner purpose of creation. Science may help us to correct the mistakes of the past, in order to enhance the spiritual and material well-being of the present and future generations. It is love for our children that will show us the path that we must follow into the future.

4. To be humble regarding the idea of ownership and to be open to the demands of solidarity. Our mortality and our weakness of judgment together warn us not to take irreversible actions with what we choose to regard as our property during our brief stay on this earth. We have not been entrusted with unlimited power over creation, we are only stewards of the common heritage.

5. To acknowledge the diversity of situations and responsibilities in the work for a better world environment. We do not expect every person and every institution to assume the same burden. Everyone has a part to play, but for the demands of justice and charity to be respected the most affluent societies must carry the greater burden, and from them is demanded a sacrifice greater than can be offered by the poor. Religions, governments, and institutions are faced by many different situations; but on the basis of

the principle of subsidiarity all of them can take on some tasks, some part of the shared effort.

6. To promote a peaceful approach to disagreement about how to live on this earth, about how to share it and use it, about what to change and what to leave unchanged. It is not our desire to evade controversy about the environment, for we trust in the capacity of human reason and the path of dialogue to reach agreement. We commit ourselves to respect the views of all who disagree with us, seeking solutions through open exchange, without resorting to oppression and domination.

7. It is not too late. God's world has incredible healing powers. Within a single generation, we could steer the earth toward our children's future. Let that generation start now, with God's help and blessing.[161]

On May 25, 2014, in Jerusalem Pope Francis and Patriarch Bartholomew issued a "Common Declaration,"[162] among whose paragraphs is the following about creation and the environment:

It is our profound conviction that the future of the human family depends also on how we safeguard—both prudently and compassionately, with justice and fairness—the gift of creation that our Creator has entrusted to us. Therefore, we acknowledge in repentance the wrongful mistreatment of our planet, which is tantamount to sin before the eyes of God. We reaffirm our responsibility and obligation to foster a sense of humility and moderation so that all may feel the need to respect creation and to safeguard it with care. Together, we pledge our commitment to raising awareness about the stewardship of creation; we appeal to all people of goodwill to consider ways of living less wastefully and more frugally, manifesting less greed and more generosity for the protection of God's world and the benefit of His people.[163]

While comparatively modest in tone and rather brief, the very fact that this paragraph is found in a statement of ten paragraphs is significant.

A STATEMENT FROM AN ECUMENICAL DIALOGUE: ROMAN CATHOLIC AND UNITED METHODIST (NATIONAL) DIALOGUE

Among the more recent documents from officially sponsored ecumenical dialogues on ecology is the joint statement of the participants in the Roman Catholic–United Methodist dialogue on the Eucharist and ecology titled "Heaven and Earth Are Full of Your Glory."[164] Meeting twice yearly from 2008 to 2012, a dozen dialogue partners officially designated by their respective church bodies worked through a number of historical, ethical, systematic, and liturgical issues surrounding the Eucharist and ecology. In the preamble, the participants stated that the joint statement drew on the historic liturgy of both churches for a framework within which to theologize about Eucharist and ecology. In this way the liturgy—*lex orandi, lex credendi*—became an important methodological statement and challenge for the dialogue partners to glean and articulate a common stance on Eucharist and ecology.

In the introductory paragraphs, the participants assert the following:

1. "Heaven and earth are full of your glory." With this acclamation, Methodists and Catholics join the whole company of heaven in praising the God of all creation. When we celebrate the Eucharist, we offer thanks to the Father for the goodness of all the things that he has made, visible and invisible, we participate in the suffering, death, and resurrection of Jesus Christ (the Paschal Mystery), and we anticipate in the Holy Spirit the time when God renews heaven and earth (cf. Rev 21:1).

2. United Methodists and Roman Catholics in the United States have been engaged in formal ecumenical dialogue for almost forty years. Often these dialogues have focused on questions of dogmatic theology. The intra-ecclesial dialogue has been crucial in defining and extending the common ground between both communions. However, in this current round the topic is not a disputed doctrine as such but a common concern. "Our two communions

are at an important crossroads. In the wake of the World Methodist Council's adoption of the Joint Declaration on the Doctrine of Justification we are being asked to consider how agreement on the doctrine of justification positions our dialogues to advance, with renewed vigor, along the path to full communion in the unity of Christ's body, the Church. One way in which we can deepen our bonds of communion is to demonstrate how our churches can speak with a common voice about one of the great moral challenges of our age. The world is impatient with our disunity, and our remaining doctrinal divergences should not prevent us from speaking together and working together on behalf of God's creation. In this way, "we seek to move from justification to justice, obedience to the divine Creator and our gratitude for the divine handiwork that finds apt from the solid ground of our common baptismal faith to a prophetic witness that shows our expression in the celebration of the Eucharist."

3. We believe that we can and should offer a joint prophetic witness on a significant challenge facing both our communions regarding the relation of humanity to the rest of the natural world. In Scripture, Jesus rejects the Pharisees' appeal for signs from heaven. Jesus chastises the Pharisees for being able to interpret the appearance of the skies while being unable to interpret the signs of the times (cf. Matt 16:3). In our time, the appearance of the skies has become a sign of the times. The threat of climate destabilization, the destruction of the ozone layer, and the loss of bio-diversity point to a disordered relation between humankind, other living beings and the rest of earth. United Methodists and Roman Catholics have interpreted the signs of these times of ecological crisis as a summons to an ecumenical response.

The balance of the statement is structured as follows:

1. The Eucharist and the Unity of Creation and Redemption
2. Creation as the Mystery of Our Origin Encountered

3. Eucharist as the Wholeness of the Christian Mystery Encountered

[The parts of the church's respective liturgies are then commented on, noting ecological resonances and expressions.]

A. Gathering
B. Word
C. Altar Table
D. Sending

4. Conclusion

Among the operating premises for the dialogue and the final statement were (1) the importance of the liturgy as expressing the church's life and belief (including the "work of human hands"), (2) the principle of sacramentality wherein the divine is manifested in nature and the human, and (3) that communion and ecclesiology are central to any appreciation for ecology in church circles. These premises as understood by the participants were not meant to be constraining but rather open-ended and inviting of the kind of high quality theology and reflection on liturgical practice this ecumenical dialogue deserved (and other ecumenical dialogues deserve).

CONCLUSION

It is very common in modern papal encyclicals that popes quote themselves, previous popes, and other documents of the magisterium (for example, church councils, and so on). That Pope Francis does the same thing in *On Care for Our Common Home* is therefore no surprise. His own contributions in the encyclical *Lumen Fidei* (understanding that it was largely Benedict XVI's effort) and especially in the postsynodal exhortation *Evangelii Gaudium* lead directly to *On Care for Our Common Home.*

As this summary has shown, there is a richness and depth to many statements of the popes preceding Pope Francis which have shaped Catholic social teaching. His immediate predecessors, John Paul II and Benedict XVI left him—and us—an important legacy in teaching on the environment that laid the groundwork for him to capitalize on their teachings and to advance on them (as will be seen in chapter 2).

However, as noted in this chapter, that the pope quotes so extensively from the documents of bishops' conferences is something very new. Whatever else can be said, it is an example of collegiality in episcopal teaching in practice. The ecclesiological lens through which Paul VI viewed the world by starting the visits of modern popes to countries outside the Vatican and his often overlooked encyclical *Ecclesiam Suam* (1964)[165] has been expanded by Pope Francis to offer us all a wide-angle lens on the church universal and international, to include emphasis on the developing world. Reliance on no fewer than a score of such documents from episcopal conferences, with many from "the periphery," indicates that this pope seeks to make a compelling case on behalf of and with teachings of the hierarchies in many parts of the developed and (especially) the developing world.

Finally, the ecumenical agenda from Vatican II was revived and directed to include the environment as a most pressing issue for the churches to face into because of the very survival of "our common home." It is no wonder that popes from John Paul II on have called this a "moral crisis" twenty-five years before the publication of *On Care for Our Common Home.*

NOTES

1. Given the breadth and depth of what Pope Francis offers in the encyclical (as can be seen by reviewing its table of contents), the review that follows is meant to express and summarize salient themes from a number of authoritative church sources. It cannot be exhaustive, however, in terms of laying out the magisterial background for the number and varied themes in the encyclical and the sources on which the pope relies (for example, theologians, spiritual writers, authors relating faith and science, and so on).

2. This list is meant to be indicative and illustrative of the wealth of theological and spiritual insight that can be gleaned from contemporary church documents on the environment. The self-imposed limitation reflects those documents that were directly influential on the pope's thought in the encyclical. The treatment of the documents from the

(American) USCCB reflects their concern about this issue and would be of particular import for American readers. The method used here could be applied by other readers who want to study and summarize documents from their native episcopal conferences.

3. See Austin Ivereigh, *The Great Reformer: Francis and the Making of a Radical Pope* (New York: Holt and Co., 2015), 122.

4. Ecumenical Patriarch Bartholomew and Archbishop of Canterbury Justin Welby, "Climate Change and Moral Responsibility" *New York Times*, op-ed (June 19, 2015), http://www.nytimes.com/2015/06/20/opinion/climate-change-and-moral-responsibility.html?_.

5. See, among others, http://www.nature.com/news/faith-and-science-can-find-common-ground-1.18083.

6. Kevin W. Irwin, *Serving the Body of Christ: The Magisterium on Eucharist and Ordained Priesthood* (New York: Paulist Press, 2013), 1–4.

7. See, for example, Joseph A. Komonchak, "*Humanae Vitae* and Its Reception: Ecclesiological Reflections," *Theological Studies* (June 1978): 221–57. In this article, Komonchak references a survey from Office of Population Research at Princeton University, published in *Family Planning Perspectives* (September/October 1977) and reported in the *New York Times* (September 26, 1977).

From my point of view, the classic article that articulates the possibility of dissent from the ordinary magisterium is Joseph A. Komonchak, "Ordinary Papal Magisterium and Religious Assent," in *Contraception: Authority and Dissent*, ed. C. Curran, 101–26 (New York: Herder & Herder, 1969) in which he summarizes the opinions of a number of theologians from the manualist theological tradition. Among others, see Richard Gaillardetz, *On Whose Authority? A Primer on the Scripture, the Magisterium, and the Sense of the Faithful* (Collegeville: Liturgical Press, 2003).

8. John Paul II, apostolic letter *motu proprio Apostolos Suos* (May 21, 1998), http://w2.vatican.va/content/john-paul-ii/en/motu_proprio/documents/hf_jp-ii_motu-proprio_22071998_apostolos-suos.html.

9. Hereafter "n." refers to the text of the encyclical unless otherwise indicated.

10. Vatican II, Decree *Christus Dominus* on the Pastoral Office of Bishops (October 28, 1965), http://www.vatican.va/archive/hist_councils/ii_vatican_council/documents/vat-ii_decree_19651028_christus-dominus_en.html.

Paul VI, apostolic letter *motu proprio Ecclesiae Sanctae* (August 6, 1966), http://w2.vatican.va/content/paul-vi/en/motu_proprio/documents/hf_p-vi_motu-proprio_19660806_ecclesiae-sanctae.html.

11. In 1966, the U.S. bishops erected two entities: the National Conference of Catholic Bishops, for issues within the church, and the United

States Catholic Conference, for matters outside the church such as immigration and international relations. In 2001, these were merged into the present structure.

12. See, for example, icelweb.org/copyright.htm.

13. It is common knowledge that this clarification by Pope John Paul II came as a reaction to the issuance by the USCCB (then called the National Conference of Catholic Bishops) of two pastoral letters, one on nuclear arms titled *The Challenge of Peace: God's Promise and Our Response* (1983) and the other on the economy titled *Economic Justice for All* (1986). A number of questions emerged after these documents were issued about the possibility that the issuance of such documents might be perceived to be a "parallel magisterium" or that they would erode the authority and responsibility of the diocesan bishop, or that the elaborate process of consultation beyond the circle of bishops and the process or this kind of collegiality of bishops might diminish the authority of the Holy See (see below).

14. U.S. National Conference of Catholic Bishops, "The Challenge of Peace: God's Promise and Our Response: A Pastoral Letter on War and Peace" (May 3, 1983), http://www.usccb.org/upload/challenge-peace-gods-promise-our-response-1983.pdf.

U.S. National Conference of Catholic Bishops, "Economic Justice for All: Pastoral Letter on Catholic Social Teaching and the US Economy" (1986), http://www.usccb.org/upload/economic_justice_for_all.pdf.

15. J. Schotte, "Vatican Synthesis," *Origins* 12 (April 7, 1983): 692.

16. *International Theological Commission: Texts and Documents 1969–1985*, ed. M. Sharkey (San Francisco: Ignatius, 1989), 285–86.

17. John Paul II, *Apostolos Suos*, 12.

18. *Ibid.*

19. See Francis Sullivan, "The Teaching Authority of Episcopal Conferences," *Theological Studies* 63 (2002): 472–93.

20. Recall the distinction that John Paul II made in *Apostolos Suos* between "collegiality" and a "collegial spirit." This distinction and these phrases are new. How well this distinction can help to clarify the actions Francis has taken toward collegiality and synodality remain to be seen.

21. These points assume some basic principles, such as the following:

- The well-known principle that particular laws must be in conformity with universal laws (except in cases when a particular law already exists and is not explicitly contradicted by a universal law; *Code of Canon Law* canon 135.2 with canon 20) returns to an exercise by universal law and so gives the weight (and indeed the binding authority) to the higher authority.

- In comparing Episcopal Conference documents to one another, documents on matters concerning an area of specific competency given by common law or special mandate of the pope are of greater weight than documents on matters concerning the general joint exercise of the episcopal ministry in responding to regional issues or circumstances (the latter would include the documents of the bishops of the Appalachian and Watershed regions, discussed below in section 4, subsection 4).
- When dealing with matters in which specific competency has been granted to an Episcopal Conference, *Code of Canon Law* canon 381.1 makes clear that, if that specific competency has been reserved to that ecclesiastical authority, that ecclesiastical authority has the proper power regarding that matter, even over the individual bishop.

See Francis Sullivan, "The Teaching Authority of Episcopal Conferences"; Francis Sullivan, *Creative Fidelity: Weighing and Interpreting Documents of the Magisterium* (Eugene: Wipf and Stock, 2003); Avery Dulles, *Magisterium: Teacher and Guardian of the Faith* (Naples: Sapientia Press, 2007); Francis Morrisey, *The Canonical Significance of Papal and Curial Pronouncements* (Washington, DC: Canon Law Society of America, 1978); and John Huels, "Assessing the Weight of Documents on the Liturgy," *Worship* 74 (2000): 117–35.

22. An additional point of interest, though less directly related to the immediate concerns here, include how letters or messages from the pope to a specific local or regional community, when he is acting in the "collegial spirit," should be compared to the letters or messages of the local bishop or bishops' conferences, the latter, significantly, being entrusted by the church with the pastoral care of that particular flock. A similar concern is how the letters or messages of individual bishops compares to those of episcopal conferences, taking note of the discussion on Episcopal Conferences in section 1, subsection 3 above and *Code of Canon Law,* canon 381.1.

23. Vatican II, Pastoral Constitution on the Church in the Modern World, *Gaudium et Spes* (December 7, 1965),http://www.vatican.va/archive/hist_councils/ii_vatican_council/documents/vat-ii_const_19651207_gaudium-et-spes_en.html.

24. In much English-language literature today, the term *environment* refers to the life context in which we live, our habitat as given us by God and for which we are responsible. *Ecology* (from the Greek *oikos*, "home") refers to our being at home on the earth, and "ecological crisis" refers to the destruction that has been worked to make the earth, our home, less inhabitable for a variety of species. *Creation* refers to the whole created

world and all living beings as gifts from God the creator. In chapter 2, we will address the distinctions that Pope Francis makes between "nature" and "creation," "ecology" and "environment."

25. This was published by the Pontifical Council for Justice and Peace (Vatican City: Libreria Editrice Vaticana, 2005) and other editions.

26. Francis, encyclical letter *Laudato Si'*, On Care for Our Common Home (May 24, 2015), http://w2.vatican.va/content/francesco/en/encyc licals/documents/papa-francesco_20150524_enciclica-laudato-si.html, n. 3.

27. While our treatment of official church teaching begins with Vatican II, John XXIII's encyclical *Mater et Magistra* contains a wealth of information, direction, and official church teaching on a number of social issues. See John XXIII's encyclical letter *Mater et Magistra* (May 15, 1961), http://w2.vatican.va/content/john-xxiii/en/encyclicals/documents/hf_j-xxiii_enc_15051961_mater.html.

28. Paul VI, encyclical letter *Populorum Progressio* (March 26, 1967), http://w2.vatican.va/content/paul-vi/en/encyclicals/documents/hf_p-vi_enc_26031967_populorum.html.

29. Paul VI, apostolic letter *Octogesima Adveniens* (May 14, 1971), http://w2.vatican.va/content/paul-vi/en/apost_letters/documents/hf_p-vi_apl_19710514_octogesima-adveniens.html.

30. Paul VI, *Message to Mr. Maurice F. Strong, Secretary-General of the Conference on the Environment* (June 1, 1972), http://w2.vatican.va/content/paul-vi/en/messages/pont-messages/documents/hf_p-vi_mess_19720605_conferenza-ambiente.html.

31. *Ibid.*

32. In noting that the environment is an urgent issue, he called for a radical commitment toward its preservation based on the biblical injunction (from Gen 1:31 and 1 Tim 4:4) that all creation was "good" and offered St. Francis of Assisi as a significant Catholic exemplar of a Christian contemplative stance that would witness to the harmony of human beings with and in nature (*ibid.*). Then, in 1979, John Paul II named St. Francis of Assisi as patron of ecology. See John Paul II's apostolic letter *Inter Sanctos* (1979), http://w2.vatican.va/content/john-paul-ii/la/apost_letters/1979/documents/hf_jp-ii_apl_19791129_inter-sanctos.html.

33. Paul VI, *Message for the Fifth World-Wide Day of Environment* (June 5, 1977), https://w2.vatican.va/content/paul-vi/en/messages/pont-mess ages/documents/hf_p-vi_mess_19770605_world-day-ambiente.html.

34. *Ibid.*

35. In addition to the documents summarized here, see Marybeth Lorbiecki's *Following St. Francis: John Paul II's Call for Ecological Action* (New York: Random House, Rizzoli Ex Libris, 2014).

36. John Paul II, encyclical letter *Redemptor Hominis* (March 4, 1979), http://w2.vatican.va/content/john-paul-ii/en/encyclicals/documents/hf_jp-ii_enc_04031979_redemptor-hominis.html.

37. *Ibid.* He also discusses redemption as a "new creation" (n. 8).

38. *Ibid.*

39. John Paul II, *Homily at Living History Farm, Des Moines [Iowa, USA]* (October 4, 1979), http://w2.vatican.va/content/john-paul-ii/en/homilies/1979/documents/hf_jp-ii_hom_19791004_usa-des-moines.html.

40. *Ibid.*

41. John Paul II, *Message to the General Assembly of the United Nations* (August 22, 1980), https://w2.vatican.va/content/john-paul-ii/en/speeches/1980/august/documents/hf_jp-ii_spe_19800822_messaggio-onu.html.

42. "L'energia è un bene universale che la divina provvidenza ha messo a servizio dell'uomo, di tutti gli uomini" (John Paul II, "Message to Participants in the Study Week on Energy and Humanity" [November 14, 1980], https://w2.vatican.va/content/john-paul-ii/it/speeches/1980/november/documents/hf_jp_ii_spe_19801114_energia-umanita.html; also available in French, Spanish, and Portuguese).

43. John Paul II, encyclical letter *Laborem Exercens* (September 14, 1981), http://w2.vatican.va/content/john-paul-ii/en/encyclicals/documents/hf_jp-ii_enc_14091981_laborem-exercens.html.

44. *Ibid.*

45. *Ibid.* "Original ordering" is an interesting phrase, especially given the more recent debates about evolution and whether one holds an evolutionary understanding of creation.

46. John Paul II, *Address to the Scientists on the Occasion of the Study Week Organized by the Pontifical Academy of Sciences* (October 2, 1984), http://w2.vatican.va/content/john-paul-ii/en/speeches/1984/october/documents/hf_jp-ii_spe_19841002_pontificia-accademia-scienze.html.

47. "Possa un più diffuso rispetto per la natura favorire anche il cammino della pace, bene di fondamentale importanza per l'uomo di oggi e di sempre" (John Paul II, *Catechesis* [June 4, 1986], http://w2.vatican.va/content/john-paul-ii/it/audiences/1986/documents/hf_jp-ii_aud_19860604.html).

48. John Paul II, *Address to the Participants in the Study Week Organized by the Pontifical Academy of Sciences* (November 6, 1987), https://w2.vatican.va/content/john-paul-ii/en/speeches/1987/november/documents/hf_jp-ii_spe_19871106_accademia-scienze.html.

49. "La creazione e la legittima autonomia delle cose create" (John Paul II, *Catechesis* [April 2, 1986], https://w2.vatican.va/content/john-paul-ii/it/audiences/1986/documents/hf_jp-ii_aud_19860402.html).

Later that same year, he referred again to *ecology* in an address to the Pontifical Academy of Sciences when speaking about the fundamental rapport between human beings and nature which is violated by the "violent alterations" in the environment. See n. 8 of John Paul II, *Address to Participants in the Plenary Assembly of the Pontifical Academy of Sciences on the 50th Anniversary of Its Foundation* (October 28, 1986), https://w2.vatican.va/content/john-paul-ii/it/speeches/1986/october/documents/hf_jp-ii_spe_19861028_pont-accademia-scienze.html.

50. "L'uomo, immagine di Dio, soggetto di conoscenza e di liberta" (John Paul II, *Catechesis* [April 23, 1986], https://w2.vatican.va/content/john-paul-ii/it/audiences/1986/documents/hf_jp-ii_aud_19860423.html).

51. John Paul II, encyclical letter *Sollicitudo Rei Socialis* (December 30, 1987), http://w2.vatican.va/content/john-paul-ii/en/encyclicals/documents/hf_jp-ii_enc_30121987_sollicitudo-rei-socialis.html.

52. It is noteworthy that in his 1989 Easter message he speaks of the reconciliation accomplished through Christ's blood, a reconciliation of human beings with God, with themselves, and with nature, and of human beings' responsibility for creation. See John Paul II, *Messaggio Urbi et Orbi Di Sua Santità Giovanni Paolo II* (March 26, 1989), https://w2.vatican.va/content/john-paul-ii/it/messages/urbi/documents/hf_jp-ii_mes_19890326_easter-urbi.html.

53. John Paul II, *Sollicitudo Rei Socialis*, n. 29.

54. *Ibid.*

55. *Ibid.*

56. John Paul II, *Peace with God the Creator, Peace with All of Creation, Message for the World Day of Peace* (January 1, 1990), http://w2.vatican.va/content/john-paul-ii/en/messages/peace/documents/hf_jp-ii_mes_19891208_xxiii-world-day-for-peace.html.

57. Especially when coupled with Pope Paul's citing St. Francis of Assisi's "contemplative stance" toward creation (see fn. 5 above) and with (what we will term) the "sacramental vision" espoused in *Centesimus Annus* (n. 37) (John Paul II, encyclical letter *Centesimus Annus* [May 1, 1991], http://w2.vatican.va/content/john-paul-ii/en/encyclicals/documents/hf_jp-ii_enc_01051991_centesimus-annus.html).

58. This document is particularly notable because it immediately preceded the World Council of Churches (Seventh) Assembly at Canberra, Australia (February 7–20, 1991), whose theme was "Come Holy Spirit—Renew the Whole Creation." See *Signs of the Spirit*, Official Report, Seventh Assembly, edited by Michael Kinnamon (Geneva: WCC Publications, 1991).

59. See John Paul II's apostolic letter *Inter Sanctos* (November 29, 1979), http://w2.vatican.va/content/john-paul-ii/la/apost_letters/1979/documents/hf_jp-ii_apl_19791129_inter-sanctos.html.

60. John Paul II, *Address to the Participants in the Study Week Organized by the Pontifical Academy of Sciences* (May 18, 1990), https://w2.vatican.va/content/john-paul-ii/en/speeches/1990/may/documents/hf_jp-ii_spe_19900518_acc-scienze.html.

61. *Ibid.*, n.3: "If an unjustified search for profit is sometimes responsible for deforestation of tropical ecosystems and the loss of their biodiversity, it is also true that a desperate fight against poverty threatens to deplete these important resources of the planet." This is a quotation of n. 3 of John Paul II, *Address to the Participants in the Study Week Organized by the Pontifical Academy of Sciences* (May 18, 1990), https://w2.vatican.va/content/john-paul-ii/en/speeches/1990/may/documents/hf_jp-ii_spe_19900518_acc-scienze.html.

62. *Ibid.*

63. John Paul II, *Message to Participants in the Symposium Sponsored by the Pontifical Academy of Sciences and the Pontifical Council for Culture* (October 4, 1991), https://w2.vatican.va/content/john-paul-ii/it/speeches/1991/october/documents/hf_jp-ii_spe_19911004_simposio-scienze-cultura.html (available in Italian and French). He also states, "science and religion...can renew culture" (n. 8).

64. *Ibid.*, n. 7.

65. John Paul II, *Address to Scholars Participating in the Study Week on 'Resources and Population'* (November 22, 1991), https://w2.vatican.va/content/john-paul-ii/en/speeches/1991/november/documents/hf_jp-ii_spe_19911122_risorse-popolazione.html. He also notes that "population problems involve jobs, education and living standards too" (n. 7).

66. *Ibid.*

67. *Ibid.*, n. 8.

68. John Paul II, *Address to the Participants in the Workshop on 'Chemical Hazards in Developing Countries'* (October 22, 1993), http://w2.vatican.va/content/john-paul-ii/en/speeches/1993/october/documents/hf_jp-ii_spe_19931022_rischi-chimici.html.

69. John Paul II, *Centesimus Annus*, n. 37.

70. John Paul II, encyclical letter *Evangelium Vitae* (March 25, 1995), http://w2.vatican.va/content/john-paul-ii/en/encyclicals/documents/hf_jp-ii_enc_25031995_evangelium-vitae.html.

71. John Paul II, *Message for Lent 1992, Called to Share the Table of Creation* (June 29, 1991), https://w2.vatican.va/content/john-paul-ii/en/messages/lent/documents/hf_jp-ii_mes_29021992_lent-1992.html.

Background

72. John Paul II, *Message for Lent 1993* (September 19, 1992), https://w2.vatican.va/content/john-paul-ii/en/messages/lent/documents/hf_jp-ii_mes_19091992_lent-1993.html.

73. John Paul II, *Message for Lent 1996, 'Give them something to eat'* (September 8, 1995), https://w2.vatican.va/content/john-paul-ii/en/messages/lent/documents/hf_jp-ii_mes_19950908_lent-1996.html.

74. John Paul II, apostolic letter *Orientale Lumen* (May 2, 1995), http://w2.vatican.va/content/john-paul-ii/en/apost_letters/1995/documents/hf_jp-ii_apl_19950502_orientale-lumen.html.

75. John Paul II, apostolic letter *Dies Domini* (May 31, 1998), https://w2.vatican.va/content/john-paul-ii/en/apost_letters/1998/documents/hf_jp-ii_apl_05071998_dies-domini.html.

76. While these hymns are still assigned as part of the revised Liturgy of the Hours (in the Latin *edition typica*), it is very common for them to be replaced by other hymns that do not express this creation/redemption motif. This is an example of where the revised liturgy in the Roman Catholic Church has invited the possibility (perhaps probability) that what is used in celebration is not what was envisioned by the architects of the reform.

77. John Paul II, *Catechesis* (January 26, 2000), http://w2.vatican.va/content/john-paul-ii/en/audiences/2000/documents/hf_jp-ii_aud_20000126.html.

78. John Paul II, *Catechesis* (August 2, 2000), http://w2.vatican.va/content/john-paul-ii/en/audiences/2000/documents/hf_jp-ii_aud_20000802.html.

79. John Paul II, *Catechesis* (January 17, 2001), http://w2.vatican.va/content/john-paul-ii/en/audiences/2001/documents/hf_jp-ii_aud_20010117.html.

80. John Paul II, encyclical letter *Ecclesia de Eucharistia* (April 17, 2003), http://www.vatican.va/holy_father/special_features/encyclicals/documents/hf_jp-ii_enc_20030417_ecclesia_eucharistia_en.html.

81. *Ibid*.

82. Benedict XVI, *Catechesis* (November 9, 2005), http://w2.vatican.va/content/benedict-xvi/en/audiences/2005/documents/hf_ben-xvi_aud_20051109.html.

83. Benedict XVI, *Homily for Corpus Christi* (June 15, 2006), http://w2.vatican.va/content/benedict-xvi/en/homilies/2006/documents/hf_ben-xvi_hom_20060615_corpus-christi.html.

84. Benedict XVI, *Address to the Diplomatic Corps* (January 8, 2007), http://w2.vatican.va/content/benedict-xvi/en/speeches/2007/january/documents/hf_ben-xvi_spe_20070108_diplomatic-corps.html.

85. Benedict XVI, *Address to the Clergy of the Diocese of Bolzano-Bressanone* (August 6, 2008), http://w2.vatican.va/content/benedict-xvi/en/speeches/2008/august/documents/hf_ben-xvi_spe_20080806_clero-bressanone.html.

86. Benedict XVI, encyclical letter *Caritas in Veritate* (June 29, 2009), http://w2.vatican.va/content/benedict-xvi/en/encyclicals/documents/hf_ben-xvi_enc_20090629_caritas-in-veritate.html.

87. Benedict XVI, *Message for the World Day of Peace 2010* (December 8, 2009), http://w2.vatican.va/content/benedict-xvi/en/messages/peace/documents/hf_ben-xvi_mes_20091208_xliii-world-day-peace.html.

88. "CCC" refers to *The Catechism of the Catholic Church* (Washington, DC: United States Catholic Conference, 1994) (among other versions).

89. Benedict XVI, *Address to the German Bundestag* (September 22, 2011), http://w2.vatican.va/content/benedict-xvi/en/speeches/2011/september/documents/hf_ben-xvi_spe_20110922_reichstag-berlin.html.

90. Francis, *Homily, Mass of Imposition of the Pallium and Bestowal of the Fisherman's Ring for the Beginning of the Petrine Ministry of the Bishop of Rome* (March 19, 2013) https://w2.vatican.va/content/francesco/en/homilies/2013/documents/papa-francesco_20130319_omelia-inizio-pontificato.html.

91. Francis, *Catechesis* (June 5, 2013), https://w2.vatican.va/content/francesco/en/audiences/2013/documents/papa-francesco_20130605_udienza-generale.html.

92. N. 34 of *Lumen Fidei* reads as follows:

The light of love proper to faith can illumine the questions of our own time about truth. Truth nowadays is often reduced to the subjective authenticity of the individual, valid only for the life of the individual. A common truth intimidates us, for we identify it with the intransigent demands of totalitarian systems. But if truth is a truth of love, if it is a truth disclosed in personal encounter with the Other and with others, then it can be set free from its enclosure in individuals and become part of the common good. As a truth of love, it is not one that can be imposed by force; it is not a truth that stifles the individual. Since it is born of love, it can penetrate to the heart, to the personal core of each man and woman. Clearly, then, faith is not intransigent, but grows in respectful coexistence with others. One who believes may not be presumptuous; on the contrary, truth leads to humility, since believers know that, rather than ourselves possessing truth, it is truth which embraces and possesses us. Far from making us inflexible, the security of faith sets us on a journey; it enables witness and dialogue with all.

Since it is born of love, it can penetrate to the heart, to the personal core of each man and woman. Clearly, then, faith is not intransigent, but grows in respectful coexistence with others. One who believes may not be presumptuous; on the contrary, truth leads to humility, since believers know that, rather than ourselves possessing truth, it is truth which embraces and possesses us. Far from making us inflexible, the security of faith sets us on a journey; it enables witness and dialogue with all.

Nor is the light of faith, joined to the truth of love, extraneous to the material world, for love is always lived out in body and spirit; the light of faith is an incarnate light radiating from the luminous life of Jesus. It also illumines the material world, trusts its inherent order and knows that it calls us to an ever widening path of harmony and understanding. The gaze of science thus benefits from faith: faith encourages the scientist to remain constantly open to reality in all its inexhaustible richness. Faith awakens the critical sense by preventing research from being satisfied with its own formulae and helps it to realize that nature is always greater. By stimulating wonder before the profound mystery of creation, faith broadens the horizons of reason to shed greater light on the world which discloses itself to scientific investigation.

(Francis, encyclical letter *Lumen Fidei*, June 29, 2013, http://w2.vatican.va/content/francesco/en/encyclicals/documents/papa-francesco_20130629_enciclica-lumen-fidei.html).

93. Francis, *Homily at Lampedusa* (July 8, 2013), https://w2.vatican.va/content/francesco/en/homilies/2013/documents/papa-francesco_20130708_omelia-lampedusa.html.

94. Francis, postsynodal apostolic exhortation *Evangelii Gaudium* (November 24, 2013), http://w2.vatican.va/content/francesco/en/apost_exhortations/documents/papa-francesco_esortazione-ap_20131124_evangelii-gaudium.html, n. 14.

95. See the following footnotes of *On Care for Our Common Home* for these references, given respectively: fnn. 33, 67, 91, 115, 119, 130, 139, 142, 151, and 155.

96. The texts read as follows:

Evangelii Gaudium, n. 56: The thirst for power and possessions knows no limits. In this system, which tends to devour everything which stands in the way of increased profits, whatever is fragile, like the environment, is defenseless before the interests of a deified market, which become the only rule.

Evangelii Gaudium, n. 181: Our mandate is to "go into all the world and proclaim the good news to the whole creation" (Mk 16:15), for "the creation waits with eager longing for the revealing of the children of God" (Rom 8:19). Here, "the creation" refers to every aspect of human life; consequently, "the mission of proclaiming the good news of Jesus Christ has a universal destination. Its mandate of charity encompasses all dimensions of existence, all individuals, all areas of community life, and all peoples. Nothing human can be alien to it." True Christian hope, which seeks the eschatological kingdom, always generates history.

Evangelii Gaudium, n. 215: There are other weak and defenseless beings who are frequently at the mercy of economic interests or indiscriminate exploitation. I am speaking of creation as a whole. We human beings are not only the beneficiaries but also the stewards of other creatures. Thanks to our bodies, God has joined us so closely to the world around us that we can feel the desertification of the soil almost as a physical ailment, and the extinction of a species as a painful disfigurement. Let us not leave in our wake a swath of destruction and death which will affect our own lives and those of future generations…[after which follows an extensive quote about this reality from the Catholic Bishops Conference of the Philippines pastoral letter *What Is Happening to Our Beautiful Land?* (January 29, 1988)].

Evangelii Gaudium, n. 257: As believers, we also feel close to those who do not consider themselves part of any religious tradition, yet sincerely seek the truth, goodness and beauty which we believe have their highest expression and source in God. We consider them as precious allies in the commitment to defending human dignity, in building peaceful coexistence between peoples and in protecting creation.

97. Francis, *Address to the FAO* (November 20, 2014), https://w2.vatican.va/content/francesco/en/speeches/2014/november/documents/papa-francesco_20141120_visita-fao.html.

98. John Paul II, Message for the Opening of the First International Conference on Nutrition (December 5, 1992), http://w2.vatican.va/content/john-paul-ii/en/speeches/1992/december/documents/hf_jp-ii_spe_19921205_conference-on-nutrition.html.

99. Francis, video *Message on the Occasion of the Meeting of National and International Representatives: "Expo of Ideas 2015—Toward the Milan Charter"* (February 7, 2015), http://w2.vatican.va/content/francesco/en/

messages/pont-messages/2015/documents/papa-francesco_20150207_
video-messaggio-expo-milano.html.

100. Francis, *Catechesis* (April 15, 2015), https://w2.vatican.va/content/
francesco/en/audiences/2015/documents/papa-francesco_20150415_
udienza-generale.html.

101. It is notable that the USCCB document "Renewing the Earth"
opens with this phrase: "At its core, the environmental crisis is a moral
challenge. It calls us to examine how we use and share the goods of the
earth, what we pass on to future generations, and how we live in harmony
with God's creation" (USCCB, "Renewing the Earth: An Invitation to
Reflection and Action on Environment in Light of Catholic Social Teaching" [November 14, 1991], http://www.usccb.org/issues-and-action/
human-life-and-dignity/environment/renewing-the-earth.cfm).

102. Recall that in *Apostolos Suos* (1998) (as noted above, section 1, subsection 3), John Paul II distinguished between "collegiality" and a "collegial
spirit." In what follows, "collegiality" in the encyclical means two things.
First, "collegiality" means that the pope utilized insights from documents
on the environment from episcopal conferences, which should be characterized as an act of collegiality. It is more than worth noting that previous
popes did not cite episcopal conference documents. More often than not,
they cited previous papal statements (their own and those of preceding
popes). Second, "collegiality" means that the pope utilized insights from
documents on the environment from other Christian traditions, especially
the Orthodox, who have more than matched the Roman Catholic Church's
efforts in the area of the environment and ecology.

103. As previously noted, what is less clear is trying to delineate a magisterial and ecclesiological framework to contextualize the relative weight
one ought to give them. While such an *a priori* clarity is normally helpful
in assessing church documents, at the same time the way documents are
valued, used, and relied on is itself its own measure of the effectiveness
and "weight" of the magisterium.

104. CELAM, *Aparecida Concluding Document* (May 2007), http://www.
celam.org/aparecida/Ingles.pdf.

105. Southern African Catholic Bishops' Conference. *Pastoral Statement on the Environmental Crisis* (September 5, 1999), http://www.inee.
mu.edu/documents/26SOUTHERNAFRICANCATHOLICBISHOPS_000.
pdf.

106. CELAM, *Aparecida Concluding Document* (May 2007), http://www.
celam.org/aparecida/Ingles.pdf.

107. Catholic Bishops' Conference of the Philippines. Pastoral letter
What Is Happening to Our Beautiful Land? (January 29, 1988), http://www.
cbcponline.net/documents/1980s/1988-ecology.html.

108. Bolivian Bishops' Conference. Pastoral Letter on the Environment and Human Development in Bolivia, *El universo don de Dios para la vida* (March 23, 2012), La Paz: Conferencia Episcopal Boliviana, 2012.

109. German Bishops' Conference, Commission for Social Issues, *Der Klimawandel: Brennpunkt globaler, intergenerationeller und ökologischer Gerechtigkeit* (September 2006), http://www.dbk-shop.de/de/ Deutsche-Bischofskonferenz/Die-deutschen-Bischoefe/Erklaerungen-der-Kommissionen/Klimawandel-.html.

110. Bishops of the Patagonia-Comahue Region (Argentina). *Christmas Message* (December 2009), http://www.fides.org/en/news/20516 -AMERICA_ARGENTINA_Christmas_Message_from_the_Bishops_of_ Patagonia_Christmas_means_saying_no_to_indifference_no_to_only_ worrying_about_one_s_own_welfare_without_being_aware_of_the_ urgent_needs_of_others_no_to_a_passive_attitude_on_many_urgent_ challenges#.VfgAIbRYXww.

111. United States Conference of Catholic Bishops, *Global Climate Change: A Plea for Dialogue, Prudence and the Common Good* (June 15, 2001), http://www.usccb.org/issues-and-action/human-life-and-dignity/ environment/global-climate-change-a-plea-for-dialogue-prudence-and-the-common-good.cfm.

112. CELAM, *Aparecida Concluding Document*.

113. German Bishops' Conference, *Zukunft der Schöpfung – Zukunft der Menschheit. Einklärung der Deutschen Bishofkonferenz zu Fragen der Umwelt und der Energieversorgung* (1980), http://www.dbk-shop.de/de/Deutsche-Bischofkonferenz/Die-deutschen-Bischoefe/Hirtenschreiben-und-Erklaerungen/Zukunft-der-Schoepfung-Zukunft-der-Menschheit.html.

114. The placement of this citation immediately next to a reference to the *Catechism* is at least intriguing. Given that the *Catechism* relies on the authority of its sources, it would appear that the use of the *Catechism*—a contemporary expression of its own sources—further supports the suggestion that these two references are primarily included to articulate the contemporaneity of the church's teaching on the dignity of all creatures, a teaching ultimately derived from scripture.

115. Canadian Conference of Catholic Bishops, Social Affairs Commission, pastoral letter *You Love All that Exists...All Things Are Yours, God, Lover of Life* (October 4, 2003), http://www.cccb.ca/site/Files/pastoralen vironment.html.

116. Catholic Bishops' Conference of Japan, *Reverence for Life: A Message for the Twenty-First Century* (January 1, 2000), http://www.cbcj.catho lic.jp/eng/edoc/01life.htm.

117. National Conference of the Bishops of Brazil, *A Igreja e a Questão Ecológica* (1992), São Paulo: Edições Paulinas, 1992.

118. Additionally, this expanded view calls for a response in addition to praise: the cultivation of "ecological virtues" (which terminology is a direct quotation from the bishops of Brazil). A quick read through the entirety of Francis's encyclical reveals this as the sole use of "ecological virtues," which leads to the question of its weight as a theological term (even within the encyclical). Nevertheless, it would appear to be related to the general thrust of *On Care for Our Common Home*—the call for dialogue and, perhaps more on point, a *new lifestyle* (for example, see the final chapter on "ecological spirituality").

119. Conference of Dominican Bishops, pastoral letter *Sobre la relación del hombre con la naturaleza* (January 21, 1987), in *"And God Saw That It Was Good": Catholic Theology and the Environment*, eds. Drew Christiansen and Walt Grazer (Washington, DC: United States Catholic Conference, 1996).

120. Paraguayan Bishops' Conference, pastoral letter *El campesino paraguayo y la tierra* (June 12, 1983), http://episcopal.org.py/news-item/el-campesino-paraguayo-y-la-tierra-12-de-junio-de-1983/.

121. New Zealand Catholic Bishops Conference, *Statement on Environmental Issues* (September 1, 2006), http://www.catholic.org.nz/nzcbc/fx-view-article.cfm?ctype=BSART&loadref=83&id=62.

122. *Love for Creation: An Asian Response to the Ecological Crisis*, Declaration of the Colloquium, sponsored by the Federation of Asian Bishops' Conferences (Tagaytay, January 31–February 5, 1993), in *Catholic International* (June 1993): 270.

123. Episcopal Commission for the Pastoral Concerns in Argentina, *Una tierra para todos* (June 2005), http://www.uca.edu.ar/uca/common/grupo68/files/Una_tierra_para_todos.pdf.

124. Portuguese Bishops' Conference, pastoral letter *Responsabilidade Solidária pelo Bem Comum* (September 15, 2003), http://www.agencia.ecclesia.pt/noticias/documentos/responsabilidade-solidaria-pelo-bem-comum/.

125. Recall what John Paul II said in *Apostolos Suos* on the need for the intervention of the Apostolic See concerning cases where Episcopal Conference comes to a decision by majority but not unanimity: "The intervention of the Apostolic See is analogous to that required by the law in order for the Episcopal Conference to issue general decrees [see Code of Canon Law, canon 455]. The *recognitio* of the Holy See serves furthermore to guarantee that, in dealing with new questions posed by the accelerated social and cultural changes characteristic of present times, the doctrinal response will favour communion and not harm it, and will rather *prepare an eventual intervention of the universal magisterium*" (emphasis added).

126. Bolivian Bishops' Conference, Pastoral Letter on the Environment and Human Development in Bolivia, *El universo don de Dios para la vida* (March 23, 2012), La Paz: Conferencia Episcopal Boliviana, 2012.

127. Mexican Bishops' Conference, Episcopal Commission for Pastoral and Social Concerns, *Jesucristo, vida y esperanza de los indígenas e campesinos* (January 14, 2008), http://caritasmexicana.org/documen tacion/ceps-caritas/1613-jesucristo-vida-y-esperanza-de-los-indigenas-y-campesinos695.

128. Australian Catholic Bishops' Conference, *A New Earth: The Environmental Challenge* (2002), http://www.socialjustice.catholic.org.au/files/SJSandresources/2002_SJSS_statement.pdf.

129. USCCB, *Renewing the Earth* (1991), http://www.usccb.org/issues-and-action/human-life-and-dignity/environment/renewing-the-earth.cfm.

130. *Ibid.*

131. *Ibid.*

132. USCCB, "Global Climate Change: A Plea for Dialogue, Prudence and the Common Good" (June 15, 2001), http://www.usccb.org/issues-and-action/human-life-and-dignity/environment/global-climate-change-a-plea-for-dialogue-prudence-and-the-common-good.cfm.

133. USCCB, *Global Climate Change* (February 2010), http://www.usccb.org/issues-and-action/human-life-and-dignity/environment/global-climate-change-2010.cfm.

134. *Ibid.*

135. Catholic Bishops of Appalachia, "This Land Is Home to Me" (1975) and "At Home in the Web of Life" (1995), http://www.ccappal.org/CCAbook040307.pdf.

136. Catholic Bishops of the Watershed Region, "The Columbia River Watershed: Caring for Creation and the Common Good: An International Pastoral Letter by the Catholic Bishops of the Watershed Region," http://www.thewscc.org/images/stories/Resources/Statements/colrvr-e.pdf.

137. Catholic Bishops of Appalachia, *This Land Is Home to Me* (1975) and *At Home in the Web of Life (1995)*, http://www.ccappal.org/CCA book040307.pdf.

138. *Ibid.*

139. Catholic Bishops of the Watershed Region, *The Columbia River Watershed: Caring for Creation and the Common Good: An International Pastoral Letter by the Catholic Bishops of the Watershed Region*, http://www.thewscc.org/images/stories/Resources/Statements/colrvr-e.pdf.

140. *Ibid.*

Background

141. The first sentence of Vatican II's Decree on Ecumenism asserts: "The restoration of unity among all Christians is one of the principal concerns of the Second Vatican Council. Christ the Lord founded one Church and one Church only" (n. 1). Later, it asserts: "Today, in many parts of the world, under the inspiring grace of the Holy Spirit, many efforts are being made in prayer, word and action to attain that fullness of unity which Jesus Christ desires. The Sacred Council exhorts all the Catholic faithful to recognize the signs of the times and to take an active and intelligent part in the work of ecumenism" (n. 4). The term "ecumenical movement" indicates the initiatives and activities planned and undertaken, according to the various needs of the church and, as opportunities offer, to promote Christian unity. These are, first, every effort to avoid expressions, judgments, and actions that do not represent the condition of our separated brethren with truth and fairness and so make mutual relations with them more difficult; then, "dialogue" between competent experts from different churches and communities. At these meetings, which are organized in a religious spirit, each explains the teaching of his communion in greater depth and brings out clearly its distinctive features. In such dialogue, everyone gains a truer knowledge and more just appreciation of the teaching and religious life of both Communions. In addition, the way is prepared for cooperation between them in the duties for the common good of humanity, which are demanded by every Christian conscience; wherever this is allowed, there is prayer in common. Finally, all are led to examine their own faithfulness to Christ's will for the church and accordingly to undertake with vigor the task of renewal and reform (see Vatican II, *Unitatis Redintegratio*, Decree on Ecumenism, November 21, 1964, http://www.vatican.va/archive/hist_councils/ii_vatican_council/documents/vat-ii_decree_19641121_unitatis-redintegratio_en.html.

142. For example, among several other instances, the pope and Patriarch Bartholomew met in Jerusalem on May 25, 2014. N. 6 of their common declaration urged ecumenical efforts for the care for creation. In June of 2014, when Pope Francis hosted political and religious leaders for a prayer service for peace, Patriarch Bartholomew served as a cohost.

143. See John Chryssavgis, ed., *On Earth as in Heaven: Ecological Vision and Initiatives of Ecumenical Patriarch Bartholomew* (Bronx, NY: Fordham University Press, 2012), 4–5.

144. Among many others, see the helpful collection *Faith-Based Statements on Climate Change* (Coronado, California: Citizens Lobby, 2015) containing documents from the Baha'i community, Buddhism, Hinduism, indigenous peoples, Islam, Judaism, Native American church, Taoism/Daoism, and the following Christian churches: Anglican, Baptist, Church of the Brethren, Eastern Orthodox, Episcopalian, Evangelical, Lutheran,

Methodist, Presbyterian, Quaker/Society of Friends, Roman Catholic, Unitarian Universalist, and the United Church of Christ.

145. Recall the observation made above that, among other initiatives, the fact that immediately after the publication of the encyclical the Archbishop of Canterbury, Justin Welby, and Patriarch Bartholomew penned an op-ed piece for the *New York Times* that was highly complimentary of the pope's text is significant. Bartholomew and Justin Welby, "Climate Change and Moral Responsibility," *New York Times* (June 19, 2014), http://www.nytimes.com/2015/06/20/opinion/climate-change-and-moral-responsibility.html?_r=0.

146. International Islamic Climate Change Symposium, *Islamic Declaration on Global Climate Change* (August 17–18, 2015), http://islamic climatedeclaration.org/islamic-declaration-on-global-climate-change/.

147. The service was published in 1991 (composed by the famous hymnographer Father Gerasimos Mikrayiannanites in Greek) and translated into English by Ephrem Lash (United Kingdom). See *Office of Vespers for the Protection of Creation* in *Orthodoxy and Ecology: Resource Book.* (Bialys tok: Syndesnis, 1996). A second English translation of the vespers service is also in *Vespers for the Protection of the Environment* (Northridge: Narthex Press, 1996). For this vespers service, also see the following: http://www. anastasis.org.uk/environm.htm and http://www.goarch.org/chapel/litur gical_texts/vespers_creation.

148. See the press release *Lettera del Santo Padre per l'istituzione della 'Giornata Mondiale di Preghiera per la Cura del Creato' (1° settembre) [Letter of the Holy Father for the Institution of the 'World Day of Prayer for the Care of Creation' (1 September)]* (August 10, 2015), http://press.vatican.va/con tent/salastampa/it/bollettino/pubblico/2015/08/10/0609/01316.html.

149. Whether or not these annual encyclicals on the environment from the patriarch will from now on be coauthored by the pope remains to be seen. If recent common statements are any indication, however, this is a well-founded hope.

150. See John Chryssavgis, "Introduction," *On Earth as in Heaven: Ecological Vision and Initiatives of Ecumenical Patriarch Bartholomew* (New York: Fordham University Press, 2012), 16.

151. Among others, see Bartholomew, *Address in Santa Barbara* where this idea is contextualized within his treatment of liturgy, offering, and communion. See *On Earth as in Heaven*, pp. 95–100.

152. Citations for 1989–2010 are from *On Earth as in Heaven*, chapter 1, "Call to Vigilance and Prayer: Patriarchal Encyclicals," pp. 23–64. Citations for 2011-2014 are from https://www.patriarchate.org/environment-messages. Citations for 2014–15 are from https://www.patriarchate. org/-/septon-patriarchikon-menyma-epi-tei-hemerai-proseuches-hyper-

tes-prostasias-tou-physikou-periballontos-01-09-2013-?inheritRedirect
=true&redirect=%2Fenvironment-messages&_101_INSTANCE_yYvX9I
5UvsXD_languageId=en_US and http://www.goarch.org/news/patriarch
messageindiction2015.

153. For a helpful summary of these meetings, see *On Earth as in
Heaven*, "Introduction," pp. 4–14.

154. Bartholomew and John Paul II, *Common Declaration of John Paul
II and the Ecumenical Patriarch His Holiness Bartholomew* (June 10, 2002),
http://w2.vatican.va/content/john-paul-ii/en/speeches/2002/june/docu
ments/hf_jp-ii_spe_20020610_venice-declaration.html.

155. See, among other sources, Bartholomew, *Message for the Day of
Prayer for the Protection of Creation* (September 1, 2012), http://www.
goarch.org/news/patriarchindiction2012.

156. Bartholomew, *Address in Santa Barbara, California* (November 8,
1997), in *On Earth as in Heaven*, p. 99.

157. Bartholomew, *Lecture at the Monastery of Utstein, Norway* (June 23,
2003), in *On Earth as in Heaven*, p. 203.

158. See https://www.patriarchate.org/bartholomew-quotes.

159. Bartholomew and John Paul II, *Common Declaration of John Paul II
and the Ecumenical Patriarch His Holiness Bartholomew*.

160. *Ibid.*

161. *Ibid.*

162. Bartholomew and Francis, *Common Declaration of Pope Francis and
the Ecumenical Patriarch Bartholomew I* (May 25, 2014), http://m.vatican.
va/content/francescomobile/en/speeches/2014/may/documents/papa-
francesco_20140525_terra-santa-dichiarazione-congiunta.html.

163. *Ibid.*

164. United States Roman Catholic-United Methodist Dialogue,
Heaven and Earth Are Full of Your Glory (April 20, 2012), http://www.
usccb.org/beliefs-and-teachings/ecumenical-and-interreligious/ecumeni
cal/ecumenical-documents-and-news-releases.cfm#CP_JUMP_106447.

165. Paul VI, encyclical letter *Ecclesiam Suam* (August 6, 1964), http://
w2.vatican.va/content/paul-vi/en/encyclicals/documents/hf_p-vi_
enc_06081964_ecclesiam.html.

CHAPTER TWO

Contributions

The purpose of this chapter is to offer a summary of the contributions which Pope Francis makes to our understanding of the environment from the perspective of Catholic (magisterial) teaching, theology, spirituality, liturgy, and practice. The term "contributions" is designed to be inclusive of the way the pope integrates now familiar themes from the prior magisterium in a new context, with added emphasis or explanation (for example, "dominion" and "stewardship," among many others) and new ideas he himself sets forth.

I. THE IMPORTANCE OF THE TITLE(S)

"Praise be to you, my Lord" (n. 1) and "Praised be to him" (n. 245) taken from St. Francis of Assisi's *Canticle of the Creatures*, are the bookends of this lengthy and comprehensive encyclical.[1] The pope uses these acclamations (and two added prayers at the end) to place this theological, spiritual, and educational document within the framework of prayer. How often do we offer words of "praise" when we pray the psalms and celebrate the liturgy? Yet, like the Book of Psalms itself, the document has its laments and challenges because of the state of the world as the pope invites us to view it. (The fact that these same words are the title and first line of a very popular song sung at many liturgies in Italian insures that there will be an immediate resonance and recognition of these words from St. Francis. Any of the searchable YouTube versions of

Contributions

Laudato si' o mi(o) Signore reflect the song's exuberance, which likely accounts for its popularity.)

The subtitle, *On Care for Our Common Home*, gives the more precise focus of the encyclical. Note these words precisely because they form the subtext of this entire document.

"CARE"

In several places the encyclical describes the state of the environment as it exists today and invites us to action to *care* for it (as opposed to being stewards, cited only twice; more on this below). This reflects a "see," "judge," "act" ("celebrate" is sometimes added) process that is commonly used in social justice methodologies and is used by Pope John XXIII in *Mater et Magistra* (noted in the previous chapter). We are invited to "see" what this earth looks like. Then we are invited to "judge" what we are to do about it, enlightened by what the best science and Catholic theology and spirituality offers us. This leads us to "act" as responsible citizens to care for creation collectively and individually, in the public square and in our personal lives, in the corridors of political power and influence, as well as in the words and actions of common prayer in our churches.

"OUR"

"Our" as opposed to "mine" is a major theme that runs through the pope's letter. True to Catholic teaching and practice, especially in social justice teaching and practice but certainly not exclusively, the pope again and again refers to the import of the *common good* (a phrase he uses over thirty times) over an *individualism* that the pope repeatedly asserts reflects negatively on and infects our contemporary culture. If the rhetoric of "our" as opposed to "mine" takes over and becomes second nature to us, then we will have moved in the direction the pope points out, a very traditional Catholic way of looking at and living life.

"COMMON HOME"

The earth is not a commodity, or a location, it is our *common home*, a home for plants, animals, and humans—all living things/

95

beings. Immediately after asserting this in the encyclical (n. 1) the pope again uses his namesake's Canticle to assert: "our common home is like a sister with whom we share our life and a beautiful mother who opens her arms to embrace us....Praise be to you, my Lord, through our Sister, Mother Earth, who sustains and governs us, and who produces various fruit with colored flowers and herbs." From the beginning of the text the pope invites us to view the earth as our common home through a wide-angle lens to include all created reality reflected by the Poverello of Assisi. One of the first (and obvious) implications here is that the use of the word "thing" should be restricted to inanimate objects and that the word "creature" should be used to refer to all animate beings on the earth.

II. DATE OF THE ENCYCLICAL: A NEW PENTECOST? A NEW CREATION?

The date when an encyclical letter is signed by the pope is important, introduced by the time-honored phrase "given at Rome." For example, John Paul II dated his encyclical on the Eucharist on Holy Thursday of 2003, the day when we commemorate the institution of the Eucharist.

PENTECOST

In 2015, Pope Francis signed *On Care for Our Common Home* on the solemnity of Pentecost, a day commemorating the coming of the Holy Spirit. The refrain for the responsorial psalm on Pentecost Sunday is "Lord, send out your Spirit, and renew the face of the earth," with verses from Psalm 104, often called a psalm of "Praise of God the Creator." This same refrain and psalm are used as the response to the first reading at the Easter Vigil from Genesis (1:1—2:2), which recounts the story of Creation. In both liturgical contexts, these texts reflect a re-creation and renewal of the earth. In addition, the traditional and present entrance antiphon for Pentecost is from the Book of Wisdom (which is frequently quoted in the encyclical), connecting the "Spirit of the Lord" with all of creation: "the Spirit of the Lord has filled the whole world and that which contains all things understands what is said, alleluia" (Wis 1:7).

CREATION

Pentecost is also a creation feast in that it derives from the Jewish feast of "Shavuoth" (also known as the Feast of Weeks), a festival that comes at the conclusion of the seven-week period of the grain harvest in early spring.

The actual beginning of the grain harvest was marked by the sacrifice at the sanctuary of the omer (the first sheaf of the newly cut barley)—the Passover. Then, fifty days later at the close of the harvest period, two loaves of bread that were baked from the wheat of the new crop were offered as a sacrifice to God. (This offering was made as a token of thanksgiving to God for making the land fertile enough to produce food.)

According to Deuteronomy 26:1–11 and 16:9–12, Shavuoth is also a time to commemorate the Exodus from Egypt, the giving of the Torah, God's self-revelation ("theophany") on Mount Sinai, and to thank God for providing land "flowing with milk and honey" (Exod 33:3). It is customary during Shavuoth to eat (leavened) bread baked from the new wheat because leavened bread symbolizes freedom, which is a product of one's own land, as opposed to unleavened bread eaten in haste during the Exodus. Traditionally, dairy products and honey are also eaten as a reminder of God's promise to the children of Israel that he would give them land flowing with milk and honey. It is a time to remember that God freed a people once in bondage, a commemoration conducted through sharing the fruit of the earth. Our continued call for God to remember his promise of freedom, lived out through our offering of the fruits of the earth, is echoed in the first words of the hymn assigned for first vespers on the solemnity of Pentecost, a ninth-century text attributed to Rabanus Maurus: *Veni Creator Spiritus*, "Come Creator Spirit."

Timing may not be everything, but when it comes to papal encyclicals, the dating of them sends strong signals. What better "signal" than a new Pentecost for the whole of creation?

III. AUTHORSHIP OF THE ENCYCLICAL

That popes ask for and receive assistance for what they write is not new. What is new with Pope Francis is that he has acknowledged the assistance of several people at the various stages of drafting this document. The clearest, authoritative statement about this came from Cardinal Peter Turkson, President of the Pontifical Council for Justice and Peace, at the press briefing announcing the encyclical, the drafting of which, he said, exemplified the kind of *dialogue* for which the pope has called (and which he uses repeatedly in homilies and addresses). Cardinal Turkson said,

> This type of dialogue was also employed as the method of preparation that the Holy Father embraced in the writing of the Encyclical. He relied on a wide range of contributions. Some, in particular those from many Episcopal Conferences from all the continents, are mentioned in the footnotes. Others who participated in the various phases of this work all the way to the complex final phases of translation and publication, remain unnamed. The Lord knows well how to reward their generosity and dedication.[2]

The accompanying footnote states,

> This is what the Pope himself said on the plane flying to Manila [on January 15, 2015] and so is already known: "Cardinal Turkson and his team prepared the first draft. Then, with some help, I took it and worked on it, then with a few theologians I made a third draft and sent a copy to the Congregation for the Doctrine of the Faith, to the second section of the Secretariat of State, and to the Theologian of the Papal Household....Three weeks ago, I got their responses back...all of them constructive. Now I will take a week of March, an entire week, to complete it. I believe that by the end of March it will be finished and sent out for translation. I think that if the work of translation goes well...then it can come out in June or July."

The reason for setting the record straight about authorship is that when a papal document says things which a reader dislikes, the parlor game that ensues is to say that the pope himself did not write that section or those words, and so they are not authoritative or binding. This preemptive strike by Cardinal Turkson clarifies issues about authorship, an invitation to dialogue and a reminder that, despite collaborators and the rather lengthy process, the (entire) document is part of the ordinary magisterium.[3] At the same time, the very fact that the pope has collaborators in drafting such a document, collaborators who come from a variety of fields (for example, theology, science, economics) and locales (for example, Europe, Africa, North and Latin America), means that there is an unofficial though very real collegiality at work in drafting this document under Francis's authorship.

IV. INTENDED AUDIENCE

As noted above, when discussing Pope Francis's drawing on the example of John XXIII (chapter 1), *On Care for Our Common Home* is addressed to "every person living on this planet." It is not addressed to Roman Catholic leaders only, as is the case with many encyclicals, or to all Roman Catholics. The letter is intended for as wide an audience as possible. This also exemplifies the way that Pope Francis sees the issue of environment as akin to how Pope John XXIII saw world peace in 1963. It is also noteworthy that Pope Francis's letter announcing the Jubilee Year of Mercy was addressed "to all who read this letter."[4]

V. A CATHOLIC ENCYCLICAL

Catholic encyclicals are letters written by the pope and reflect Catholic teaching. But *On Care for Our Common Home* is also particularly and decisively Catholic in the worldview it expresses and presumes. Central tenets of Catholicism such as the role of theology, the celebration of sacraments and liturgy, and concepts such as collegiality, community, the common good, interrelationships, and belonging (among many others) are all strong suits that underlie Roman Catholicism. An example of the "thick" identity of Roman Catholicism is the way the text courses through the world, all that dwell on and in it, the church as communion, common worship, prayer, saints, and so on. The radical inclusivity and universality of Catholicism is seen on every page of the document.

VI. BREADTH OF THE ENCYCLICAL

The breadth of the document is stellar and stunning:

- from environment to immigration, from the dangers of climate change to the urgency of food distribution,
- from political action on behalf of our common home to prayer and spirituality steeped in an awareness of God's gift of creation,
- from actions to stop pollution and deforestation to contemplation of the goodness of and praise for the God of all creatures great and small,
- from placing the poor at the center of our lives—not the periphery—to our concern for the entire cosmos in which we live.

VII. CHAPTER SUMMARIES

The encyclical is divided into six chapters:

CHAPTER ONE: WHAT IS HAPPENING TO OUR COMMON HOME?

The method of "see, judge, act" seen in the Aparecida document (n. 19) is reflected in the structure of the encyclical. It is a method well appropriated and used by Pope Francis. Chapter 1 sets out the contours of the present ecological crisis. Thus, the document opens with a description of why this document is needed now. We are invited to "see" what is occurring and to "see" the beginnings of a theological response in the chapter that follows. It is at least notable that the Canadian Jesuit theologian Bernard Lonergan began his book *Method in Theology* with the admonition, "be attentive" (along with "be intelligent," "be reasonable" and "be responsible"). An underlying theme of the encyclical is that we need to "be attentive" and to "see" what is around us inspiring awe and gratitude, as well as sadness and action. That the encyclical begins by quoting St. Francis of Assisi's *Canticle of the Creatures* is no mere stylistic or clever introduction. It lays the foundation for the encyclical's explicit and implicit understanding that all created beings are just that, beings in relationship with one another. Specific issues here concern climate change, water, biodiversity, and global inequality.

CHAPTER TWO: THE GOSPEL OF CREATION

The use of the term *gospel* ("good news") widened under John Paul II with his encyclical *Evangelium Vitae* ("The Gospel of Life"). As noted above, it was then adopted in the *Aparecida Document* to refer to "the good news" "of human dignity," "life," "family," and of "human activity" (specifically work). In the encyclical the pope delineates the "gospel" of creation from biblical roots in both the Old and New Testaments, emphasizing the creation accounts in the Book of Genesis and "the gaze of Jesus." He also reiterates previous papal teachings about the common destination of goods.[5]

CHAPTER THREE: THE HUMAN ROOTS OF THE ECOLOGICAL CRISIS

Technology and globalization are facts of life. The pope here assesses their strengths and weaknesses in terms of what they contribute to the good of society and how they can also be harmful. One of the factors addressed repeatedly in the encyclical is the wide-angle lens the pope uses to view all of reality as interconnected and as God's creation. This is a deliberate attempt to balance out the often-presumed (and sometimes extreme?) anthropocentrism of Catholic theology and life. In n. 68, the pope adapts the phrase "tyrannical anthropocentrism" from the 1980 document of the German bishops conference[6] and notes that it can lead to being "unconcerned for other creatures." (Again, note the use of the word "creatures.")

CHAPTER FOUR: INTEGRAL ECOLOGY

This chapter contains the most distinctive contribution of the encyclical. The combining of "environmental," "economic," "social," "cultural" ecology with the "ecology of daily life" clearly advances on prior magisterial statements and reflects the inclusiveness of the pope's view of creation. These are then coupled with reiterating two of the foundational concepts in Catholic social teaching—the common good and justice—and applying them to the current ecological crisis.

Part of the pope's integral vision is to connect issues and fields of expertise not often understood together: morality, economics, science, spirituality, theology, liturgy, and sacraments.

While there is an inherent logic in the way the encyclical unfolds, there is something to recommend reading this chapter first because it contains key aspects of Pope Francis's contributions to the debate. This argument is in accord with the "judge" phase of the pope's method.

CHAPTER FIVE: LINES OF APPROACH AND ACTION

As the pope moves to the third of his methodological triad—"act"—the worldwide audience for this Roman Catholic encyclical is reiterated, that is, all of humanity in the international, national, and local realms. His repeated invitation to a "dialogue" is important, given the dialogical stance the pope takes throughout the text. In effect, he is "thinking outside the box" in terms of international bodies, politics, the economy, and the relationship of faith and science—sometimes adversaries, but now recalled as partners for Catholic thinking. The call for "transparency in decision making" is a direct challenge to those who argue from preconceived positions at their self-interest, sometimes because of the funding they offer for the research undertaken.

CHAPTER SIX: ECOLOGICAL EDUCATION AND SPIRITUALITY

This final chapter focuses the "action" part of the previous chapter and extends it to a fourth imperative, "celebrate," by calling on strong suits of Catholicism: conversion to a new lifestyle, to deeper engagement in liturgy, sacraments, and the Sabbath, to an awareness and appreciation of the trinitarian communion of all creatures within all of creation, and to deeper prayer. These are part and parcel of the Catholic imagination where a binary "either... or" is replaced by an inclusive "both...and"—"prayer and work," "contemplation and action."

VIII. HOW TO INTERPRET CATHOLIC SOCIAL TEACHING

One of the premises of the study of hermeneutics is that each of us brings our own educational background, insights, life experience, and, yes, prejudices to the interpretation of what we read, hear, or view. In an Internet world where the "news cycle" is 24/7, "breaking news" can be interpreted differently depending on the worldview of the editors of the TV station, radio show, or online news service. Similarly, in the print media often the editorial policies (articulated or not articulated) of newspapers and periodicals interpret the same news differently. Sometimes this means leaving out some of the facts. At other times it takes data and spins it for a preconceived agenda.

Church documents are themselves often interpreted according to preconceived ideas or ideological perspectives. Unfortunately, words such as "liberal" and "conservative" are thrown around often to criticize a differing position, very often not without conviction and passion. One of the difficulties today for an American public is that often the prejudices of those interpreting church documents reflect the various sides of the American political debate, with numberless categories and labels used—liberal, conservative, progressive, neoconservative, and so on. This leads to the reminder that we need to read church documents in full, on their own terms and not filtered by any ideological preconceptions. Yet even here those who study hermeneutics remind us that this is almost impossible. The continual challenge is to allow ourselves to be convinced and converted by church documents and not by the arguments of commentators on them.

For example, the fiftieth anniversary of the close of the Second Vatican Council has provided an opportunity for scholars, theologians, church leaders, pastoral ministers, and all the baptized to reread and rediscover what the Council taught and ways to continue to implement its teachings a half-century later. A fruitful interpretation of these teachings today requires attention to the documents in their full context, including the content of the Council debates, the subsequent revisions of the drafts, promulgation of the final texts, implementation and reception, and the relationship of Council documents among one another and with other documents before and after the Council. While some commentators have posited the interpretive approach of a "hermeneutic of continuity" over against a "hermeneutic of discontinuity," such a debate does not reflect precisely what Pope Benedict XVI said in his 2005 Christmas address to the Roman Curia, in which he emphasized a "hermeneutic of reform, of renewal in the continuity of the one subject-Church" and stated that the true spirit of the Council is "in the impulses toward the new that are contained in the texts."[7] Decrying a hermeneutic of discontinuity, some today criticize the interpretation Giuseppe Alberigo, his five-volume *History of Vatican II*,[8] and "the Bologna School" of interpreting Vatican II. However, my own sense is that the individual essays of Alberigo's multivolume work stand alongside Herbert Vorgrimler's *Commentary on the Documents of Vatican II*[9] as mutually enriching. Attempts to counterbalance the Bologna School interpretation include Agostino Marchetto's *The Second Vatican Ecumenical Council*[10] and Roberto De Mattei's *Il concilio Vaticano II*,[11] although I am unable to recommend the latter due to its imbalances and inaccuracies. An independent voice on interpreting Vatican II that deserves wider readership is Massimo Faggioli, especially his books *Vatican II: The Battle for Meaning* and *True Reform: Liturgy and Ecclesiology in Sacrosanctum Concilium.*[12] Finally, English-speaking authors Ormond Rush (*Still Interpreting Vatican II*),[13] Richard Gaillardetz (*The Church in the Making*),[14] and John O'Malley (*What Happened at Vatican II*)[15] are very useful in interpreting and implementing Vatican II today.[16]

When it comes to Catholic social teaching, the issue of interpretation looms large, especially today. One example on a practical level concerns the right of workers to unionize, as taught from

Leo XIII through Pope Francis. Some ignore this teaching outright. On a more theoretical level, one question has to do with how to understand "solidarity" and "subsidiarity," words that are part of that same trajectory of social justice teachings. Authors such as Robert Putnam, Robert Bellah, and Alan Ehrenhalt have indicated how and where solidarity is under pressure in American society today. Philosophers like Alasdair MacIntyre and Charles Taylor have traced the theoretical origins of the challenges to solidarity in our age. Collectively, they have chronicled how solidarity has been spiraling down in a long retreat in our age.

From a totally different perspective are the theories and groups that actually rejoice in the decline of solidarity—libertarians, devotees of Austrian economics' methodological individualism, Ayn Rand's objectivists, and varieties of anarchists. Among them are those who absolutize private choice and who radicalize egoistic independence— those who find something romantic about the storybook character of the rugged individual who subsists without use or need for others. For all of these worldviews that celebrate unencumbered individualism, solidarity is viewed with suspicion, viewed as a sort of weakness at best or (nodding to F. A. Hayek) serfdom at worst.[17]

Among others, libertarians like Charles Murray would argue against any emphasis on solidarity for what he perceives as the problem of dependency. The interdependency that is at the heart of solidarity is judged to compromise the autonomy and liberty of the individual. Institutions based on solidarity are imagined to weaken the development of self-sufficiency and self-reliance that are celebrated by libertarians like Murray. Solidarity is suspicious for its alleged coddling of individuals, which is thought to under-cut the personal responsibility that libertarians presume is the basis for an effective citizenry.

For those who subscribe to Austrian economics, including such thinkers as Murray Rothbard and Ludwig von Mises, the problem with solidarity is its interference with market forces. Theorists of this sort idolize the free competition of the market and associate solidarity with the collusion of interests that can interfere with such competition. Ideally, workers and consumers should be individuals who do not organize collectively in pursuit of their interests. Labor unions, in particular, are derided for compromising the free competition of and for labor in production.

In Catholic circles, those who militate against an emphasis on institutions of solidarity often do so with reference to the idea of subsidiarity (more on this in chapter 3). As if subsidiarity were in some fashion opposite to solidarity. As if subsidiarity were compatible with Austrian economics, libertarianism, and Ayn Rand. By any fair reading, the church's teaching about subsidiarity is not really compatible with such thinking.

Subsidiarity refers to the appropriate balancing of responsibilities and functions among the parts of a social order. It has its origin in the Catholic understanding of community, which perceives a community not as so many individuals connected by contracts, but as a corporate whole—a moral and cultural body that, like any body, is comprised of limbs and parts, the differences of which contribute to the good of the whole. The ethic that pertains to the unity of the body is called solidarity. The ethic that pertains to the role of the parts is subsidiarity. The good of the whole by which solidarity and subsidiarity are measured is called the common good. Among others, the writings and teaching of John A. Ryan at The Catholic University of America interpreted, for an American context, the Catholic social teaching of Leo XIII and Pius XI. The center of his thought was human dignity and human welfare, and his core values were thinking, knowing, communing, loving, serving, and giving as opposed to "having."[18]

Given the breadth and depth of the encyclical allow me to reiterate that openness to "conversion" needs to be among the ways we read, study, and pray over the document. Sound bites and summaries should always cede to studying the text (and any other church document) so that its wisdom can guide our thoughts and actions ("see, judge, act, celebrate").

IX. MAJOR THEMES

A COMPREHENSIVE, INCLUSIVE THEOLOGY OF CREATION AND ECOLOGY

Again and again the pope reminds us that all who dwell on this good earth are interrelated and interconnected. The pope reiterates throughout the document that everything and everyone are interrelated, and that while we can and do make distinctions, there is an overriding unity and integrity to facing the ecological issues before us in an integral and integrated way. He argues against unhealthy dualisms (n. 98), which might prevent us from appreciating the unity of body and spirit and of the importance of all creatures as gifts from God the Creator.

One of the reasons that the document is comparatively long, especially when compared with other papal encyclicals, is precisely the issue of the breadth and depth of the interconnectedness of the number of realities living on the earth and of the disciplines involved in a comprehensive discussion—scripture, theology, ethics, science, economics, spirituality, liturgy, sacraments, and the practical.

The pope teaches us well from the scriptures, the Catholic theological tradition, and in particular to our social justice tradition, the wisdom of the mendicant traditions personified by his patron, the *poverello* St. Francis of Assisi, and the church's whole spiritual tradition. Not surprisingly, he also draws on his own Jesuit spiritual tradition.

CATHOLICISM: A THEOLOGICAL, NOT A FUNDAMENTALIST TRADITION[19]

At the beginning of chapter 1, Pope Francis asserts (n. 17), "Theological and philosophical reflections on the situation of humanity and the world can sound tiresome and abstract unless they are grounded in a fresh analysis of our present situation, which is in many ways unprecedented in the history of humanity. So, before considering how faith brings new incentives and requirements with regard to the world of which we are a part, I will briefly turn to what is happening to our common home." This assertion and what follows in the encyclical are simply the "stuff" of Roman Catholicism. We are a theological tradition. We are not fundamentalists (meaning those who repeat the scriptures or any other kind of authoritative document alone and juxtapose them to contemporary life). At our best we assess the "signs of the times" in the light of the scriptures and respond, for example, at an ecumenical council to define our doctrines about Christ (fourth century), or in the face of the Protestant reformers at Trent to assert true Catholic doctrines about a number of things such as the sacrificial character of the Mass (six-teenth century), or the role of the church in the modern world at Vatican II (twentieth century). Sometimes this means a wholesale "rethink" of what Catholic theology is, as was done in a stellar and long lasting way by St. Thomas Aquinas, St. Bonaventure, and others. In this document, Pope Francis assesses the changed and pressing world context in chapter 1 of the encyclical and offers insights (not cures!) based on the biblical revelation and our existing body of teaching, and then he offers ideas of his own about deepening those insights and applying them to the present. In this sense, the pope follows the path set by his predecessors and faces into current problems rather than shying away and repeating formulas from the past. Part of the genius of Catholicism is the ability to build on our theological tradition (teaching and practice) in new and exciting ways. Like many of his predecessors, that is what the pope has done with this encyclical. This is the best of what Catholicism always does in facing into the pressing questions of the day.

THE GOD OF CREATION, OF THE COVENANTS, AND OF REDEMPTION

The God we believe in is a God who acts. We believe in the biblical God who created and creates, who forges relationships in terms of covenants and who redeems specifically through his Son's dying and rising. Ever since God invited Abraham and Sarah into a covenant relationship (Gen 15) and continued to forge other covenants in the bible, all of us in the Judeo-Christian tradition are related to one another and to every living creature as sharers in the covenant. The particularity of the covenant with Noah (Gen 9:8 ff.) is its inclusion of animals, not just human beings. In fact, it was the sin of human beings that required the purgation of the earth with redemption offered first to Noah, his wife, their sons, their sons' wives, and selected animals. The biblical phrase "the God of Abraham, the God of Isaac and the God of Jacob" is really a shorthand way of saying that God is a relational God and that we are related to each other and to all creatures on this good earth, as Pope Francis reminds us again and again in *On Care for Our Common Home*.[20] One of his particular contributions in the encyclical is placing such emphasis on God's creative love and action.

108

When the priest takes the bread and wine and places it on the altar at Mass he says:

Blessed are you, *Lord God of all creation,*
for through your goodness we have received
the bread we offer you:
fruit of the earth and work of human hands
it will become for us the bread of life....

Blessed are you, *Lord God of all creation,*
for through your goodness we have received
the wine we offer you:
fruit of the vine and work of human hands
it will become our spiritual drink.

Blessed be God forever.

In the section of the encyclical on the bible the pope reminds us that "the God who liberates and saves is the same God who created the universe, and these two divine ways of acting are inseparably connected" (n. 73). This key insight raises up the way that in the prayers of the Catholic liturgy we regularly call on God using a number of names and images, as well as demonstrations of God's "mighty deeds" of redemption (*magnalia Dei*), which were accomplished in the past and are experienced anew in and through the liturgy until they are fulfilled in the kingdom of heaven.[21] One centrally important and classic place is in the (preface and) Eucharistic Prayer at Mass. Perhaps the clearest example is in the Fourth Eucharistic Prayer, which acclaims,

It is truly right to give you thanks,
truly just to give you glory, Father most holy,
for you are the one God living and true.

Other prefaces elaborate on these titles and begin with "Lord, holy Father, almighty and eternal God."

This cluster of names surrounding the title "Father" reflects a number of aspects about God at the beginning of this great prayer of thanksgiving as articulated in the scriptures:

Gen 12:4: we pray along with Abraham, who obeyed God's call and whom we acclaim as "our father in faith" in the Roman Canon;

Gen 18:8: we pray with the mysterious visitors to Abraham who shared the food Sarah prepared for them;

Exod 19:20: we pray with Moses who received the Torah;

John 1:1, 14: we pray with Jesus named the (incarnate) Word of God who was made flesh and dwelt among us;

Luke 24:13–35: we pray with the disciples on the road to Emmaus on that Sunday night when they recognized the risen Lord in the breaking of the bread (the Eucharist).

...existing before all ages and abiding for all eternity,
dwelling in unapproachable light;
yet you, who alone are good, the source of life,
have made all that is,
so that you might fill your creatures with blessings
and bring joy to many of them by the glory of your light.
And so, in your presence are countless hosts of Angels,
who serve you day and night
and, gazing upon the glory of your face,
glorify you without ceasing.
With them we, too, confess your name in exultation,
giving voice to every creature under heaven,
as we acclaim:

Holy, Holy, Holy Lord God of hosts.
Heaven and earth are full of your glory.
　　　Taken from Isa 6:3, an explicit acclamation for creation

Hosannah in the highest.
Blessed is he who comes in the name of the Lord.
　　Taken from Matt 21:9, quoting Ps 118:26, the acclamation
　　　　of the crowd when Jesus enters Jerusalem (the incarnate
　　　　God of redemption to begin his paschal self-offering)

Hosannah in the highest.

The juxtaposition of these biblical texts means that the "Holy,

holy, holy" acclamation always names and acclaims the God of creation and redemption.

> *We give you praise, Father most holy,*
> *for you are great*
> *and you have fashioned all your works*
> *in wisdom and love.*

A feature of all such prayers in the eucharistic liturgy is the way they acclaim the *magnalia Dei*, the mighty deeds God has done for us in creation and redemption.

> *You formed man in your own image*
> *and entrusted the whole world to his care,*
> *so that in serving you alone, the Creator,*
> *he might have dominion over all creatures.*

Recall here the special place of humanity in creation and that "dominion" in the encyclical (nn. 66–67, more below) explicitly means "tilling" the land (as in cultivating, ploughing, and working) and "keeping" (as in caring, protecting, overseeing, and preserving).

> *And when through disobedience he had lost your friendship*
> *you did not abandon him to the domain of death.*
> *For you came in mercy to the aid of all,*
> *So that those who seek might find you.*
> *Time and again you offered them covenants*
> *and through the prophets*
> *taught them to look forward to salvation....*

The God of creation and redemption is the God of the several biblical covenants forged with Noah and his family, including animals in Genesis 9 (most notable in relation to this encyclical stressing our vocation as "companions"); Abraham, Sarah, and their progeny in Genesis 11; Moses in Exodus 34; Aaron in Numbers 25; David in 2 Samuel 7; and the "new" covenant promised in Jeremiah 31, which is understood to be fulfilled in Jesus Christ.

TRINITARIAN COMMUNION

Fundamentally, the biblical God is a God of relationships and relatedness. God's overarching concern is to invite us, followers and fellow believers, into a relationship with the triune God. As previously noted, the Old Testament repeatedly recounts how God's chosen people responded to the "God of Abraham, Isaac and Jacob" and thereby underscores the abiding union into which God invites us as followers.

Some of the names assigned to God in the Old Testament are not nouns, but are really verbs. For example, in Exodus 3:14 God says that his name is "I am who I am." The often-used name "Emmanuel" means "I will always be there for you." Jesus came to put a face on God, and the New Testament authors give us a variety of names, including Christ, Lord, Messiah, and Son of God. That same New Testament gives us a number of names for the Holy Spirit, including Paraclete and Advocate. As early as the mid-second-century, Christians were engaged in searching for appropriate names for the God of the scriptures to carry over to the ever new cultural circumstances in which the church found itself.

The work of "naming God" makes its way into every liturgy that the Christian church celebrates by calling on God as Father, Son, and Holy Spirit, and by countless other terms describing the three persons in God and the attributes of the triune God.

Toward the end of the encyclical, Pope Francis writes of what is perhaps the most important theological foundation for this document, especially from a Roman Catholic creedal perspective. It sets forth a comprehensive (and admittedly somewhat dense) summary of the notion of trinitarian communion (nn. 238–40).[22] This "fills out" what we profess weekly at Sunday Mass when in the Nicene Creed we say:

> I believe in one God
> the Father almighty,
> *maker of heaven and earth*, of all things visible and invisible.
> I believe in one Lord Jesus Christ,
> the Only Begotten Son of God,
> born of the Father before all ages.
> …*through him all things were made*.…

Contributions

I believe in the Holy Spirit, the Lord, *the giver of life....*
[emphasis added]

As one reads the encyclical it would be important to have *trinitarian communion* as one of the lenses through which to view it. The faith we profess in the triune God is faith in a God of relationships within God (Father-Son-Spirit) and of relationships with each other in and through the living God. Fidelity to the Judeo-Christian tradition in the Catholic theological tradition requires that we view the Trinity as the "communion" of Father, Son, and Spirit into whom we are incorporated through baptism and sustained in the ecclesiology of "communion" in the faith, life, and worship of the church.

This premise about "the three-personed God" in whom we believe and into whom we are drawn is the foundation for the pope's assertions:

- that we have hope for full ecclesial communion with the Orthodox (n. 5);
- that as Christians, quoting Patriarch Bartholomew, we are "to accept the world as a sacrament of communion" (n. 9);
- that human beings enter into communion with each other (n. 65);
- that creation is a gift from God who calls us into universal communion (n. 76);
- that as part of the universe we are called into a "universal family and a sublime communion" (n. 89);
- that a deep sense of communion cannot be felt without "tenderness, compassion and concern for our fellow human beings" (n. 91);
- that this "communion excludes nothing and no one" (n. 92);
- that human beings have not always appropriated what is necessary to live "in communion with all that surrounds us" (n. 216);
- that we should be grateful for this universal communion (n. 220);
- and that care for creation is part of the gift of communion (n. 228).

In his famous speech at the Areopagus (Acts 17:22–34), St. Paul uses the phrase now summarized in Sunday Preface VI: "in you we live and move and have our being." This is one way to describe the communion in the God of the Trinity in which we now share here on earth since we "possess the pledge of eternal life." We hope to share final and complete communion in the triune God in heaven.

A UNIVERSAL, GLOBAL, AND INTERNATIONAL CHURCH

The fact that the Catholic church professes to be *catholic* in the sense of being *universal* requires that the pope always look beyond any individual nation or church or group of nations (for example, Europe) to focus on the needs of the worldwide church and the world itself, its populations and creation itself.

The pope's firsthand experience of economic injustice caused by multinational corporations raping the land and the pollution caused by trashing the earth causes him to be a voice for the voiceless. The Latin American pope teaches from his experience and challenges those corporations who have ravaged the land.

Under Pope Francis, this universality means global and international. His repeated use of the word "periphery" indicates his preferential option for places often regarded as not that important and truly "peripheral." The pope's vision, however, is really reflected in the shift of the Catholic population itself. A century ago, eighty percent of the Catholic population lived in Europe and the Americas. Today, the shift is moving in exactly the opposite direction. The election of the first Latin American pope (admittedly with Italian parents who immigrated in Argentina) reflects the shift in the Catholic population.

Put somewhat differently, those who find the Francis papacy striking different chords and raising different questions might well be reflecting a knee jerk Eurocentric and American reaction to this pope from Latin America. In fact, the College of Cardinals may well have reflected "the signs of the times" in the election and now in the ministry of Pope Francis.

An example of this global reality is that for generations dioceses in the United States welcomed clergy born and raised in Ireland to these shores to engage in pastoral ministry. At the very same time U.S. Catholics have been very generous in offering themselves for ministry in the foreign missions, for example, Maryknoll. At the present time, with the comparative shortage of ordained priests to serve in the United States, diocesan bishops here are welcoming increasing numbers of international priests on a regular basis to serve the pastoral needs of the (arch)dioceses in the United States.[23]

With regard to issues about ecology and environment, the pope continues the Vatican precedent and practice of working with international bodies, for example, by having an official Vatican "observer" at the United Nations in New York City and in the United Nations office in Geneva, Switzerland. In the encyclical, the pope speaks about the importance of holding "world summits" (n. 166) on the environment.

THE SACRAMENTAL PRINCIPLE

Intimately connected to "trinitarian communion" and ecclesial belonging, as the pope asserts, is the communion we experience in the celebration of the liturgy (nn. 233–37), especially the Eucharist (nn. 235–36). It is often said that Catholicism is "a sacramental church." Recent studies of American Catholics indicate that among the highest factors influencing self-identification as Catholics is the liturgy, principally the Mass. The Eucharist is generously cited in the encyclical. It is "the summit and source" of Catholic life.

This summit and source, however, is based on the underlying principle of sacramentality—that we raise up gifts from nature and the work of human hands derived from this good earth to worship God.[24] This needs more exposition in a technological culture where worshippers live in (sub)urban settings and are further and further removed from nature and the actual "work of human hands." These paragraphs in the encyclical take on an ecumenical significance when read in light of Patriarch Bartholomew's numerous references to the liturgy and sacraments as an important underlying current in theologizing about the environment (as noted in chapter 1).[25]

The paragraphs on the Eucharist[26] deserve careful attention (again, as previously noted) not to say contemplation. They reflect the intersection of theology with the highest form of our worship of God. They remind us that the grammar of the liturgy is not only words, but the world and all creatures on it, including the primal elemental gifts of earth, air, fire, and water.[27] This is the sacramental principle which undergirds the celebration of the liturgy and the sacraments. In the act of the liturgy, we take what God has given to us as gifts and offer them back to God through, with, and in his Son's paschal mystery. This is to say that there is a primal quality to the worship that human beings offer to God.

For example, each day we are given the light of day and the ability to engage in human work. At Morning Prayer, we acknowledge the light of day and consecrate our work to God in its intercessions. At Evening Prayer, we acknowledge the lengthening shadows of evening and offer thanks for all that was done well during the day. Morning and Evening Prayer are thus cosmic events that confirm and by the very celebration of the liturgy reestablish our place on the earth and our role in the world. They are the "bookends" of the Christian liturgical day. One distinct example and contribution of how the liturgy articulates this is the hymns about the days of creation assigned to evening prayer.

Another example is the way we offer "the work of human hands" to God in the Eucharist. The bread and wine we offer in the Eucharist comes from the cycle in nature of planting, harvesting, milling, and fermenting. These then become the bread and wine we offer to God in order that they might become the "bread of life" and the "cup of eternal salvation." The process of dying and rising that produces the bread and wine fittingly become the consecrated bread and wine on which we dine in order to participate in the paschal dying and rising of Christ.

The sacramental principle links this world and the world that will never end; it links time with the timeless; it links the ordinary with the extraordinary; it links the here and now with the forever in God; and it links human work and "the work of our redemption" (a phrase that is repeatedly prayed in the Roman liturgy to assert and describe what the act of liturgy "accomplishes").[28] Sacramentality grounds the celebration of sacramental liturgy. The celebration of the liturgy sets us in proper relationship with God and each other through the use of creatures and companions on this good earth.

Of particular is "bodiliness" in the way we worship and to valuing all creatures as revelations of God. The self-expression of our bodies and all our faculties in the act of worship respects and actualizes all that we are as human beings who choose to worship God and to be immersed in God through the liturgy.

In addition, the principle of sacramentality means that we experience God in liturgy in a mediated way[29] through the earth, its gifts, our companions on earth and each other in the participating community and in the church universal. At the same time, sacramentality means that whatever we commemorate and celebrate in and through the liturgy is always provisional. We experience God through a glass darkly (1 Cor 13:12), aware that we will experience the fullness of triune *communio* in the kingdom of heaven forever. What is sacramental is revelatory of God's fullness and our full lives in God, but it never fully discloses God until we meet the triune God face-to-face and forever.

FROM "NATURAL" AND "HUMAN" (OR "SOCIAL") ECOLOGY TO "INTEGRAL ECOLOGY"

One can well argue that *On Care for Our Common Home* makes a number of contributions to understand ecology and the environment from a specifically theological point of view. There can be little argument, however, that the most important theological insight about ecology in the document is summarized in the phrase *integral ecology*, noted in several places but argued fully in chapter 4 of the encyclical (as noted above). This combines what is often called *natural* and *human* ecology. (It is notable that Benedict XVI's phrase "ecology of peace" is not part of the pope's argument. Does this indicate that one can only stretch the meaning of "ecology" so far?[30]) Pope Francis asserts that "since everything is closely interrelated, and today's problems call for a vision capable of taking into account every aspect of the global crisis, I suggest that we now consider some elements of an integral ecology, one which clearly respects its human and social dimensions" (n. 137).

As noted in the first chapter, one of the contributions which John Paul II made to this issue was his highly anthropomorphic stance toward responsibility for and care for creation.[31] Among the reasons why Benedict XVI took a similar stance was to nuance the church's understanding of ecology away from "nature conservancy" only. From his first encyclical *Redemptor Hominis* (note the title, "On the Redemption of Man") through *Evangelium Vitae* ("The Gospel of Life"), John Paul II had been very concerned to support the intrinsic worth of the human person and concomitantly to articulate responses human beings owe both to God, their Creator, and to fellow human beings. It is in this connection that contemporary papal teaching up through Pope Francis stresses responsibility for creation. This teaching can be characterized as overwhelmingly theocentric and anthropological. Creation is God's good work; human beings must respect it and preserve it for future generations. Positively put, this means that ecological destruction needs to be addressed today as one of the significant contemporary disasters and moral issues of our time. This anthropocentric vision grounds a contemporary rereading of the scriptural theme of stewardship. As Pope Francis stresses very clearly (nn. 66–67, 74–75), "dominion" means responsibility for creation. Negatively assessed this is to say that ecological destruction is not treated as sinful in itself, but rather as a byproduct of sin. At the same time in this connection, it is useful to recall that Pope Francis cited Patriarch Bartholomew, who stated that "by stripping the earth of its natural forests or destroying its wetlands; for human beings to contaminate the earth's waters, its land, its air, and its life—these are sins" (n. 8). Similarly, the problem with destruction of nature is not that nature itself is injured, but that it is a symptom of our lack of obedience to God, of sin, of the perversion of what *our* human nature ought to be—rational, sensible, and humble.[32] Given the fact that creation itself has traditionally had a privileged place in Catholic theology and belief, and that in several other religions due acknowledgment is paid to God the Creator, it would be helpful if this conventionally presumed anthropological foundation could be broadened to include respect for the world's resources precisely because they are resources from the world as created and blessed by God as "good."

Pope Francis complements and expands on this very directly. In commenting on the Book of Genesis, he asserts the rupture in the order planned by God and its effects in our relationships with God, our neighbor, and the earth.[33] In addition, the pope asserts very directly, "clearly, the Bible has no place for a tyrannical anthropocentrism unconcerned for other creatures" (n. 68), that there is no place for a "distorted anthropocentrism" (n. 69, as mentioned in chapter 1), and that "the crisis and effects of modern anthropo-centrism" are very real (nn. 115–22). The pope then writes, simply and directly, "Since everything is closely interrelated, and today's problems call for a vision capable of taking into account every aspect of the global crisis, I suggest that we now consider some elements of an integral ecology, one which clearly respects its human and social dimensions" (n. 137).

At the same time, Pope Francis argues that there cannot be a solid ecology without a solid anthropology, which therefore brings responsibilities. He asserts that the uniqueness of human beings is our ability to reason, develop arguments, be inventive, interpret reality, and to create art (n. 81).

An integral ecology[34] is inclusive and integrative of a way that we are invited to view, care for, and nurture all living beings on this good earth. Thus, any separation between "natural" ecology and "human" ecology (a phrase crafted by Benedict XVI, as noted above[35]) is transcended. This approach also reflects the best of the "both…and" rhetoric that marks much of the Catholic theological tradition.

FROM "STEWARDSHIP" TO "CARE"

When discussing the proper understanding of "dominion" in the Genesis text, the pope quotes the document from the Federation of Asian Bishops' Conferences (1993) (noted above), which stated that any understanding of "dominion" should mean "responsible stewardship."[36] This section is a direct response and correction that human beings can "use" and "abuse" the land and all that dwells on it.[37] It is more than notable that "stewardship" is used only when discussing what "dominion" really means in n. 116 and when speaking about being "stewards of creation" as a response to celebrating the Eucharist in n. 236.

In fact, the preferred term in the encyclical is not "steward" or "stewardship," but rather "care," as clearly seen in the document's title and throughout its text. The "act" part of the pope's discussion of integral ecology (again: "see," "judge," "act" [and "celebrate"]) concerns our *care* for creation. The term "care" is used over thirty times in the document to advise and remind us of our common responsibilities. When one's vocation is to "care" for creation,

119

one does not stand outside or apart from all that dwells on this good earth—plants, animals, fish, human beings, and so on—and its land and oceans themselves. One stands alongside them and works to protect them in the imagery from St. Francis with which Pope Francis begins the encyclical: "Praised be to you, my Lord, through our Sister, Mother Earth, who sustains and governs us, and who produces various fruit with colored flowers and herbs" (n. 1). He goes on to say that "we have forgotten that we ourselves are dust of the earth (Gen. 2:7); our very bodies are made up of her elements; we breathe her air and we receive life and refreshment from her waters" (n. 2). The primary and foundational assertion here is relatedness and relationships. From this perspective, we can say that the world is composed of living beings, all created good by God. The responsibility that human beings have is to nurture and care for all.

Important texts on "care" include care for the vulnerable (n. 10), a responsibility that all of us have (n. 14), healthcare (n. 28), care on behalf of biodiversity (n. 42), positive examples of what care can do (n. 58), that care is a particular (but not exclusive) Christian responsibility (n. 64), care is part of our proper responsibility for our neighbor (n. 70), care helps to redirect any notion of power (nn. 78–79), the need to be as flexible and dynamic as the modern world (n. 144), care for the indigenous communities (n. 146), which communities serve the land when they can stay and inhabit it (n. 146), care for our own bodies (n. 155), care for the ecosystem of the entire earth (n. 167, echoing the 1972 Stockholm Declaration), care for our brothers and sisters and our natural environment (n. 208) as an intrinsic part of ecological education (n. 210), the nobility of daily actions of care in very concrete circumstances of daily life (n. 211), which we learn this from our families (n. 220), care as related to inner peace (n. 225), care as part of living together and "communion" (n. 228), the need for a genuine culture of care for the environment (n. 229), care as a civic and political responsibility (n. 231), and that social (not "just" individual) love encourages us to a "culture of care" (n. 213).

One might say by way of summary that he insightfully invites us to an openness to regard other creatures as "thou" (n. 110).

MAKING DISTINCTIONS

Nature and Creation. Throughout the text, the pope uses such words as "world," "nature," "earth," "creation," "planet," "universe," "ecology," and "environment." However, he makes an important distinction between "creation" and "nature" when he says in n. 76:

> In the Judeo-Christian tradition, the word "creation" has a broader meaning than "nature," for it has to do with God's loving plan in which every creature has its own value and significance. Nature is usually seen as a system which can be studied, understood and controlled, whereas creation can only be understood as a gift from the outstretched hand of the Father of all, and as a reality illuminated by the love which calls us together into universal communion.

This moving yet direct statement can be said to characterize the understanding of the environment that runs through the encyclical.

Ecology and Environment. The pope goes on to describe both "ecology" (n. 138) and "environment" (n. 139):

> 138. Ecology studies the relationship between living organisms and the environment in which they develop. This necessarily entails reflection and debate about the conditions required for the life and survival of society, and the honesty needed to question certain models of development, production and consumption. It cannot be emphasized enough how everything is interconnected.

> 139. When we speak of the "environment," what we really mean is a relationship existing between nature and the society which lives in it. Nature cannot be regarded as something separate from ourselves or as a mere setting in which we live. We are part of nature, included in it and thus in constant interaction with it. Recognizing the reasons why a given area is polluted requires a study of the workings of society, its economy, its behaviour patterns, and the ways it grasps reality.

Given the scale of change, it is no longer possible to find a specific, discrete answer for each part of the problem. It is essential to seek comprehensive solutions which consider the interactions within natural systems themselves and with social systems. We are faced not with two separate crises, one environmental and the other social, but rather with one complex crisis which is both social and environmental. Strategies for a solution demand an integrated approach to combating poverty, restoring dignity to the excluded, and at the same time protecting nature.

CLIMATE CHANGE AND GLOBAL WARMING IN CONTEXT

From the earliest stages of discussion about what should be included in the encyclical (recall the discussion of "authorship" above), it was clear that the encyclical would not be about "climate change" or "global warming" only. Rather, it was to be a fairly comprehensive document about a host of issues which are germane to Catholic theology, teaching, spirituality, and practice. That is, in effect, what the pope gave us. At the same time the timing of the encyclical (May of 2015) was deliberate in order to be in place and known well before the global warming talks held in Paris in November and December of 2015.

With regard to the text of the encyclical, there was some debate during the drafting stages about whether or how to specify the issue of global warming and whether to assert that it is caused by human beings. The terms of the argument concerned whether including "science" might open the pope to the criticism that this is not his field of expertise (which did in fact happen in some initial negative assessments of the document). Others, who won the day, argued that without "science" an encyclical on the environment could be regarded as a pious exhortation and nothing more and, in effect, not invite much needed negotiations and decisions about climate change.

In the end, the pope took a *via media* approach by way of strategy and in sections of chapter 5 of the encyclical (nn. 164–202). I suggest that *via media* be understood in three ways: that climate change was addressed, that climate change was not the only thing addressed in the encyclical, and that there was no specification about the number of degrees that should be the goal sought for to "cool" the planet (that is, two degrees centigrade is often spoken as the goal). The pope faced into these issues in nn. 22–26 of the encyclical, more specifically at nn. 24–25.[38]

In terms of strategy of moving toward these positions, the Vatican's Pontifical Council of Sciences[39] and the more recently established Pontifical Council of Social Sciences[40] became forums about the issue of ecology, sustainability, and climate change in 2014 and 2015. Among the most important workshops were those on *Sustainable Humanity and our Responsibility* (May of 2014)[41] and on *Protect the Earth, Dignify Humanity: The Moral Dimensions of Climate Change and Sustainable Humanity* (April of 2015).[42] The fact that this second meeting was cosponsored by the Pontifical Council of Social Sciences and the group Religions for Peace is "Vatican-speak" to say that this is very high level. That the keynote addresses were given by Ban Ki-moon, the United Nations Secretary-General, and Cardinal Peter Turkson, President of the Pontifical Council for Justice and Peace, indicates that the work of the Pontifical Academy had gained the attention and respect of international leaders. The presence and contribution of Professor Jeffery Sachs, the Director of Earth Institute at Columbia University and the Director of the UN Sustainable Solutions Network, which caused some controversy because of his decided (and deliberate) approach to climate change and to ending world poverty, is notable.[43] On the other hand, the fact that Professor Sachs is so well versed on these issues would make him a likely candidate to address this conference. In the Vatican's judgment, the preponderance of scientific data indicates that human beings (in a number of guises, for example, multinational corporations) are a major cause of climate change.

At the same time, as the April 2015 meeting of the Pontifical Councils was held in Rome, there was a protest meeting also in Rome sponsored by the Chicago-based Heartland Institute. Decidedly "free market" in its orientation, the Institute was covered in some international press but made no inroads on Vatican thinking.[44]

The underlying debates, dialogue, and careful thought on these issues becomes apparent toward the end of this section of the encyclical, where the pope asserts (n. 188):

There are certain environmental issues where it is not easy to achieve a broad consensus. Here I would state once more that the Church does not presume to settle scientific questions or to replace politics. But I am concerned to encourage an honest and open debate so that particular interests or ideologies will not prejudice the common good.

While it is important to reiterate that the document is about much more than climate change, climate change is an urgent issue which the pope wants us to face. That is among the reasons why he addressed the environment in such a rich, interconnected way, especially in terms of world poverty and the destruction of the environment, in his September 2015 address to the General Assembly of the United Nations.[45]

At the same time, it is important to underscore that despite very many media descriptions, the document is about much more than "climate change." In effect what the pope offers us is a "primer" about a truly Catholic theology of God, ourselves, and all that dwell on this earth, as well as a "primer" in a truly Catholic spirituality where we are not taken out of the world to pray and worship God, but are immersed more and more fully in and on this good earth to see God in all things and to worship God above all things, even as we await our return to the Lord to see him face-to-face.

INTERCONNECTEDNESS

The very length of the document illustrates that in it the pope wants to include a number of ideas and practices that are often (regrettably) understood as separate. Early on and regularly throughout the document, the pope refers to a number of ways that everything is interconnected and the challenges that this presents: "the intimate relationship between the poor and the fragility of the planet, the conviction that everything in the world is connected, the critique of new paradigms and forms of power derived from technology, the call to seek other ways of understanding the economy and progress, the value proper to each creature, the human meaning of ecology" (n. 16).

That the pope will emphasize poverty and assert, along with the Bolivian bishops that all attacks on the environment affect the poorest (n. 48) fits in perfectly with his repeatedly stated and frequently reiterated understanding of our responsibility for each other and the earth itself. He says, "Today…we have to realize that a true ecological approach always becomes a social approach; it must integrate questions of justice in debates on the environment, so as to hear both the cry of the earth and the cry of the poor" (n. 49). Both are fragile. Because the earth and the poor have no voice we need to give voice to their life threatening concerns. We need to be the voice of the voiceless. He goes on to say that wealthier nations have the responsibility to help solve problems of poorer countries (n. 52) to the point of reasserting the now familiar claim in Catholic social teaching that we must always exercise the "preferential option for the poor" (n. 158).

In point of fact, the notion of "interconnectedness" underlies the broad scope of the document in terms of theology, economics, spirituality, science, and so on. He repeatedly links environmental and human degradation (nn. 48, 49, 56). The task of seeing all these things as related extends to a number of ethical issues, as well, such as the right to drinkable water and the plight of immigrants, among other things. The pope himself is a "walking parable" in the way he exemplifies and illustrates this integration in his teachings in practice. Just four months after beginning his Petrine ministry (March 19, 2013), when he spoke about care for creation in his homily, the pope traveled to the island of Lampedusa, a place where many immigrants seek to come on shore and begin a new life in Europe. The pope's message in word and action was and remains clear—ecology, immigration, poverty, economics, and so on are all intertwined. (This topic will be further discussed in chapter 3).

RIGHT TO LIFE AND TO A LIVING

The phrase "right to life" has been used from the early 1970s onward in American politics and society at large to speak about one's right to birth and, when applied to political processes, to putting an end to what are called "abortion rights." Once again seeing things as intrinsically interconnected, the pope places the preservation of the planet in relation to the preservation of every human life and every human embryo (n. 120).

That Francis cites abortion as one of the elements of the conversation is significant, writing the following (n. 120):

> Since everything is interrelated, concern for the protection of nature is also incompatible with the justification of abortion. How can we genuinely teach the importance of concern for other vulnerable beings, however troublesome or inconvenient they may be, if we fail to protect a human embryo, even when its presence is uncomfortable and creates difficulties?

> If personal and social sensitivity towards the acceptance of the new life is lost, then other forms of acceptance that are valuable for society also wither away.

Further along, he links abortion, sexual exploitation of children, and abandonment of the elderly (n. 123), which is yet another example of interconnectedness.

The pope raises up a number of human behaviors that lead to mitigating human life in all its forms: undrinkable water, lack of access to the world's goods, lack of access to food, lack of a home or shelter, polluted air, issues of hygiene, and so on. The issue of human healthcare from womb to tomb is, in the Catholic magisterium and tradition, named a "right" for everyone. All too often politicians frame the "right to life" debate as the "right" to an abortion or not. The pope skillfully frames the debate differently and argues that if we value life in all its forms, we are responsible for all its manifold forms.

In the contemporary politicized American culture, the "right to being born" is backed by some politicians who then deny access to childcare and education for the child's parent(s). On the other hand, many who favor postnatal care and training for parents also favor legislation that allows abortion. Because, at least in the United States, this issue is capsulized politically in the phrase "right to life," the question is asked whether and who are "pro life." The problem with "pro life" as a phrase, however, is that it is often taken to mean "antiabortion." Taking our lead from Pope Francis about interconnectedness, we might well want to ask who is truly "pro life" in terms of decrying abortion as well as decrying limiting postnatal care for families unable to pay for it or childcare for working mothers or food for the working poor, whose numbers are rising at an alarming rate. There is a holistic framework which the pope repeatedly invites us into through the encyclical, especially when it comes to "life" issues.

Pope Francis's wide framework extends to the right to a living and to a job that produces sufficient income. The right to a living wage was among the first papal pronouncements about social issues at the end of the nineteenth century in Pope Leo XIII's *Rerum Novarum*, n. 20. The fact that it remains a mantra (through Vatican II's *Gaudium et Spes*, n. 67 and the *Catechism of the Catholic Church*, n. 2434) indicates just how insightful Pope Francis is in linking environment with the economy. At the same time, it should be remembered that Pope Leo XIII's "just wage" teaching was revolutionary at the time and defamed by many. That Pope Francis has been criticized by many, especially American capitalists and some "conservative" religious commentators, whose view of capitalism is through a free market lens and whose experience of capitalism is to earn money from unregulated markets puts him in the company of Pope Leo XIII and many popes since. Here again the pope from Latin America takes his stand with the poor. The lack of a good economy gives rise to migration from poorer countries to richer ones. In this connection, the talk which Pope Francis gave in Bolivia within weeks of the encyclical's publication indicates his passion for a worldwide economy that is inclusive and just.[46]

In the end, one of the more important contributions that Pope Francis makes in *On Care for Our Common Home* is to frame the debate about human life in a wide context with a number of hitherto separate issues now seen as intrinsically interconnected and interrelated.

VOCATION AND VALUE OF HUMAN WORK

Pope Francis stands firmly in continuity with and yet deepens the thought which John Paul II expressed in *Laborem Exercens*,[47] issued on the eightieth anniversary of Leo XIII's *Rerum Novarum*. In characteristically personalist terms, John Paul II argues that part of the human vocation is to engage in work that is productive, yet at the same time humanly satisfying. In fact, he insists that labor not be subservient to capital gain, that people not be subservient to things. He continues and deepens the church's support for full employment (n. 13), that workers should receive just wages and benefits (n. 19), that workers have the right to unions (n. 20), that the disabled have the same rights as other workers (n. 22), and that there is a decidedly (Catholic) "spirituality" that should inform and sustain human beings so that work not be drudgery, but rather part of one's commitment to the common good and of all humanity (n. 25).

Pope Francis deepens these themes by commenting on the "till and keep" commands from Genesis 1:28 and 2:15 in two specific contexts. He asserts in n. 67 that "tilling" refers to cultivating, ploughing, or working, while "keeping" means caring, protecting, overseeing, and preserving. Thus, he implies a relationship of mutual responsibility between human beings and nature.[48] Fully in line with St. Bonaventure (whom he cites specifically in the text of n. 67), the pope asserts that the vocation "to till and to keep" is our responsibility in order to heal the rupture between human beings and nature, and that this should lead us to reconciliation with every creature. One of Pope Francis's key contributions is the way he contextualizes and understands "dominion" as a privilege and responsibility to care for the earth, as opposed to dominating over it in any way.

Later on in sections specifically devoted to employment, the pope speaks of the need to protect employment so that human beings may continue to "keep and till" the earth (n. 124). He reminds us of the value of labor (n. 128), that business is a noble vocation (n. 129), and that the creation and keeping of jobs is part of the common good of all. He cites in n. 156 the commonly accepted definition of the common good from n. 26 of Vatican II's *Gaudium et Spes* when he asserts that the common good "is the sum of those conditions of social life which allow social groups and their individual members relatively thorough and ready access to their own fulfillment." It is not surprising that Pope Francis asserts that "underlying every form of work is a concept of the relationship which we can and must have with what is other than ourselves" (n. 125). The now familiar themes of interconnectedness and "integral ecology" logically move toward this kind of assertion and theology.

In characteristic forthright language, Francis makes the following appeal in the first chapter of the encyclical (n. 13):

The urgent challenge to protect our common home includes a concern to bring the whole human family together to seek a sustainable and integral development, for we know that things can change. The Creator does not abandon us; he never forsakes his loving plan or repents of having created us. Humanity still has the ability to work together in building our common home. Here I want to encourage and thank all those striving in countless ways to guarantee protection of the home which we share. Particular appreciation is owed to those who tirelessly seek to resolve the tragic effects of environmental degradation on the lives of the world's poorest. Young people demand change. They wonder how anyone can claim to be building a better future without thinking of the environmental crisis and the sufferings of the excluded.

In addition, and on another level, the pope repeatedly refers to "beauty"—in particular the beauty of art, music, (even) skyscrapers, and so on (n. 103)—as powerful attestations against "tedious monotony" (n. 113). Like his patron St. Francis, he praises the "Creator of such beauty" and affirms in a holistic way that "rather than a problem to be solved, the world is a joyful mystery to be contemplated with gladness and praise" (n. 12).

Given the prosperity of the developed countries of the world and the presumption that manufactured goods can be at everyone's fingertips at any time of the day or night, one does wonder about where we put our resources and what aspects of our construction can truly be called "beautiful." Have shopping malls become our new cathedrals because materials for construction include marble, fine wood, and glass in spaces that are airy and light filled, and on occasion have pianists performing on fine instruments? Are these the houses in which we worship the god of consumption? What of houses of worship that are constructed by the cheap and the ephemeral because people do not see well-constructed, beautiful churches as part of the way we glorify God? (This is further discussed below.)

Finally, while the terms "sustainable" and "sustainability" are used over thirty times in the text, among the more poignant and pertinent for owners of small farms is the assertion that we need to work for sustainable agriculture as well as renewable and less polluting forms of energy, encouraging a better management of marine and forest resources, and ensuring universal access to drinking water" (n. 164, more on this below). The challenge the pope lays out for architects is that their designs reflect profound and constant concern for quality of life and mutual assistance for all who live on the earth (n. 150), especially when people experience "urban chaos, poor transportation and visual pollution and noise" (n. 44).

THE CHALLENGE OF "RIGHTS" LANGUAGE

In line with his predecessor Benedict XVI,[49] Pope Francis speaks about our *absolute* right to potable water (nn. 27–30) and our *relative* right to private property (n. 93). With regard to safe drinking water, the encyclical italicizes the following assertion (n. 30): *"Access to safe drinking water is a basic and universal human right, since it is essential to human survival and, as such, is a condition for the exercise of other human rights…[and that regrettably, not to say scandalously, the poor] are denied the right to life consistent with their inalienable dignity."* Regarding property, Pope Francis links this relative "right" to the "universal destination of goods" (seen in the papal magisterium outlined in chapter 1 above), asserting that "the principle of the subordination of private property to the universal destination of goods, and thus the right of everyone to their use, is a golden rule of social conduct and 'the first principle of the whole ethical and social order'" (n. 93).

On one level, the right to water seems to be easily understood in much of the United States because water is commonly (though not universally) available. Thus, the pope's statement is perfectly logical. At the same time, the second assertion about the relative right to private property seems to be diametrically opposed to the American dream of having and possessing what we want, not just what we need, and to invest for our own futures by having possessions, houses, and investment plans. The "right" to private property, however, is a relative one.

When it comes to "rights" language, it is important to recall our assertions above about the "universal, global and universal church." To my knowledge, the Catholic church is the only religion that divides up the world into parishes. This is to say that, in the end, wherever we live on this earth we belong to a territory over which the Catholic church claims responsibility for the spiritual welfare and well-being of its inhabitants. Simply put, wherever we Catholics live, we belong. This is what it means to belong to an interconnected network of parishes that comprise a diocese and an interconnected network of dioceses that forms a truly global church. One example of this is in our (hopefully instinctive) sense of charity and giving to others. If we begin from the premise and experience of belonging to each other in a parish, in a diocese, and in a worldwide church, then "rights" language can be an important reminder of what we stand for and who we are. Once we understand that we are in fact part of one another, then we will be very concerned when some of us do not have access to potable water or access to property.

Our response, therefore, will be institutional and personal. Institutional because we Catholics can rely on an international group of charitable agencies that assess damages and disburse goods, services, and money to victims, especially after "natural" disasters such as earthquakes and hurricanes, as well as "manmade" disasters such as genocide, human trafficking, war (repeatedly noted by Pope Francis), and their consequences, which media coverage of refugees across the world brings to us in vivid color. Even within our own nation, the very fact that the American bishops in Appalachia considered it their responsibility to address the land, water, and the right to both in their pastoral letters[50] reminds us who live in one part of the country that the "they" who have no water or food are really the other part of "us." Free and easy access to potable water in much of our nation should not cloud out our responsibility to share those resources with others, not just within our nation, but internationally. Just as the pope speaks about the danger of "tyrannical anthropocentrism" (n. 68), we might want to think of the danger of "tyrannical nationalism," a particular scandal for members of a global church.

An offshoot of "tyrannical nationalism" with regard to water, its allotment, and its use might well be in those parts of the United States where gated communities of the "haves" squander water on perfectly green and manicured lawns where others who live nearby have to ration their water use. The issue of "water rights" certainly affects international relations, in particular between Israel and Palestine. Catholic social teaching has consistently asserted the right to water.[51] Contemporary theologians have worked on this topic in an inclusive and challenging way.[52]

To the criticism that this might be "socialism" as opposed to (American) "capitalism," one could easily counter that being our brother's brother and our sister's sister is a fundamental biblical and Catholic tenet, whereas "capitalism" is nowhere found as part of our foundational beliefs or practices, except where the official church has critiqued its excesses. Capitalism has never been condemned by the church, but unregulated laissez-faire capitalism has repeatedly been the target of magisterial critiques from *Rerum Novarum* (1891) through Pope Francis.

PRECAUTIONARY PRINCIPLE

To those who would deny (or mitigate) that human beings cause climate change, the pope directly cites the 1992 Declaration from the "Rio" Conference in his encyclical, which conference asserted the importance of the "precautionary principle." The pope writes in n. 186,

> The Rio Declaration of 1992 states that "where there are threats of serious or irreversible damage, lack of full scientific certainty shall not be used as a pretext for postponing cost-effective measures" which prevent environmental degradation. This precautionary principle makes it possible to protect those who are most vulnerable and whose ability to defend their interests and to assemble incontrovertible evidence is limited. If objective information suggests that serious and irreversible damage may result, a project should be halted or modified, even in the absence of indisputable proof. Here the burden of proof is effectively reversed, since in such cases objective and conclusive demonstrations will have to be brought forward to demonstrate that the proposed activity will not cause serious harm to the environment or to those who inhabit it.

This would affect such practices as mountaintop drilling for coal and fracking. Both practices are very much debated today, and both offer almost immediate financial gain when practiced. Here is the place for an "honest" debate—that is, one not sponsored by special interests who already know the judgment they want, that is, the businesses that sponsor such actions—and for taking precautions where any doubt can arise about the long-term impact of such practices. One excellent example of the way the Catholic social justice teachings can be applied to fracking is the Ohio Catholic Conference.

While raising the issue of the long-term effects of practices was raised by John Paul II,[53] the "precautionary principle" and a consistent factoring in of long-term consequences when considering present actions is a keystone of Pope Francis's teaching and is a central part of his wide-angle lens through which he views the world, its resources, and especially those who are deprived of them (or who do not have their fair share of them).

Along with his immediate predecessors in the papacy, Pope Francis asserts that the market cannot guarantee integral human development (n. 109). Wise, careful, and selfless decisions can foster integral human development. In many cases, that means invoking the precautionary principle since the results of some actions may not be known immediately, but disastrous effects can become known over time. Pope Francis succinctly reminds us of the danger of short-term financial gain (n. 129).

One of the classical themes of Catholic theology related to this is eschatology (from the Greek term *eschatos*, meaning the study of "the last things" or the end of an individual life, of the world as we know it and the return of Christ at the end of time to bring time to an end). What we experience on this good earth is a foretaste of future perfection, the kingdom that will have no end. In the meantime, as we "wait in joyful hope for the coming of our Savior," we live in this world and are to appreciate that creation is "on loan" to each generation. We are to care for and till the earth, not rape it. Our responsibility is an inter-generational and intra-generational solidarity (n. 162) for what we have received and what we are then to pass on. Eschatology, then, becomes a wake-up call not only for the end of life or the world but for living carefully, responsibly, and well in the "in between" times.

FAITH AND SCIENCE

One of the hallmarks of John Paul II's papacy was the repeated initiatives he took to foster the reconciliation of faith and science, especially after the infamous Galileo debacle and succeeding evidences of the same mentality. His efforts were an important legacy for Pope Francis to inherit. In fact, the important interrelationship between faith and science becomes a presumption in the encyclical (and other writings). It must be asserted, however, that not everyone welcomed this conversation. Some scientists judged that this this a recent development, which, in fact, it is not.

Catholic tradition has always possessed the resources to embrace science. Early Christian tradition made a promising start when it interpreted ancient stories of creation as a nonliteral, yet theistic, account of the origin of the cosmos. Despite the development of a strain of theology marked by supernaturalism, the philosophical approach associated with Thomas Aquinas made it possible for Catholic teaching to accommodate and even sponsor scientific discoveries. Well before the waning of antimodernism in the twentieth century and the decrees of Vatican II, Catholic teaching learned to accommodate evolution and scientific biblical inquiry, tempering its conservatism with an openness to progressive scholarship. The social encyclicals beginning with Leo XIII highlight this development. Even though many critics of the church claim to discern an affinity between church teachings and fundamentalism's rejection of such scientific bulwarks as evolution, the highest-level institutions of the church put the lie to such a connection.[54]

With regard to the Vatican specifically, the concern about the sciences stretches as far back as 1603 with the establishment of the Pontifical Academy of Science. It is comprised of eighty academicians from a variety of fields, locales, and religions. It is headed by a president (elected from among the members), a council, and a chancellor, who is appointed by the pope. The present chancellor is Archbishop Marcello Sanchez Sorondo. His involvement in the pope's assessment of climate change has been clear since his Pontifical Academy cosponsored meeting on April 28, 2015, titled "Protect the Earth, Dignify Humanity: The Moral Dimensions of Climate Change and Sustainable Humanity," at which meeting (as noted above) the two keynote presentations were delivered by United Nations Secretary-General Ban Ki-moon and Cardinal Peter Turkson, President of the Pontifical Council for Justice and Peace.

It is clear that Pope Francis wants to continue the fruitful dialogue with scientists and the sciences, the dialogue of science and religion. At the beginning of chapter 2 of the encyclical ("The Gospel of Creation") the pope asserts, "nonetheless, science and religion, with their distinctive approaches to understanding reality, can enter into an intense dialogue fruitful for both" (n. 62). Evident here is the pope's now characteristic stance of humility and his keen desire for "dialogue." Simply put, the church does not have all the answers, but it has much to contribute to the conversation.

NOTES

1. From what was argued in chapter 1, it is notable that in the *Aparedica Document* of 2007 the CELAM bishops quote St. Francis (n. 125) when they speak about "our sister, mother earth." The longer version with which Pope Francis begins the encyclical is the centerpiece of a talk which Benedict XVI gave to students participating in a meeting promoted by the "Sister Nature Foundation" on November 28, 2011, http://w2.vatican.va/content/benedict-xvi/it/speeches/2011/november/documents/hf_ben-xvi_spe_20111128_sorella-natura.htm.

2. Vatican Press, "Conferenza Stampa per la presentazione della Lettera Enciclica 'Laudato si' del Santo Padre Francesco sulla cura della casa commune" [Press Conference for the Presentation of the encyclical letter *Laudato Si'* of the Holy Father Francis on the Care for Our Common Home], *Bulletin* (June 18, 2015), http://press.vatican.va/content/sala stampa/en/bollettino/pubblico/2015/06/18/0480/01050.html#eng.

3. A recent example are those who rejected, out of hand, parts of Benedict XVI's *Caritas in Veritate*. This dissecting and dissent is skillfully countered by Christiana Peppard in "Commodifying Creation? Pope Benedict XVI's Vision of the Goods of Creation Intended for All," in *Environmental Justice and Climate Change: Assessing Pope Benedict XVI's Ecological Vision for the Catholic Church in the United States*, ed. Jame Schaefer and Tobias Winright (Lanham: Lexington Books, 2013), 93–96.

4. Francis, Bull of Indiction for the Year of Mercy *Misericordiae Vultus* (April 11, 2015), https://w2.vatican.va/content/francesco/en/apost_let

ters/documents/papa-francesco_bolla_20150411_misericordiae-vultus.
html.

5. See the discussion in chapter 1 above, especially section 3, subsection 5 on Pope Francis's writings and section 4, subsection 1 on CELAM.

6. See chapter 1, section 4, subsection 2.

7. Benedict XVI states the following:

> On the one hand, there is an interpretation that I would call "a hermeneutic of discontinuity and rupture"; it has frequently availed itself of the sympathies of the mass media, and also one trend of modern theology. On the other, there is the "hermeneutic of reform," of renewal in the continuity of the one subject-Church which the Lord has given to us. She is a subject which increases in time and develops, yet always remaining the same, the one subject of the journeying People of God.
>
> The hermeneutic of discontinuity risks ending in a split between the pre-conciliar Church and the post-conciliar Church. It asserts that the texts of the Council as such do not yet express the true spirit of the Council. It claims that they are the result of compromises in which, to reach unanimity, it was found necessary to keep and reconfirm many old things that are now pointless. However, the true spirit of the Council is not to be found in these compromises but instead in the impulses toward the new that are contained in the texts (Benedict XVI, *Address to the Roman Curia, Christmas Greeting*, December 22, 2005, http://w2.vatican.va/content/benedict-xvi/en/speeches/2005/december/documents/hf_ben_xvi_spe_20051222_roman-curia.html).

8. Giuseppe Alberigo, ed. *The History of Vatican II*, 5 vol., English edition ed. Joseph A. Komonchak (Leuven: Peeters/Maryknoll: Orbis Books, 1995–2006). The shadow cast over this multivolume work may be a result of Alberigo's more editorialized pieces, which were excised and published in one volume as *A Brief History of Vatican II*, trans. Matthew Sherry (Maryknoll: Orbis Books, 2006).

9. Herbert Vorgrimler, ed., *Commentary on the Documents of Vatican II* (New York: Herder and Herder, 1967–69); original German, *Zweite Vatikanische Konzil. Dokumente und Kommentar*.

10. Agostino Marchetto, *Il concilio ecumenico Vaticano II: Contrappunto per la storia* (Rome: Libreria Editrice Vaticana, 2005); *The Second Vatican Ecumenical Council: A Counterpoint for the History of the Council*, trans. Kenneth D. Whitehead (Scranton: University of Scranton, 2010).

11. Roberto De Mattei, *Il concilio Vaticano II: Una storia mai scritta* (Turin: Lindau, 2010).

12. Massimo Faggioli, *Vatican II: The Battle for Meaning* (New York/ Mahwah: Paulist Press, 2012); Massimo Faggioli, *True Reform: Liturgy and Ecclesiology in Sacrosanctum Concilium* (Collegeville: Liturgical Press, 2012).

13. Ormond Rush, *Still Interpreting Vatican II: Some Hermeneutical Principles* (New York/Mahwah, NJ: Paulist Press, 2004).

14. Richard Gaillardetz, *The Church in the Making: Lumen Gentium, Christus Dominus, Orientalium Ecclesiarum* (New York/Mahwah, NJ: Paulist Press, 2006).

15. John W. O'Malley, *What Happened at Vatican II* (Cambridge: Belknap Press of the Harvard University Press, 2008); see also his article "'The Hermeneutic of Reform': A Historical Analysis," *Theological Studies* 73 (September 2012): 517–46.

16. Some examples of this ongoing, necessary, and very fruitful debate about how to interpret the Council include The Catholic University of America's four-day symposium "Reform and Renewal: Vatican II after Fifty Years" in September of 2012, as well as the same institution's symposia marking the anniversaries of some significant conciliar documents.

17. The arguments against solidarity from its critics take several forms. Ayn Rand's novels, for example, depict the basic responsibilities of association with others as corruptions and constraints on the creative authenticity of her protagonists, like John Galt. Solidarity, for Rand, is synonymous with a sort of phoniness; a life lived for the concerns of others is viewed as shameful and cowardly. Among Catholic (arch)bishops who have criticized the theories of Ayn Rand's individualism, calling it "poison," is Cardinal Sean O'Malley's Christmas Message, http://www.bostoncatholic.org/Utility/News-And-Press/Content.aspx?id=31957.

18. See John Ryan's *A Living Wage* (London: Macmillan, 1906) and *Distributive Justice* (New York: Macmillan, 1916, 1927, 3rd ed. 1942).

19. Among my own efforts to articulate the issue, see "The Development of Sacramental Doctrine in the Church," in *Recovering the Riches of Anointing: A Study of the Sacrament of the Sick* (Collegeville: Liturgical Press, 2002), 59–64, where I rely on the work of Thomas O'Meara, *Fundamentalism: A Catholic Perspective* (New York/Mahwah, NJ: Paulist Press, 1990). Also see part 1 of my own, *The Sacraments: Historical Perspectives and Liturgical Theology* (New York/Mahwah, NJ: Paulist Press, 2016), 1–167, which treats of the historical evolution of the church's sacramental rites and prayers. That Catholicism is a "both…and" and not an "either…or" theological tradition is exemplified in my own, *Models of the Eucharist* (New York/Mahwah, NJ: Paulist Press, 2005).

20. This is a rich and recurring theme in *On Care for our Common Home*, and one that requires that we rethink and reimage how we understand plants, animals, and all other living things as companions.

21. This is a major part of my thesis on developing a liturgically grounded and inspired Catholic sacramental theology. See my own, *The Sacraments: Historical Perspectives and Liturgical Theology* (New York/Mahwah, NJ: Paulist Press, 2016).

22. See the following paragraphs from *On Care for Our Common Home*:

N. 238. The Father is the ultimate source of everything, the loving and self-communicating foundation of all that exists. The Son, his reflection, through whom all things were created, united himself to this earth when he was formed in the womb of Mary. The Spirit, infinite bond of love, is intimately present at the very heart of the universe, inspiring and bringing new pathways. The world was created by the three Persons acting as a single divine principle, but each one of them performed this common work in accordance with his own personal property. Consequently, "when we contemplate with wonder the universe in all its grandeur and beauty, we must praise the whole Trinity" (citing John Paul II).

N. 239. For Christians, believing in one God who is trinitarian communion suggests that the Trinity has left its mark on all creation. Saint Bonaventure went so far as to say that human beings, before sin, were able to see how each creature "testifies that God is three". The reflection of the Trinity was there to be recognized in nature "when that book was open to man and our eyes had not yet become darkened." The Franciscan saint teaches us that each creature bears in itself a specifically Trinitarian structure, so real that it could be readily contemplated if only the human gaze were not so partial, dark and fragile. In this way, he points out to us the challenge of trying to read reality in a Trinitarian key.

N. 240. The divine Persons are subsistent relations, and the world, created according to the divine model, is a web of relationships. Creatures tend towards God, and in turn it is proper to every living being to tend towards other things, so that throughout the universe we can find any number of constant and secretly interwoven relationships. This leads us not only to marvel at the manifold connections existing among creatures, but also to discover a key to our own fulfilment. The human person grows more, matures more and is sanctified more to the extent that he or she enters into relationships, going out from themselves to live in communion with God, with others and with all creatures. In this way, they make their own that trinitarian dynamism which God imprinted in them when they were created. Everything is interconnected, and this invites us to develop a spirituality of that global solidarity which flows from the mystery of the Trinity.

23. That this is not without its problems is clear in terms of a long-term commitment to a diocese when international priests are on year-by-year contracts, language differences that impact a priest's effectiveness with a vernacular liturgy, or cultural differences in terms of expectations of parishes regarding priestly ministry. These and many other issues are discussed in, among others, Dean R. Hoge and Aniedi Okure, *International Priests in America: Challenges and Opportunities* (Collegeville: Liturgical Press, 2006) and Mary Gauthier, et. al., *Bridging the Gap: The Challenges and Opportunities of International Priests Ministering in the United States* (Washington, DC: Center for Applied Research in the Apostolate, 2014).

24. Among others, see my own: "The Sacramentality of Creation and the Role of Creation in Liturgy and Sacraments," in *Preserving the Creation: Environmental Theology and Ethics*, ed. Kevin W. Irwin and Edmund J. Pellegrino, 67–111 (Washington, DC: Georgetown University Press, 1994); "The Theology of Creation in the *Missale Romanum* of Paul VI," in *Unum Omnes in Christo: In Unitatis Servitio: Miscellanea in Honor of Gerardo J. Bekes*, 109–26 (Pannonhalma: Bences Foapatsag, 1995); "Discovering the Sacramentality of Sacraments," *Questions liturgiques* 81 (2000): 171–83; "Sacramentality and the Theology of Creation: A Recovered Paradigm for Sacramental Theology" *Louvain Studies* 23 (1998): 159–79; "The Sacramental World: The Primary Language for Sacraments," *Worship* 76, no. 3 (May 2002): 197–211; "Sacramental Theology," in *New Catholic Encyclopedia*, vol. 12, 2nd rev. ed., 465–79 (Washington, DC: CUA Press, 2002); "Cosmic Mass," in *Models of the Eucharist*, 39–66; "Sacramentality: The Fundamental Language for Liturgy and Sacraments," in *Per Ritus et Praeces: Sacramentalita della Liturgia*, 131–60, Analecta Liturgica 28 (Rome: Studia Anselmiana, 2010); "The Sacramental Principle," in *What We Have Done, What We Have Failed To Do*, 89–113; and "Sacramentality," in *The Sacraments: Historical Perspectives and Liturgical Theology*, 209–30.

25. See chapter 1, section 5, subsection 1 on Orthodox initiatives, especially Patriarch Bartholomew's annual September 1 encyclicals.

26. See nn. 235–36 of *On Care for Our Common Home*:

N. 235. The Sacraments are a privileged way in which nature is taken up by God to become a means of mediating supernatural life. Through our worship of God, we are invited to embrace the world on a different plane. Water, oil, fire and colours are taken up in all their symbolic power and incorporated in our act of praise. The hand that blesses is an instrument of God's love and a reflection of the closeness of Jesus Christ, who came to accompany us on the journey of life. Water poured over the body of a child in Baptism is a sign of new life. Encountering God does not mean fleeing from this world or turning our back on nature. This is especially clear in the spirituality of the Christian East. "Beauty, which in the East is one of the best loved names expressing the divine harmony and the model of humanity transfigured, appears everywhere: in the shape of a church, in the sounds, in the colours, in the lights, in the scents." For Christians, all the creatures of the material universe find their true meaning in the incarnate Word, for the Son of God has incorporated in his person part of the material world, planting in it a seed of definitive transformation. "Christianity does not reject matter. Rather, bodiliness is considered in all its value in the liturgical act, whereby the human body is disclosed in its inner nature as a temple of the Holy Spirit and is united with the Lord Jesus, who himself took a body for the world's salvation."

N. 236. It is in the Eucharist that all that has been created finds its greatest exaltation. Grace, which tends to manifest itself tangibly, found unsurpassable expression when God himself became man and gave himself as food for his creatures. The Lord, in the culmination of the mystery of the Incarnation, chose to reach our intimate depths through a fragment of matter. He comes not from above, but from within, he comes that we might find him in this world of ours. In the Eucharist, fullness is already achieved; it is the living centre of the universe, the overflowing core of love and of inexhaustible life. Joined to the incarnate Son, present in the Eucharist, the whole cosmos gives thanks to God. Indeed the Eucharist is itself an act of cosmic love: "Yes, cosmic! Because even when it is celebrated on the humble altar of a country church, the Eucharist is always in some way celebrated on the altar of the world." The Eucharist joins heaven and earth; it embraces and penetrates all creation. The world which came forth from God's hands returns to him in blessed and undivided adoration: in the bread of the Eucharist, "creation is projected towards divinization, toward the holy wedding feast, towards unification with the Creator himself." Thus, the Eucharist is also a source of light and motivation for our concerns for the environment, directing us to be stewards of all creation.

27. The comments of Rowan Williams about the trajectory from *Evangelii Gaudium* to the encyclical deserve inclusion and reflection: "A final

point: If I had a single reservation about *Evangelii Gaudium* it would have been that an understandable desire to avoid any churchy preciousness about liturgy made the brief remarks about the sacramental life in that document feel just a little perfunctory. This encyclical more than makes up for that in the eloquent reflections on the sacraments in its concluding pages" (Rowan Williams, "Embracing Our Limits: The Lessons of *Laudato Si'*," *Commonweal* [September 23, 2015], https://www.commonwealmag azine.org/embracing-our-limits).

28. This classic phrase is found in the first (theological) section of the Constitution on the Sacred Liturgy, n. 2 (to whose footnote to the Prayer over the Offerings on the Ninth Sunday after Pentecost from the Tridentine Missal should be added that it is now in the Prayer over the Offerings for the Second Sunday of the Year and in the Evening Mass of the Lord's Supper). Among many others, see Anscar J. Chupungco, *Handbook of Liturgical Studies*, vol. 1 (Collegeville: Liturgical Press, 1997), 345–46; and Jordi Pinell, "I testi liturgici voci di autorita nella Costizione 'Sacrosanctum Concilium.'" Congregazione per il culto dinivo (ed.,) *Costizione liturgica* "Sacrosanctum Concilium," *Studi* (Roma: Vaticano, 1986) 331–41.

29. I rely here on the phrasing of Edward Kilmartin that the liturgy is "mediated immediacy" which he adapts from the classic work by Heribert Mühlen, *Una Mystica Persona*. (Munchen, Paderborn, Wien: Schoningh, 1964). See Edward Kilmartin, "The Catholic Tradition and Eucharistic Theology: Towards the Third Millennium," *Theological Studies* 55 (1994): 435; *The Eucharist in the West*, ed. R. Daly (Collegeville: Liturgical Press, 1998), 357.

30. See nn. 8 ff. of Benedict XVI, Message for the World Day for Peace (January 1, 2007), https://w2.vatican.va/content/benedict-xvi/en/mes sages/peace/documents/hf_ben-xvi_mes_20061208_xl-world-day-peace. html.

31. See chapter 1, section 1, section 3, subsection 3.

32. On the limits of anthropocentrism of this teaching, see Daniel M. Cowdin, "Toward an Environmental Ethic," in *Preserving the Creation*; Daniel M. Cowdin, "John Paul II and Environmental Concern, Problems and Possibilities," *The Living Light* 28 (Fall 1991): 44–52; Sean McDonagh, *Passion for the Earth*, 124–46 (Maryknoll: Orbis, 1994); and Peter C. Phan, "Pope John Paul II and the Ecological Crisis," *Irish Theological Quarterly* 60 (1994): 59–69.

33. See the *On Care for Our Common Home*, nn. 66–67:

N. 66. The creation accounts in the book of Genesis contain, in their own symbolic and narrative language, profound teachings about human existence and its historical reality. They suggest that human life is grounded in three fundamental and closely intertwined relationships: with God, with our neighbour and with the earth itself. According to the Bible, these three vital relationships have been broken, both outwardly and within us. This rupture is sin. The harmony between the Creator, humanity and creation as a whole was disrupted by our presuming to take the place of God and refusing to acknowledge our creaturely limitations. This in turn distorted our mandate to "have dominion" over the earth (cf. Gen 1:28), to "till it and keep it" (Gen 2:15). As a result, the originally harmonious relationship between human beings and nature became conflictual (cf. Gen 3:17–19). It is significant that the harmony which Saint Francis of Assisi experienced with all creatures was seen as a healing of that rupture. Saint Bonaventure held that, through universal reconciliation with every creature, Saint Francis in some way returned to the state of original innocence. This is a far cry from our situation today, where sin is manifest in all its destructive power in wars, the various forms of violence and abuse, the abandonment of the most vulnerable, and attacks on nature.

N. 67. We are not God. The earth was here before us and it has been given to us. This allows us to respond to the charge that Judaeo-Christian thinking, on the basis of the Genesis account which grants man "dominion" over the earth (cf. Gen 1:28), has encouraged the unbridled exploitation of nature by painting him as domineering and destructive by nature. This is not a correct interpretation of the Bible as understood by the Church. Although it is true that we Christians have at times incorrectly interpreted the Scriptures, nowadays we must forcefully reject the notion that our being created in God's image and given dominion over the earth justifies absolute domination over other creatures. The biblical texts are to be read in their context, with an appropriate hermeneutic, recognizing that they tell us to "till and keep" the garden of the world (cf. Gen 2:15). "Tilling" refers to cultivating, ploughing or working, while "keeping" means caring, protecting, overseeing and preserving. This implies a relationship of mutual responsibility between human beings and nature. Each community can take from the bounty of the earth whatever it needs for subsistence, but it also has the duty to protect the earth and to ensure its fruitfulness for coming generations. "The earth is the Lord's" (Ps 24:1); to him belongs "the earth with all that is within it" (Dt 10:14). Thus God rejects every claim to absolute ownership: "The land shall not be sold in perpetuity, for the land is mine; for you are strangers and sojourners with me" (Lev 25:23).

34. Some commentators have asserted that the pope's approach to "integral ecology" follows that of Leonardo Boff. See Boff's article at http://www.earthcharterinaction.org/content/articles/1149/1/Article-by-Leonardo-Boff-on-the-Popes-Encyclical/Page1.html; also his *Cry of the Earth, Cry of the Poor*, trans. Phillip Berryman (Maryknoll: Orbis, 1997).

35. See chapter 1, section 3, subsection 4.

36. See *Care for Our Common Home*, n. 116, fn. 94.

37. For English-speaking audiences, this will resonate with the criticism by Lynn White in his article "The Historical Roots of our Ecological Crisis," *Science* 155 (1967): 1203–07.

38. See *On Care for Our Common Home*, nn. 24–25:

N. 24. Warming has effects on the carbon cycle. It creates a vicious circle which aggravates the situation even more, affecting the availability of essential resources like drinking water, energy and agricultural production in warmer regions, and leading to the extinction of part of the planet's biodiversity. The melting in the polar ice caps and in high altitude plains can lead to the dangerous release of methane gas, while the decomposition of frozen organic material can further increase the emission of carbon dioxide. Things are made worse by the loss of tropical forests which would otherwise help to mitigate climate change. Carbon dioxide pollution increases the acidification of the oceans and compromises the marine food chain. If present trends continue, this century may well witness extraordinary climate change and an unprecedented destruction of ecosystems, with serious consequences for all of us. A rise in the sea level, for example, can create extremely serious situations, if we consider that a quarter of the world's population lives on the coast or nearby, and that the majority of our megacities are situated in coastal areas.

N. 25. Climate change is a global problem with grave implications: environmental, social, economic, political and for the distribution of goods. It represents one of the principal challenges facing humanity in our day. Its worst impact will probably be felt by developing countries in coming decades. Many of the poor live in areas particularly affected by phenomena related to warming, and their means of subsistence are largely dependent on natural reserves and ecosystemic services such as agriculture, fishing and forestry. They have no other financial activities or resources which can enable them to adapt to climate change or to face natural disasters, and their access to social services and protection is very limited. For example, changes in climate, to which animals and plants cannot adapt, lead them to migrate; this in turn affects the livelihood of the poor, who are then forced to leave their homes, with great uncertainty for their future and that of their children. There has been a tragic rise in the number of migrants seeking to flee from the growing poverty caused by environmental degradation. They are not recognized by international conventions as refugees; they bear the loss of the lives they have left behind, without enjoying any legal protection whatsoever. Sadly, there is widespread indifference to such suffering, which is even now taking place throughout our world. Our lack of response to these tragedies involving our brothers and sisters points to the loss of that sense of responsibility for our fellow men and women upon which all civil society is founded.

39. The Pontifical Academy of Sciences, http://www.casinapioiv.va/content/accademia/en.html.

40. The Pontifical Academy of Social Sciences, http://www.pass.va/content/scienzesociali/en.html.

41. The Pontifical Academy of Sciences, *Sustainable Humanity and our Responsibility* (May 2014), http://www.casinapioiv.va/content/accademia/en/publications/extraseries/sustainable.html.

42. The Pontifical Academy of Sciences, *Protect the Earth, Dignify Humanity: The Moral Dimensions of Climate Change and Sustainable Humanity* (April 2015), http://www.casinapioiv.va/content/accademia/en/events/2015/protectearth.html.

43. Among several others, see Jeffrey Sachs, *The End of Poverty: Economic Possibilities for Our Time* (New York: Random House, 2006).

44. The Heartland Institute, https://www.heartland.org/.

45. Francis, Address to the Members of the General Assembly of the United Nations Organization (September 25, 2015), http://w2.vatican.va/content/francesco/en/speeches/2015/september/documents/papa-francesco_20150925_onu-visita.html.

46. Francis, "Address to the Second World Meeting of Popular Movements" (July 9, 2015), http://w2.vatican.va/content/francesco/en/speeches/2015/july/documents/papa-francesco_20150709_bolivia-movimenti-popolari.html.

47. See chapter 1, section 3, subsection 3.

48. The English translation "mutual responsibility" is somewhat weaker than the Spanish, which reads "una relacion de reciprocal" or the Italian which reads "una relazione di reciprocita responsabile," which

can be rendered "a reciprocal relation" and "a relation of reciprocal responsibility."

49. Among others, see Pope Benedict XVI's message, delivered by Cardinal Renato Martino, for the International Exposition on Water and Sustainable Development in Zaragoza, Spain, June 14–September 14, http://w2.vatican.va/content/benedict-xvi/en/letters/2008/documents/hf_ben-xvi_let_20080710_expo-zaragoza.html.

50. See chapter 1, section 4, subsection four.

51. Among others, see Pontifical Council for Justice and Peace, *Water, an essential Element for Life* (Vatican City: Pontifical Council for Justice and Peace, 2003), as well as other more recent statements such as that prepared for the 2012 international forum on water, http://www.vatican.va/roman_curia/pontifical_councils/justpeace/documents/rc_pc_just peace_doc_20120312_france-water_it.html.

52. Among others, see Christiana Z. Peppard, *Just Water: Theology, Ethics, and the Global Water Crisis* (Maryknoll: Orbis, 2014). The pope asserts how water poured over a child at baptism brings new life (n. 235). The end of the prayer for blessing water at the Easter Vigil is "springs of water, bless the Lord, praise and exalt him above all for ever." Among the "praise" psalms in the Liturgy of the Hours is Psalm 148:7–8: "Praise the Lord from the earth, / you sea monsters and all deeps, / fire and hail, snow and frost, stormy wind fulfilling his command!" The refrain in the Canticle from Daniel (3:57–88) is "bless the Lord," for example, "Cold and chill, bless the Lord, / Dew and rain, bless the Lord, / Frost and chill, bless the Lord, / Ice and snow, bless the Lord."

53. Recall the assertions by John Paul II cited in chapter 1, section 3, subsection 3, which include the following:

- Encyclical Letter *Redemptor Hominis* (4 March 1979), in which he emphasizes "people over things";
- *Homily at Living History Farm, Des Moines [Iowa, USA]* (October 4, 1979), in which he speaks on humanity's responsibility toward conservation;
- the 1984, 1987, 1991, and 1993 addresses to the participants of the Study Week Organized by the Pontifical Academy of Sciences, where he calls for responsible use of technology (1984, 1987), argues against irrational use of nature (1991), and calls for human responsibility and self-control (1993);
- Encyclical Letter *Sollicitudo Rei Socialis* (December 30, 1987), in which he argues for limits to indiscriminate possession and products of human industry;

- Encyclical Letter *Centesimus Annus* (May 1, 1991), in which he decries contemporary focus on possession of things and asserts the need, instead, to relate them to the truth;
- *Catechesis* (January 17, 2001), in which he observes that man, in pursuing his own prerogatives, places himself into conflictual tension with his mission from God.

54. See Robin Darling Young, "Does the Earth Have Rights? Hopes and Expectations Ahead of the Next Encyclical *Commonweal* (April 30, 2015), https://www.commonwealmagazine.org/does-earth-have-rights.

CHAPTER THREE

Implementation

The purpose of this chapter is to delineate and expand on a number of issues which Pope Francis raises for reflection and action. Fidelity to the "see, judge, act (and celebrate)" methodology is the requirement that what we now "see" in a new light through papal teaching requires that we make judgments based on that teaching that together lead to new or changing patterns of "action" and "celebration" communally, collegially, and personally. Some issues are joined together because the pope himself argues repeatedly about "interconnectedness," and in my opinion they seem to be both interconnected and intertwined. Others topics (for example, liturgical practice) are intrinsically linked together.

I. TEACHING AND DIALOGUE

As has been noted more than once, this encyclical is addressed to all persons, but in addition, and quite strikingly, this document is an invitation to *dialogue* with all persons. The reality of "dialogue" has marked the post–Vatican II church, specifically dialogue with other churches and other religions. That Pope Francis invites all to such a posture of give-and-take is highly laudable. Many find this in accord with the manner with which the pope teaches many things—by word and example. Like Jesus in Matthew 7:29, he teaches "with authority," not with "power." The pope argues, most often very persuasively, and engages his hearers in a dialogue. This is specified, invited, and even required from reading the encyclical.

However, one temptation that can confront those in dialogue

is to water down positions for the sake of commonality. A principle of all ecumenical dialogue should be that the partners not only dialogue with each other across denominational lines, but that they always need to check back with their own colleagues to make sure that positions taken are faithful to their church or religious group. This temptation is particularly acute in multilateral dialogues. If what is achieved is "the least common denominator," then neutrality masks depth and a neutral color masks the many hues of Catholic thought and theology.

With regard to climate change, for example, in September of 2014 there was an interfaith summit at Union Theological Seminary in New York City followed by an interfaith march the following Sunday on the streets in Manhattan. At the end of the weekend, thirty-two signatories signed off on a document titled "The Statement," subtitled "Climate, Faith and Hope: Faith Traditions Together for a Common Future."[1] My own assessment is that it made some fine assertions about climate change from a religious vantage point. Yet as a Roman Catholic, I wonder whether it was too generic and was so broad in its origins and intentions that, in effect, it was not so much a theological statement as a statement for all people of goodwill from a number of people of goodwill. My sense is that it was a disappointment and ultimately could lead us back to the "broad but not deep" place many of us found ourselves in during the early 1990s (recall this assertion in the Preface). In addition, that it addressed climate change and not other aspects of the full range of issues that are related to the environment, especially from a religious perspective, was equally disappointing.

The pope addresses every person on the planet and invites us to a dialogue about the present ecological crisis and the contribution which Roman Catholicism can offer. In particular, while offering a comprehensive presentation from the Catholic perspective, he invites an ecumenical conversation as he generously cites the work of Patriarch Bartholomew and the Orthodox church.

We need to be willing to adopt new perspectives even as we nuance our own. Among the issues involved in dialogue is that we bring to bear all of what we believe and offer it for reflection and discussion. Dialogue also means that we recognize that we do not have all the answers and that we are to be open and docile to the dialogue process. It also means that in this area, among many others as cited in the encyclical, we need to practice *humility*. This virtue is seen in the tone of the document and in the tone which the pope adopted in his speech to the U.S. Congress (September 24, 2015)[2] and to the United Nations (September 25, 2015).[3]

In addition to humility, the encyclical calls for sobriety (n. 224) and urges that a "less is more" conviction mark our thought about and actions toward our common home. Clearly these are ancient tenets of the Christian tradition (see more in the next chapter about monasticism). They are meant to be liberating. However, the pope judges that "sobriety and humility were not favorably regarded in the last century" (n. 224), with ensuing dire consequences.[4] The pope argues that part of sobriety and humility is being at peace with oneself (n. 225). Part of an authentic Catholic spirituality includes the cultivation of inner peace.[5] While endorsing Pope John Paul II's call for an "ecological conversion" (especially in all of chapter 6, where he reflects on the profound way that Catholic spirituality relates to ecology), he combines this with his repeated call for an "integral ecology" (n. 225).

II. INTELLECTUAL HONESTY AND ACADEMIC FREEDOM

From the very beginning of the encyclical, the pope calls for an "honest" debate about ecology (nn. 16, 138, 184, 188, 229) and for researchers to be allowed to continue their studies in full "academic freedom" (n. 140). He specifies this more fully in chapter 5, which is given the subtitle "dialogue and transparency in decision-making." This reference to "transparency" reflects the pope's experience of witnessing corruption and the exchange of favors regarding construction projects at the risk of harming the environment (n. 182). The pope applauds the practice of what we often call "environment impact studies" (his phrase is "environment impact assessment") so that honest, proper assessments can be made up front (n. 183). He also adopts a "preferential option for the poor" approach when he asserts that "the local population should have a special place at the table; they are concerned about their own future and that of their children, and can consider goals transcending immediate economic interest. We need to stop thinking in terms of 'interventions' to save the environment in favor of policies developed and debated by all interested parties" (n. 183). The pope's principle of interconnectedness is exemplified when he enumerates the factors that should be included in making such an assessment: the use of natural resources, levels of emission or discharge, the amount of refuse, changes to the landscape, and the habitats of protected species or public spaces. He pointedly asserts that "some projects, if insufficiently studied, can profoundly affect the quality of life of an area due to very different factors such as unforeseen noise pollution, the shrinking of visual horizons, the loss of cultural values, or the effects of nuclear energy use." He concludes this paragraph by combining his frequent critique of consumerism with transparency: "the culture of consumerism, which prioritizes short-term gain and private interest, can make it easy to rubber-stamp authorizations or to conceal information."

The pope invokes the absolute right to potable water with "the precautionary principle," with making a decision to stop a project. In n. 185 he states, "in this discernment ["discernment" is a word that is central to Jesuit spirituality], some questions must have higher priority. For example, we know that water is a scarce and indispensable resource and a fundamental right which conditions the exercise of other human rights." He then says in n. 187:

> If objective information suggests that serious and irreversible damage may result, a project should be halted or modified, even in the absence of indisputable proof. Here the burden of proof is effectively reversed, since in such cases objective and conclusive demonstrations will have to be brought forward to demonstrate that the proposed activity will not cause serious harm to the environment or to those who inhabit it.

In addition to presuming that all people of goodwill would want to enter such a debate this way, the pope is also signaling that outside influences such as multinational corporations, politicians, and people under the influence of outside money might try to influence the debate and should be called out and not included.

The corruption and compromise caused by financial pressure cannot be ignored.

At the same time as there are places with no potable water, there are also places where the presumed potable water was found to be contaminated. For example, in January of 2014 the water for 300,000 West Virginia residents was polluted because of a chemical spill in the Elk River. Nine months later, six officials of the coal mining company whose cleaning plant is on the riverbank were indicted for violations to the Clean Water Act. Another example is the water crisis in Flint, Michigan. In April of 2014, the city of Flint changed its water source from treated Lake Huron water (via Detroit) to the Flint River. Almost immediately its drinking water had a series of problems that culminated with lead contamination, creating a serious public health danger. The corrosive Flint River water caused lead from aging pipes to leach into the water supply, causing extremely elevated levels of lead. As a result, between 6,000 and 12,000 residents had severely high levels of lead in the blood and experienced a range of serious health problems. In November of 2015, four families filed a federal class action lawsuit (the first of many lawsuits) in the United States District Court for the Eastern District of Michigan in Detroit against Governor Rick Snyder and thirteen other city and state officials. Separately, the United States Attorney's Office for the Eastern District of Michigan and the Michigan Attorney General's office opened investigations. On January 5, 2016, the city was declared to be in a state of emergency by the Governor of Michigan, before President Obama declared the crisis as a federal state of emergency, authorizing additional help from the Federal Emergency Management Agency and the Department of Homeland Security less than two weeks later.

Four government officials—one from the City of Flint, two from the Michigan Department of Environmental Quality, and one from the Environmental Protection Agency—resigned over the mishandling of the crisis. Snyder issued an apology to citizens and promised to fix the problem, and later sent $28 million to Flint for supplies, medical care, and infrastructure upgrades. Subsequently, it was revealed that the majority of the people affected were African American and Latinos many of whom were undocumented. It was judged that given their skin color and status that there would be no repercussions from the decision to change the source of the water. Among other factors social media and mainstream media broke and carried the story to the embarrassment of city officials. That Michigan Governor Rick Snyder met with President Obama about the crisis at the White House attests to the urgency of this health issue (and, some have argued, to the power of the media in the United States).[6]

That the church must teach humbly is reflected in the pope's assertion that the church is by no means opposed to technology, and that "there are certain environmental issues where it is not easy to achieve a broad consensus. Here, I would state once more that the church does not presume to settle scientific questions or to replace politics, but I am concerned to encourage an honest and open debate so that particular interests or ideologies will not prejudice the common good" (n. 188). Such assertions reflect and apply bedrock Catholic principles and theology.

III. SOLIDARITY, SUSTAINABILITY, SUBSIDIARITY

Especially because of what was noted in chapter 2 about how to interpret Catholic social justice teaching, it is important to cite and apply the way Pope Francis uses these terms. In effect, he adopts the usages of previous Catholic teaching and adds important applications to the environment.

SOLIDARITY

Again, as noted in chapter 2, the notion of "solidarity" has received generous application by previous popes and Catholic teaching. No fewer than fourteen times does Pope Francis refer to "solidarity." Again, not surprisingly, he cites two of his predecessor's teachings. The first is his use of Benedict XVI's teaching that "every violation of solidarity and civic friendship harms the environment"[7] in the context of arguing (in n. 142) his now familiar position that "everything is related" and "social ecology is necessarily institutional, and gradually extends to the whole of society, from the primary social group, the family, to the wider local, national and international communities." Further along he cites

Benedict on intergenerational and intragenerational solidarity,[8] and Pope Francis notes "intergenerational" solidarity two more times in n. 159.

At the very beginning of the encyclical, the pope argues that "we require a new and universal solidarity" (n. 14)[9] and goes on to say that "for all our limitations, gestures of generosity, solidarity and care cannot but well up within us, since we were made for love" (n. 58). In that same paragraph, he cites improvements made to the environment and later argues that such acts of solidarity continue to be practiced by the poor in places of dense population, whose density can cause a feeling of asphyxiation (n. 148).[10] A bit further along he offers a summons to solidarity and reiterates the church's "preferential option for the poor" and the long established principle of "the common good" (n. 158). Among his more specific recommendations here is that the poor have access to and use solar energy for their own sake now and for the sake of future generations. In line with the rest of the document, he links concern for the poor with education about and care for our common home (nn. 210, 232). He encourages all to daily expressions of gratitude, especially at grace before and after meals, and to acknowledge and thank God, in particular for the gifts of creation (n. 227).[11]

SUSTAINABILITY

Pope Francis joins his voice with many others in religious circles and outside of them (for example, in the world of engineering and development, as the pope himself notes in n. 102) for a kind of development that is both "integral" and "sustainable." At the beginning of the encyclical the pope makes this "appeal" by asserting (n. 14):

> the urgent challenge to protect our common home includes a concern to bring the whole human family together to seek a sustainable and integral development, for we know that things can change. The Creator does not abandon us; he never forsakes his loving plan or repents of having created us. Humanity still has the ability to work together in building our common home.

He links integral and sustainable development with the common good in n. 18. That he links sustainable development with the notion of the world as a "sacrament of communion" from Patriarch Bartholomew's 2012 address at Halki—(again, as noted in chapter 1 titled "Global Responsibility and Ecological Sustainability")—reflects his indebtedness to and reliance on the work of the Patriarch (and by extension to the Orthodox church).[12]

Among the ways the pope uses "sustainability" are his concerns for the use of fresh drinking water (n. 28), that one of the reasons why some argue for a reduction of the birth rate is regrettably the lack of a sustainable use of the environment (n. 50), that multinational corporations often "use" resources in developing countries (n. 51) and often "leave behind great human and environmental liabilities such as unemployment, abandoned towns, the depletion of natural reserves, deforestation, the impoverishment of agriculture and local stock breeding, open pits, riven hills, polluted rivers and a handful of social works which are no longer sustainable."[13] To this the pope adds what developed countries owe to the developing world as a result (n. 52). Both "intergenerational solidarity" (n. 159) and planning for the agricultural needs of the "international community" (n. 164, 180) reflect the pope's global vision and his responsibility to offer insight about our responsibility for each other on this good earth. The pope names and counters the positions of those who argue that placing emphasis on sustainability in planning and practice is "a waste of money" (n. 190). Toward the end of this section of the document he makes this urgent and poignant appeal (n. 194):

> Put simply, it is a matter of redefining our notion of progress. A technological and economic development which does not leave in its wake a better world and an integrally higher quality of life cannot be considered progress. Frequently, in fact, people's quality of life actually diminishes—by the deterioration of the environment, the low quality of food or the depletion of resources—in the midst of economic growth. In this context, talk of sustainable growth usually becomes a way of distracting attention and offering excuses. It absorbs the language and values of ecology into the categories of finance and technocracy, and the social and environmental responsibility

of businesses often gets reduced to a series of marketing and image-enhancing measures.

That the pope refers to the efforts of the United Nations in this regard from the Stockholm Summit (1972) and the Earth Summit in Rio (1992) is notable, specifically the latter's assertion that "human beings are at the centre of concerns for sustainable development." This phrasing gets beyond the "natural" versus "human" ecology divide. At the same time, the pope is not shy about critiquing national and international efforts about the environment (see, for example, n. 54).[14]

SUBSIDIARITY

The pope uses the term "subsidiarity" in two places in the encyclical, both of which stand in line with the social justice teachings of the church, as well as contain a wealth of tersely worded insight. The first (n. 157) links the common good with respect for persons, especially the family, and a distributive justice that works toward social peace, security, and stability.[15] The second (n. 196) restates the principle of subsidiarity and weighs the pros and cons where economic issues play a dominant role and offers his own critique.[16]

IV. LINKING ECOLOGY, MIGRATION, ECONOMICS, AND POLITICS

Pope Francis's repeated assertion in the encyclical about things being "interconnected" is exemplified in the way he argues about the intrinsic relationship among ecology, migration, economics, and politics. One reference to migration in the encyclical is a quotation from Benedict XVI's *Caritas in Veritate*, in which Benedict himself cites John XXIII. Part of n. 175 of the encyclical reads,

> As Benedict XVI has affirmed in continuity with the social teaching of the Church: "To manage the global economy; to revive economies hit by the crisis; to avoid any deterioration of the present crisis and the greater imbalances that would result; to bring about integral and timely disarmament, food

security and peace; to guarantee the protection of the environment and to regulate migration: for all this, there is urgent
need of a true world political authority, as my predecessor
Blessed John XXIII indicated some years ago."[17]

A major focus of Pope Francis's teaching and practice ("see, judge,
act") has been how migration and its causes (for example, the
economy, civil wars, and religious persecution) effects the breakup
of families. As noted in the previous chapter, Pope Francis's first
trip outside of mainland Italy was to the island of Lampedusa,
a destination for tens of thousands migrating to Europe through
Italy. The liturgy he celebrated there was utterly simple, with
artifacts reflecting a nautical motif, and the pope's homily began
with these stark words:

> Immigrants dying at sea, in boats which were vehicles of hope
> and became vehicles of death. That is how the headlines put
> it. When I first heard of this tragedy a few weeks ago, and
> realized that it happens all too frequently, it has constantly
> come back to me like a painful thorn in my heart. So I felt
> that I had to come here today, to pray and to offer a sign of
> my closeness, but also to challenge our consciences lest this
> tragedy be repeated. Please, let it not be repeated![18]

Sadly, "this tragedy" has been repeated again and again with
one million immigrants arriving in Europe during 2015, tens of
thousands dying in the attempt. That the pope made immigration
a major priority for the Vatican is clear in his so-called "state of the
world" address to diplomats accredited to the Holy See in January
of 2016.[19]

At the center of his homily at Lampedusa, he reminded his lis-
teners of the dialogue between God and Adam in Genesis when
God asks, "Where are you?" and between God and Cain when
God asks, "Where is your brother?" The pope then said,

> God's two questions echo even today, as forcefully as ever!
> How many of us, myself included, have lost our bearings; we
> are no longer attentive to the world in which we live; we don't
> care; we don't protect what God created for everyone, and

we end up unable even to care for one another! And when humanity as a whole loses its bearings, it results in tragedies like the one we have witnessed.

This text forms a bridge between the pope's emphasis on caring for each other and all of creation, expressed in the homily he delivered at the inaugural Mass of his pontificate (2013) and his more developed teachings on linking ecology and migration, witnessed in his address to the European Parliament, to the United States Congress, and to the United Nations (2015).[20] The people of Lampedusa gave the pope a photo album as a souvenir gift of his visit. It was a large photo album containing black and white photos of immigrants arriving at Lampedusa, all in makeshift vessels, all huddled together. Half of the photos were of smiling, obviously very happy (mostly African) refugees as they arrived safely. The other half were of vessels arriving with all of the passengers dead. When the pope arrived back in Rome, he gave the album to Cardinal Peter Turkson, President of the Pontifical Council for Justice and Peace, who regularly shows the photos to visitors. If pictures are worth a thousand words, some words— like migration—are worth a thousand pictures. They resonate and reflect the pope's plea, "Let it not be repeated."

At the risk of oversimplification, it is argued that the migration issues in 2015 concerned fleeing the civil war in Syria and the economy of many African countries. Hence, it is no surprise that the pope regularly links ecology with the economy, and more specifically with the poor. Again he credits his predecessor Benedict XVI, who offers this challenge to members of the diplomatic corps assigned to the Holy See, challenging them to work toward "eliminating the structural causes of the dysfunctions of the world economy and correcting models of growth which have proved incapable of ensuring respect for the environment" (n. 6). That the poor and the root causes of poverty are at the heart of Francis's papacy is reflected on almost every page of the encyclical. Among the most pertinent and poignant summaries of this issue are the pope's arguments about "global inequality." At the beginning of n. 49, he asserts, "It needs to be said that, generally speaking, there is little in the way of clear awareness of problems which especially affect the excluded." This assertion obviously comes from his association with and ministry to the poor in Buenos Aires. He ends the same paragraph by indicating one of the implications of his "integral ecology" when he asserts succinctly and pointedly: "Today, however, we have to realize that a true ecological approach always becomes a social approach; it must integrate questions of justice in debates on the environment, so as to hear both the cry of the earth and the cry of the poor."[21] With regard to business itself, the pope boldly asserts in n. 195 that "the principle of the maximization of profits, frequently isolated from other considerations, reflects a misunderstanding of the very concept of the economy."

That the pope relies on the cooperation of national leaders and international bodies like the European Union and the United Nations is clear. Yet he is also not unwilling to criticize them and to invite other bodies into conversations about ecology and the environment. He argues for international agreements about care for the earth (n. 173) and governance for oceans (n. 174). For example, his address to European Parliament in November of 2014 reflects this challenging call to dialogue. He assessed that, although the European Union seems to have grown larger and stronger over the last 25 years (when Pope John Paul II last addressed the same body), the increasing interconnectedness of the globe has led to less "Eurocentrism" and the impression that Europe itself is "somewhat elderly and haggard, feeling less and less a protagonist in a world which frequently regards it with aloofness, mistrust and even, at times, suspicion."[22] In that address, he praised Europe for being a leader in efforts of ecology, while at the same time calling on European leaders to engage once more in dialogue and "to abandon the idea of a Europe which is fearful and self-absorbed, in order to revive and encourage a Europe of leadership, a repository of science, art, music, human values and faith as well."[23] In this same manner of praise for ecological efforts and critique of their limited success, Francis reminds us in the encyclical (n. 166):

> Worldwide, the ecological movement has made significant advances, thanks also to the efforts of many organizations of civil society. It is impossible here to mention them all, or to review the history of their contributions. But thanks to their efforts, environmental questions have increasingly

found a place on public agendas and encouraged more far-sighted approaches. This notwithstanding, recent World Summits on the environment have not lived up to expectations because, due to lack of political will, they were unable to reach truly meaningful and effective global agreements on the environment.

Such World Summits included in this discussion are, among others, the 1992 Earth Summit in Rio de Janeiro.

Moving further into his concern for dialogue in the section on "dialogue for new national and local policies," the pope argues (n. 175):

The twenty-first century, while maintaining systems of governance inherited from the past, is witnessing a weakening of the power of nation states, chiefly because the economic and financial sectors, being transnational, tends to prevail over the political. Given this situation, it is essential to devise stronger and more efficiently organized international institutions, with functionaries who are appointed fairly by agreement among national governments, and empowered to impose sanctions.

When it comes to articulating some of the avenues that might be taken on national and international levels to deal with the environmental crisis, as the pope directly calls it (in n. 101), the pope is not shy. He says (n. 53):

The problem is that we still lack the culture needed to confront this crisis. We lack leadership capable of striking out on new paths and meeting the needs of the present with concern for all and without prejudice towards coming generations. The establishment of a legal framework which can set clear boundaries and ensure the protection of ecosystems has become indispensable; otherwise, the new power structures based on the techno-economic paradigm may overwhelm not only our politics but also freedom and justice.

In n. 175, Pope Francis asserts,

As Benedict XVI has affirmed in continuity with the social teaching of the Church: "To manage the global economy; to revive economies hit by the crisis; to avoid any deterioration of the present crisis and the greater imbalances that would result; to bring about integral and timely disarmament, food security and peace; to guarantee the protection of the environment and to regulate migration: for all this, there is urgent need of a true world political authority," as my predecessor Blessed John XXIII indicated some years ago.

Diplomacy also takes on new importance in the work of developing international strategies which can anticipate serious problems affecting us all.

That Pope Francis judges the involvement of the Vatican at the Paris conference on climate change (November and December of 2015, sometimes cited as "COP21) to have been an important "success" is reflected in his statement for the World Day of Peace (2016) when he says,

Some events of the year now ending inspire me, in looking ahead to the new year, to encourage everyone not to lose hope in our human ability to conquer evil and to combat resignation and indifference. They demonstrate our capacity to show solidarity and to rise above self-interest, apathy and indifference in the face of critical situations.

Here I would mention the efforts to bring world leaders together at COP21 in the search for new ways to confront climate change and to protect the earth, our common home. We can also think of two earlier global events: the Addis Ababa Summit for funding sustainable development worldwide and the adoption of the United Nations 2030 Agenda for Sustainable Development, aimed at ensuring a more dignified standard of living for all the world's peoples, especially the poor, by that year.[24]

V. CONSUMERISM AND THE "THROWAWAY CULTURE"

Pope Francis cites Benedict XVI (n. 6) who cautions against viewing everything as "our property" to be used "for ourselves alone."[25] This kind of statement is bold on its own and deeply challenging, but it needs to be recalled that the pope is writing for a global audience with varied societal systems with varying kinds of support for things like education and pensions. This includes countries with repressive, communist-based (or at least inspired) regimes where ownership is really unknown. It would seem that Americans need to be reminded of this principle even as we need to deal day-to-day with the costs of (especially higher) education and financial planning for retirement.

This is followed by the rhetorically poignant challenge that the pope cites from Patriarch Bartholomew, who asks us "to replace consumption with sacrifice, greed with generosity, wastefulness with a spirit of sharing, an asceticism that entails learning to give, and not simply to give up. It is a way of loving, of moving gradually away from what I want to what God's world needs. It is liberation from fear, greed and compulsion."[26]

By way of introducing "consumerism" and "consumption" (and other variations on these words, occurring over sixty times in the encyclical), Pope Francis refers to the example of St. Francis in combining contemplation and action: "If we approach nature and the environment without this openness to awe and wonder, if we no longer speak the language of fraternity and beauty in our relationship with the world, our attitude will be that of masters, consumers, ruthless exploiters, unable to set limits on their immediate needs" (n. 11).

Pope Francis adopts and develops what his immediate predecessors and Patriarch Bartholomew have said about consumerism and human consumption. In n. 5, for example, Francis generously quotes John Paul II's *Redemptor Hominis* that human beings frequently seem "to see no other meaning in their natural environment than what serves for immediate use and consumption."[27] Subsequently, John Paul II would call (in his *Catechesis of January 17, 2001*) for a global "ecological conversion" and noted (in his encyclical *Centesimus Annus*, n. 38) that little effort had been made to "safeguard the moral conditions for an authentic human ecology." Later in *Centesimus Annus* (n. 58), John Paul II exhorted that "every effort to protect and improve our world entails profound changes in lifestyles, models of production and consumption, and the established structures of power which today govern societies."[28]

The pope reiterates the insights of his predecessors by linking consumerism and rampant individualism, for example, n. 162.[29] Like his predecessors, he argues that a change in lifestyle is necessary on the part of those who consume far more of the world's resources than could be judged to be their "fair share." He cites Benedict XVI (in n. 193), who argued that "technologically advanced societies must be prepared to encourage more sober lifestyles, while reducing their energy consumption and improving its efficiency." One example of his demonstration of "collegiality in practice" by citing documents from episcopal conferences reflects this same concern when he cites the statement of the bishops of New Zealand who asked what the commandment "Thou shall not kill" means when "twenty percent of the world's population consumes resources at a rate that robs the poor nations and future generations of what they need to survive."[30] The pope reiterates traditional Catholic teaching against abortion (as previously noted) and argues that equitable distribution of resources is the real issue which some use to argue about diminishing the birth rate (n. 50).[31]

While we will deal with the pope's concerns about "markets" in the next section, it is worth noting that he links the market with consumerism in n. 123 when he addresses the particularly vulnerable in a "culture of relativism"

> which drives one person to take advantage of another, to treat others as mere objects, imposing forced labour on them or enslaving them to pay their debts. The same kind of thinking leads to the sexual exploitation of children and abandonment of the elderly who no longer serve our interests. It is also the mindset of those who say: Let us allow the invisible

forces of the market to regulate the economy, and consider their impact on society and nature as collateral damage. In the absence of objective truths or sound principles other than the satisfaction of our own desires and immediate needs, what limits can be placed on human trafficking, organized crime, the drug trade, commerce in blood diamonds and the fur of endangered species? Is it not the same relativistic logic which justifies buying the organs of the poor for resale or use in experimentation, or eliminating children because they are not what their parents wanted? This same "use and throw away" logic generates so much waste, because of the disordered desire to consume more than what is really necessary. We should not think that political efforts or the force of law will be sufficient to prevent actions which affect the environment because, when the culture itself is corrupt and objective truth and universally valid principles are no longer upheld, then laws can only be seen as arbitrary impositions or obstacles to be avoided.

He links these ideas with the wisdom of Romano Guardini in *The End of the Modern World*[32] when he states (n. 203),

Since the market tends to promote extreme consumerism in an effort to sell its products, people can easily get caught up in a whirlwind of needless buying and spending. Compulsive consumerism is one example of how the techno-economic paradigm affects individuals. Romano Guardini had already foreseen this: "The gadgets and technics forced upon him by the patterns of machine production and of abstract planning mass man accepts quite simply; they are the forms of life itself. To either a greater or lesser degree mass man is convinced that his conformity is both reasonable and just." This paradigm leads people to believe that they are free as long as they have the supposed freedom to consume. But those really free are the minority who wield economic and financial power. Amid this confusion, postmodern humanity has not yet achieved a new self-awareness capable of offering guidance and direction, and this lack of identity is a source of anxiety. We have too many means and only a few insubstantial ends.

Part of the solution to rampant consumerism is living a modest lifestyle. The Quakers' question, "Do I want it, do I need it, can I live without it?" might well be adopted by us all. The presumption that we can "shop till you drop" and "buy till you cry" may well be a cynical indictment of the culture of consumerism, especially in the face of those in developing countries who regularly go without. A wise abbot counseled his monks that if they had not worn an article of clothing in a year it was time to give it to the poor (more on monasticism in the next chapter). Two practices to which the pope himself calls attention is unrecycled paper (n. 22) and the use of air conditioning (n. 55).[33] A third concerns the use of cars and transportation.[34] (More in section 7 below.)

Not surprisingly, however, the pope broadens his concern about consumerism to be based in part on global interconnectedness and interdependence: "An interdependent world not only makes us more conscious of the negative effects of certain lifestyles and models of production and consumption which affect us all; more importantly, it motivates us to ensure that solutions are proposed from a global perspective, and not simply to defend the interests of a few countries. Interdependence obliges us to think of one world with a common plan" (n. 164). The pope's global vision[35] combines with his premise about teaching and *dialogue* when he refers specifically to discussions about consumerism in n. 134 (especially), as well as nn. 169 and 183. He argues for international policies encouraging the use of renewable energy (n. 26),[36] challenges politicians reluctant to change (n. 174), and even while asserting that there are no uniform solutions, he offers ideas on what can and should be undertaken (n. 180).[37]

That Pope Francis frames part of his discussion of this issue in terms of the "rich-poor" divide is clear in such paragraphs as those about present levels of consumption (n. 27), the self-examination regarding the consumerism of wealthier countries (n. 34), the warming caused by the huge consumption by richer countries (n. 51),[38] and the imperative that the developed countries should assist in reversing a system where the poorer countries lose their "goods and resources" (n. 52). At the same time, the pope nuances these assertions by noting that the issue is consumption by the few even in poorer countries (n. 172).[39]

The pope offers something of a preemptive strike when he

addresses potential critics when he discusses what "progress" means in n. 191:

Whenever these questions are raised, some react by accusing others of irrationally attempting to stand in the way of progress and human development. But we need to grow in the conviction that a decrease in the pace of production and consumption can at times give rise to another form of progress and development. Efforts to promote a sustainable use of natural resources are not a waste of money, but rather an investment capable of providing other economic benefits in the medium term. If we look at the larger picture, we can see that more diversified and innovative forms of production which impact less on the environment can prove very profitable. It is a matter of openness to different possibilities which do not involve stifling human creativity and its ideals of progress, but rather directing that energy along new channels.[40]

That the pope regards the pace of consumption as a major crisis is poignantly asserted in n. 161:

Doomsday predictions can no longer be met with irony or disdain. We may well be leaving to coming generations debris, desolation and filth. The pace of consumption, waste and environmental change has so stretched the planet's capacity that our contemporary lifestyle, unsustainable as it is, can only precipitate catastrophes, such as those which even now periodically occur in different areas of the world. The effects of the present imbalance can only be reduced by our decisive action, here and now. We need to reflect on our accountability before those who will have to endure the dire consequences.

Finally, Francis also speaks against what he terms the "throwaway culture," a concern he has articulated from the beginning of his papacy.[41] In the encyclical (n. 22), he links the problems of pollution with the throwaway culture by arguing that our propensity to discard what we use daily (for example, paper)—instead of recycling or reusing—demonstrates that we have not accepted the natural processes of the earth, which processes (decomposition, synthesis of nutrients, plant growth, and so on) cannot keep up with the high levels of waste produced by today's industrial and technological society. He acknowledges that attempts to counteract the throwaway culture have thus far achieved only limited success, and he challenges all to consider new and more fruitful ways of overcoming the culture of waste (nn. 22, 43).

VI. BUSINESS, CAPITALISM, AND FREE MARKETS

In an American context, the assertions by Milton Friedman that "the business of business is business," that the "responsibility of business is to make money," and that any challenges to business to improve the social landscape and lives of citizens is wrongheaded are all challenged by the assertions of Pope Francis in this encyclical. They have also been critiqued by popes before him (as noted in chapter 1, section 3).

As previously noted, businesses create jobs and jobs create income and provide resources on which to live, but some businesses support the common good more than others. Is there a debate to be had about which? What are the contours and the frame of this debate? Issues about the common good and human dignity should be coupled with Pope Benedict XVI's critique of the chaos that unregulated markets can cause, all of which need to be in the quotient according to which we assess the value of businesses. In *Caritas in Veritate*,[42] Benedict XVI argued that the market cannot guarantee the kind of integrity and development which Pope Francis envisions throughout the encyclical, for example, in n. 109: "By itself the market cannot guarantee integral human development and social inclusion."[43] Another related question is how wealth is shared, among whom and by what criteria and formula.

It is often said today that capitalism has brought more prosperity to more people and brought more people out of poverty in the last few years than ever before. Therefore, why criticize it? That the pope sees it differently is clear in the encyclical. The rebuttal to this assertion asks the question at what other costs has capitalism increased prosperity. The pope speaks specifically of water and air pollution, and his initial statement under the title "pollution, waste and the throwaway culture" is stunning and searing (n. 20):

> Some forms of pollution are part of people's daily experience. Exposure to atmospheric pollutants produces a broad spectrum of health hazards, especially for the poor, and causes millions of premature deaths. People take sick, for example, from breathing high levels of smoke from fuels used in cooking or heating. There is also pollution that affects everyone, caused by transport, industrial fumes, substances which contribute to the acidification of soil and water, fertilizers, insecticides, fungicides, herbicides and agrotoxins in general. Technology, which, linked to business interests, is presented as the only way of solving these problems, in fact proves incapable of seeing the mysterious network of relations between things and so sometimes solves one problem only to create others.

This is but a glimpse into his reiterated and detailed concern about pollution. It is cited here as a reminder that there are high costs to be paid, not necessarily in dollars, to foster job creation for which ecological factors and care for our common home should never be neglected.

The pope offers a direct challenge when he says that we need to adopt a new lifestyle (nn. 203–8) that opens the possibility of "bringing healthy pressure to bear on those who wield political, economic and social power" (n. 206). This shift manifests when consumer choices are able "to change the way businesses operate, forcing them to consider their environmental footprint and their patterns of production" (n. 206). Francis's call to a new lifestyle (in nn. 203–8) is, in fact, built upon the entire encyclical, which throughout develops a sharp challenge to problem of situations when financial, social, or political interests are prioritized to the detriment of the human person and the earth (nn. 54–56, 109, 169, 182, 197). He repeatedly calls for local, regional, and international associations to employ "legitimate means of pressure, to ensure that each government carries out its proper and inalienable responsibility to preserve its country's environment and natural resources, without capitulating to spurious local or international interests" (n. 38; also see nn. 179, 181–88, 197).

In addition, one needs to raise the question, under what kind of working conditions do laborers work? What is the number of hours they must work, especially in countries without the benefit of regulations to prevent worker abuse? The soaring rates of unemployment and underemployment in many countries make the American problem with unemployment pale in comparison. How many families are separated for long periods of time because a spouse needs to work away from her or his family? This, in turn, puts more than a strain on married life and the family unit.

When it comes to multinational corporations and their problematic behavior in developing countries, the pope relies on the wisdom of his fellow bishops from the Patagonia-Comahue Region of Argentina who assert tersely, "They do here what they would never do in developed countries" (cited in n. 51).[44] Who is responsible for "checks" and "balances" to this kind of behavior?

This concern for the poor goes far back in Catholic social justice teaching. Pope Francis begins no fewer than two dozen references to "justice" by citing his patron's example (by word and action).[45] For example, St. Francis "was a mystic and a pilgrim who lived in simplicity and in wonderful harmony with God, with others, with nature and with himself. He shows us just how inseparable the bond is between concern for nature, justice for the poor, commitment to society, and interior peace" (n. 10). He adds, "Today, however, we have to realize that a true ecological approach always becomes a social approach; it must integrate questions of justice in debates on the environment, so as to hear both the cry of the earth and the cry of the poor" (n. 49). These and several others throughout the encyclical will likely be "hard sayings" for some American "think tanks," "institutes," lobbyists, and corporations today, but it is especially here where the pope's arguments remind us that he is speaking to and for a worldwide church where the United States is not the center of the universe.

Finally, one way that the Vatican has concretized its concerns about "business" is in the document from the Pontifical Council on Justice and Peace on the *Vocation of the Business Leader: A Reflection*.[46] Some pertinent questions for Catholic institutions to ask are the following: Are Catholic business schools any different from other business schools? On what basis? What elements of Catholic law schools are based on Catholic social teaching? It is notable that in recent years a number of Catholic universities have founded schools for business and economics. Hopefully, they will be noted for fidelity to the church's social justice teachings.

VII. THE SABBATH: RELIGIOUS PRACTICE, WORK, AND HUMAN RELATIONSHIPS

In the encyclical's second chapter on "the gospel of creation" and in the last chapter on an ecological "spirituality," Pope Francis refers to the theology and practice of the Sabbath. After delineating the gift of creation by God's creative work and largesse, the pope recalls the other truths from Genesis, namely, that "although 'the wickedness of man was great in the earth' (Gen 6:5) and the Lord 'was sorry that he had made man on the earth' (Gen 6:6), nonetheless, through Noah, who remained innocent and just, God decided to open a path of salvation. In this way he gave humanity the chance of a new beginning. All it takes is one good person to restore hope!" (n. 71). This assertion has enormous merit of its own and continues the motif of how original sin is passed on. It also underlies the importance of the Noahic covenant, which is useful for dialogue among the monotheistic religions about the environment.[47]

The pope then goes on to assert that "the biblical tradition clearly shows that this renewal entails recovering and respecting the rhythms inscribed in nature by the hand of the Creator. We see this, for example, in the law of the Sabbath. On the seventh day, God rested from all his work. He commanded Israel to set aside each seventh day as a day of rest, a Sabbath, (cf. Gen 2:2–3; Ex 16:23; 20:10)" (n. 71). Later on in the document, the pope argues that the practice of the Sabbath rest has a number of meanings, including that it is a day that heals our relationships (n. 237). The requirement of the Sabbath observance derives from the Old Testament and is a hallmark of Jewish observance to this day. In an accommodated way, it is also experienced and practiced in Christian and Muslim faiths.

In his classic work *The Sabbath*, Abraham Heschel argues, "The meaning of the Sabbath is to celebrate time rather than space. Six days a week we live under the tyranny of things of space; on the Sabbath we try to become attuned to *holiness in time*. It is a day on which we are called on to share what is eternal in time, to turn from the results of creation to the mystery of creation; from the world of creation to the creation of the world."[48] That the Sabbath begins at table in the evening by invoking "Lord, God of all creation" is poignant and rich for Jews and Christians theologically, spiritually, and liturgically.

There is a fairly new shopping center just outside of the New Gate in the city of Jerusalem. It is filled with a variety of stores and is a remarkable architectural achievement. What is very poignant, especially for a Western Christian, is to see the neon sign that says "24/6!" That is the Sabbath in the present day "up in lights," but as we all know the Sabbath rest is not that simple, especially in a "24/7" Internet culture. I often wonder whether the sweatshops where mass-produced goods result in a dehumanization of too many of our brothers and sisters in the nineteenth century (and scandalously still in some places today, even as was countered as early on as Pope Leo XIII) are replaced in our culture and in other cultures with the "electronic sweatshops" of our Internet-linked machines that lead to an equally dehumanized society. Thinking about Joseph Pieper's book *Leisure, the Basis of Culture*, I truly wonder what the basis of our culture is without the presumption of leisure, which leisure is meant to lead to personal integration and societal cohesion. The Sabbath means a day for restoration with creation and all creatures—indeed, a renewal of relationships.

The Sunday celebration of the Eucharist as the center of the "Christian Sabbath" is meant to be framed by leisure, the kind of sacred leisure that the Sabbath prescriptions insured. To celebrate the Eucharist with and for each other is part and parcel of the kind of "human" ecology that popes have called for since John Paul II and the integral ecology so forcefully and cogently argued by Francis in the encyclical (n. 237).[49]

Prophetically and poignantly, Pope Francis takes this to another level when he speaks of the Internet and the quality of human relationships. Clearly some cultures continue the tradition of family gathering and sharing meal as cornerstones of the Sabbath. Equally clear is the fact that many so-called "developed" cultures do not. While one must be careful not to "finger wag" at families who cannot take a day to rest together because of work or family obligations (for example, to care for elderly relatives so that other caregivers can themselves experience a Sabbath day), one can also legitimately ask the question about how this fundamental principle and practice, including religious practice, of refraining from work, and healing human relationships can be preserved and restored.

RELIGIOUS PRACTICE

At about the same time as the liturgical reforms from Vatican II were studied and implemented, there was a certain reassessment underway about how the Christian Sunday differed from the Jewish Sabbath. More specifically the questions raised concerned whether any of the Sabbath prescriptions in the Old Testament were required for Christians.[50] The Sabbath "rest" was sometimes replaced by Sunday worship, with the "rest" allowed to either be presumed, not emphasized or ignored. The basis of the argument was that the New Testament and patristic sources emphasized the celebration of the Eucharist on the "day of the Lord."[51] However, the methodological deficiency here was to take this data on its own and not to contextualize the practice of Sunday Eucharist in cultural contexts that were hostile to Christianity. For example, the gathering for an evening Eucharist was because the early Christians observed Sunday (not Saturday) as a day of commerce and work. That in America the Sunday ("Sabbath") practice of common worship was accompanied by having to observe Sunday "blue laws," among others, might not have been a bad thing. The phenomenon of a decided decline in Sunday worship observance needs to be faced into where for so many "monthly is the new weekly." (More on this in chapter 4, final section.)

WORK

Pope Francis cites John Paul II when he argues for the value of labor. In n. 124, he states that "any approach to an integral ecology, which by definition does not exclude human beings, needs to take account of the value of labor, as St. John Paul II wisely noted in his Encyclical *Laborem Exercens*."

In *Laborem Exercens*, Pope John Paul II wrote movingly about the Christian vision of the dignity and meaning of human work. He argued that we live in an age that has all but lost this Christian vision of the meaning of work. There was a certain dehumanization of human work from the Industrial Revolution, which demanded that human beings be subjects in the process of manufacture and production. While John Paul II asserted that this is not a new problem, it is tragically part of a larger social and individual malady, a bad fruit of the rupture of human integrity and solidarity wrought by sin. John Paul II begins *Laborem Exercens* by asserting the following:

> Man is made to be in the visible universe an image and likeness of God himself, and he is placed in it in order to subdue the earth. From the beginning therefore he is called to work. Work is one of the characteristics that distinguish man from the rest of creatures, whose activity for sustaining their lives cannot be called work. Only man is capable of work, and only man works, at the same time by work occupying his existence on earth. Thus work bears a particular mark of man and of humanity, the mark of a person operating within a community of persons. And this mark decides its interior characteristics; in a sense it constitutes its very nature.[52]

In section 6 of this encyclical, John Paul II asserts that however true it may be that man is destined for work and called to it, in the first place work is "for man" and not man "for work." Pope Francis adopts and deepens John Paul II's assertions about the command (Gen 2:15) "to keep" and "to till" the earth. He then broadens this idea to include not only manual or agricultural labor, but "any activity involving a modification of existing reality, from producing a social report to the design of technological development" (n. 125). What follows is the principled reminder that "underlying every form of work is a concept of the relationship which we can and must have with what is other than ourselves." Further along, he asserts that "work is a necessity, part of the meaning of life on this earth, a path to growth, human development and personal fulfillment" (n. 128). Characteristically, he cites the plight of the poor when he asserts that helping them financially should always be a provisional solution: "The broader objective should be to allow them a dignified life through work" (n. 128). He ends this section of the encyclical by arguing that "Business is a noble vocation, directed to producing wealth and improving our world. It can be a fruitful source of prosperity for the areas in which it operates, especially if it sees the creation of jobs as an essential part of its service to the common good" (n. 129).

These astute assessments about labor, work, and business place before us the responsibility and opportunity to insure that working conditions foster these transcendent realities and that any dehumanization of the human being, who is as the pinnacle of God's creation, be avoided and human beings be respected and revered. It also requires that we have the vision to see beyond material goods to where they came from on the earth, that the human creativity in designing them be respected and that what is manufactured be seen to be the result of a process of human interaction and community. All too often in a consumerist culture, argues Vincent Miller, "we nourish ourselves on food from nowhere and dress in clothes made by no one."[53]

HUMAN RELATIONSHIPS

One of the foundations upon which the Sabbath meal was predicated was the coming together of the family for the event. The notion of a Sabbath "meal" meant a social occasion for conversation, prayer, and sharing food, focused on the family that gathers and invited guests. It was not about the ingesting of foods (or food groups) for the sake of nutrition to support the body. Volumes have been written on table fellowship in the scriptures presuming the "bondedness" of human and religious relationships expressed through meal taking among family, friends, and disciples. This presumption was so strong in the bible that to be invited to table meant to experience a relationship as profound as being blood relatives. Hence, for example, the paradox of the settings in which the earthy Jesus shared meals with the "least likely"—the outcasts, tax collectors, and sinners (for example, the meal taking in the Gospel of Luke, especially the parables of the lost coin, the lost sheep, and the prodigal son in Luke 15 introduced by vv. 1–2 about his audience of "tax collectors and sinners," "Pharisees and scribes").

This kind of presumption about dining is the exact opposite of what some commentators today call "sink dining." This means that in some industrialized societies individuals stand at their kitchen sink and dine alone, not unlike the famous Robert Putnam thesis in *Bowling Alone*.[54] Closely related to this is the phenomenon of "carry/take-out" meals prepared by others for consumption by any and every one, anywhere. Given the changes in family life with both parents working, after school care and many extracurricular activities, it is not uncommon that families find it hard to eat meals together and to cook meals on the day they are consumed. Any antidote to these practices that attempts to restore the humanity and humanness in the dining process should be welcomed and encouraged, but again without oppressive prejudgments. The balance to be struck here is about human creativity and ingenuity, which need time and effort, and the way that dining together can be a part of the (hopefully daily but certainly weekly) healing of human relationships.

A Catholic theology of creation and ecology is an integral theology of the earth, all creatures on this earth and of the family and other human relationships, of our communal relatedness to God, and our weekly common worship of God. Regarding (inter)relationships the pope says, "Disregard for the duty to cultivate and maintain a proper relationship with my neighbor, for whose care and custody I am responsible, ruins my relationship with my own self, with others, with God and with the earth. When all these relationships are neglected, when justice no longer dwells in the land, the Bible tells us that life itself is endangered" (n. 70).

VIII. ASSESSMENT AND ADJUSTMENTS IN LITURGICAL PRACTICE

In 1964, Romano Guardini penned a letter to the bishops of Germany about how Europe's inheriting a nineteenth-century individualism would offer a challenge to implementing the reformed liturgy as a "liturgical act" of the church.[55] In light of the encyclical and our common experience is this not the same today? Theologically, it could not be truer that the liturgy is a communal, public act. This is something that is reasserted in the Constitution on the Sacred Liturgy from Vatican II and is the presumption in all liturgy, especially in the reformed liturgical rites of the church. Yet how often does the kind of individualism that Guardini speaks of still plague our appreciation of the celebration of the liturgy? Issues of ecclesiology loom large in sacramental practice today. In my estimation, among the salient examples are the following.

CONFIRMATION

Timothy Gabrielli's *Confirmation: How a Sacrament of God's Grace Became All about Us*[56] raises and assesses the question "What have we done to confirmation?" in the United States in the last century. He argues that the various mutations which confirmation has undergone were religious education and faith formation driven, not theologically driven. The emphasis about individual choice placed the emphasis on the self and the preparation required for confirmation so that "I" can renew "my" faith. Most regrettably confirmation, when celebrated apart from baptism, is no longer seen as a communal sacrament of initiation celebrated within the presumed context of the ongoing communal celebration of faith with regular liturgical participation and practice presumed. How often is the rite of "mature commitment" an exit strategy from regular liturgical participation and practice? One step in the direction of righting this wrong is the restoration of the order of initiation sacraments for all: baptism, chrismation/confirmation, and Eucharist.[57] The emphasis would then have to be on renewing and upgrading faith formation apart from holding out sacraments as "goals." It would also insure that sacramental preparation not be a new Pelagianism, the observance of which "earns" us sacraments.

WEDDINGS

The decline in the number of marriages taking place in the Catholic church in America is cause for legitimate alarm. Pastoral strategies by the United States Conference of Catholic Bishops and individual dioceses reflect important initiatives not only to "stem the tide," but also to reintroduce the value of a sacramental marriage celebrated in the church.[58] Some phrases, such as the requirement that Catholics must be married "in the church," need explanation so that these are not seen to prohibit ecumenical marriages, and so on.

At the same time, does not the celebration of marriage today carry individualist overtones? In addition to the danger of falling into consumerism (as previously noted) "destination weddings" raise major ecclesiological issues. The relatively recent phenomenon of "destination weddings" reflects both the "believers not belongers" phenomenon, as well as the issue of consumerism. What happens, in fact, is that people choose not to celebrate major turning points in their lives as sacraments in their parish churches (or other places of worship) in favor of flying elsewhere to wed on beaches or in gardens by an officiant of no particular faith or civic tradition in the presence of relatives and friends who have expended enormous amounts of money to be there. Very often these are three-day affairs (or more) with planned activities and more than sufficient food and drink, usually no problem with running out of wine as did Jesus' friends at Cana (John 2)!

In America, the "wedding industry" is sadly just that, and not just for destination weddings. The seduction of consumerism is just below the surface that motivates all too many people who earn their living from inducing couples to expend exorbitant amounts of money even to the point of going into debt. Exorbitant sums are spent, sometimes by people who have to borrow the money, on outlandish parties whose monies could have been spent far more wisely, as in a down payment for a house. Or more tragically, in light of the honesty that Gospel living should be based on, have wedding receptions become aspirational and not really reflect who the couple are? Related to this expenditure of money is the cultural presumption that this is the way weddings must be conducted. Some dioceses have faced into this squarely by offering group weddings of several couples together with a reception for all families and friends in a social hall. This spares the couple any embarrassment about the inability "to keep up with the Joneses." Yet if people do insist on this exorbitant outlay of money might they consider the biblical injunction of a tithe for the church's "Cana fund" to be used to feed and clothe the poor?

In addition to arguing for the value of being married in one's parish (or regular place of worship), what would happen if couples requesting a nuptial Mass were offered the opportunity to have their vows witnessed at a regularly scheduled weekend Mass?

ORDINATIONS

Of late, an artifact used in the pre–Vatican II rite has returned: the *manutergeon,* the white linen that covers the hands of the newly ordained after being anointed with, in the former rite of ordination, the oil of the catechumens. In fact, it is no longer in the Roman Rite, but it has made its return at the request of many of those to be ordained. Certainly the origin and presence of the *manutergeon* in the ordination rite was to focus attention on the hands that will consecrate, raise up, and distribute the sacred species. It also underscored that no one but the ordained could touch the sacred species. Now that communion in the hand is common, the presumed emphasis on the priest's hands is no longer the case. I judge that the revival of the *manutergeon* places an emphasis on the individual at odds with the fundamental ecclesial sense of the reformed rite.[59] (This is often done by those who are sticklers for rubrical precision and fidelity.) The real issue after ordination is not who receives the cloth (the new priest or his mother), but where and how the ordained use their hands in ministry—clearly to hold up the most sacred species, but also to wash feet, to haul in groceries for the elderly, to write well prepared homilies on office computers, to hold the hands of aging parishioners on sick calls, and to hold the hands of people as they die literally in their arms. Might one counter the emphasis on the priests' hands during the ordination simply by insisting that the post–Vatican II rite of ordination be followed?

RCIA PROCESS

Another example concerns the popularity of the process involved in the Rite for the Christian Initiation for Adults. In the revision of these rites, the prescriptions of Vatican II to bring into prominence the twofold character of Lent—penitential and baptismal—and to restore the catechumenate were taken very seriously, as have been the revised rites themselves. These revised rites mark the progressive assimilation of catechumens and candidates into the body of Christ through the Rite of Election, Scrutinies, rites of preparation for the Easter Vigil, and the Vigil itself. Cathedrals, parishes, and campus ministries put forth enormous energy into the weekly or even twice weekly meetings with catechumens and candidates, and their sponsors, throughout this process.

In these practices, however, there is a danger of promising a level of personal intimacy that may not be able to be maintained after sacramental initiation. That is, does the RCIA process, which presumes a high level of intimacy in the weekly or twice weekly meetings, ultimately disappoint when the newly initiated are introduced into the larger community? Do the newly initiated then "fall away" when intimacy needs cannot be met in the larger parish community? More specifically there should be great concern that the RCIA process does not prepare catechumens and candidates for the liturgical life of the local church as the sustaining action of the church. In terms of "making" or "fostering" a sense of community, are the newly initiated confronted with a Sunday celebration of the Eucharist which cannot uphold their expectations for intimacy and belonging, especially given the large size of some of our worshipping assemblies (and as compared with smaller Protestant congregations)? Finally, it is important to raise the question of how well catechumens and candidates are formed to belong, not only to their local parish community, but also to the church universal, the communion of saints.

A PERSONAL RELATIONSHIP WITH JESUS

Placing emphasis on having a "personal relationship with Jesus" has its limitations in Catholicism, principally because we believe that the earthly Jesus died, rose, and is now seated at the right hand of the Father, interceding for us as the risen and exalted Lord. Nothing less than a conciliar document teaches us that liturgy is the "summit and source" of the Christian life (Constitution on the Sacred Liturgy, n. 10). If so, that means that any immediate and direct contact with the divine is always mediated in at least two ways: (1) it is mediated through and within the community of the church, and (2) it is mediated through commonly agreed-upon ritual structures of word, gesture, symbol, creation, and so on. Liturgy (especially in Orthodox and Catholic contexts) articulates and names the cosmos by its very celebration. It also contextualizes the proclamation of the word and active participation. In the words of Edward Kilmartin (adapted from Heribert Mühlen), liturgy is mediated immediacy.[60] To this I would add that liturgy is always multivalent/polyvalent and that by its nature as a ritual, its possible understandings and appropriations are never predictable or fully explainable.

One example of this is the way Catholic liturgy uses the psalms in our worship. While this is easily seen in the case of praying the psalms in the Liturgy of the Hours, it may well be less easily seen in the Eucharist where hymns and other popular music more often than not replaces the psalms in practice.[61] That Roman Catholic worship has incorporated into itself hymns from other Christian traditions has its deficiencies, which are often unnoticed and yet nonetheless can erode the genius of Catholic liturgy—a liturgy that has relied on the psalms in a fulsome way to accompany processions and as responses to scripture readings. The issue is not a style of music. As the same Vatican II document states, "The Church has not adopted any particular style of art as her very own."[62] The issue is how far the texts we sing veer from the words of the Psalter and what content takes its place. When hymns of the "me and Jesus" genre, or hymns that use the "I" as opposed to the "we" pronoun become appropriated in Catholic worship, the gathered assembly's active participation is skewed away from the baseline and fundamental principle that *we* worship and are a church that responds to God's gracious invitation among and with each other in the *communion* of the church.

PRIMALNESS REEMPHASIZED

In catechesis about the liturgy, the principle of sacramentality and the use of nature and living things need to be understood to be strong suits of Catholic worship.[63] One example of reemphasizing the primalness of Catholic worship would be to restore the emphasis on "ashes" and "dust" on Ash Wednesday. This is to say that the traditional formula at the distribution of ashes, taken from Gen 2:7, is about our being dust and returning to the earth after death: "Remember that you are dust, and to dust you shall return."

This is taken up in the very first words of the encyclical where the pope reminds us, "We have forgotten that we ourselves are dust of the earth (see Gen 2:7); our very bodies are made up of her elements, we breathe her air and we receive life and refreshment from her waters" (n. 2). The alternate form at the distribution, "repent, and believe in the Gospel," was added to the Roman liturgy by Paul VI to coincide with the Holy Year of Renewal and Reconciliation (1975). On that Ash Wednesday, he advised his masters of ceremonies at the evening Mass at St. Peter's[64] to ask the priests who were distributing ashes to use this new, more evangelically oriented admonition. This was to support the more biblically oriented notions of renewal and reconciliation he addressed during that holy year (for example, in this same year the two Eucharistic Prayers for Reconciliation were provided). Would a return to the traditional formula about dust not be a subtle reiteration of Pope Francis's point?

In addition, it is notable that *The Roman Missal* contains the following Mass formulas under the title "Masses and Prayers for Various Needs and Occasions": For the Sanctification of Human Labor, At Seed Time and After the Harvest (as well as "In Times of Bushfires," "In Time of Draught," "In Time of Floods," and "In Time of Cyclone" for the dioceses in Australia). These can be used whenever another Mass formula is not required on a weekday.

IX. TECHNOLOGY, ENERGY, AND RECYCLING

TECHNOLOGY

Pope Francis is no Neanderthal when it comes to the issue of technology. In the encyclical he acknowledges the importance of technology in general and the Internet more specifically (see, for example, n. 103).[65] At the same time, he would agree in general terms with (and make his own applications from) the rather grim assessments in parts of Romano Guardini (again in *The End of the Modern World*) about the powerful influence and negative uses of technology, especially when it comes to a certain depersonalization and commodification of persons (see, for example, nn. 104–5).[66]

In the encyclical he speaks of the information overload that can come with an overuse of the Internet and whether true and real relationships are fostered in a culture so thoroughly influenced by "instant access," "instant message," and social media. One could also ask whether the overuse of the Internet is caused by or leads to boredom (or both). One of the issues in a culture that so values productivity and information is a certain one-dimensionalism that disregards the breadth of society and the true humanity as we together form the human community.[67] His sober words in n. 47 are worth serious reflection:

> True wisdom, as the fruit of self-examination, dialogue and generous encounter between persons, is not acquired by a mere accumulation of data which eventually leads to overload and confusion, a sort of mental pollution. Real relationships with others, with all the challenges they entail, now tend to be replaced by a type of internet communication which enables us to choose or eliminate relationships at whim, thus giving rise to a new type of contrived emotion which has more to do with devices and displays than with other people and with nature. Today's media do enable us to communicate and to share our knowledge and affections. Yet at times they also shield us from direct contact with the pain, the fears and the joys of others and the complexity of their personal experiences. For this reason, we should be concerned that, alongside the exciting possibilities offered by these media, a deep and melancholic dissatisfaction with interpersonal relations, or a harmful sense of isolation, can also arise.

Furthermore, his assessment of "what is happening to our common home" at the beginning of the encyclical contains something of the same warnings.[68]

Data varies about the percentage of Americans who do not have access or use the Internet (note that "access" and "use" are not the same). That the number has declined precipitously over the past ten years is clear; that the numbers are about the same over the past three years seems to be the case.[69] Those of us who live in urban or suburban areas are likely to find lack of Internet access unimaginable, but that is the case in many parts of rural America and the experience of many poor people in our country and worldwide. Access to the Internet has enormous ramifications for education and literacy. Governmental initiatives in this regard are to be applauded and supported.[70]

ENERGY

With regard to energy, the pope repeatedly issues cautions about its overuse in many parts of the developed world and its comparative scarcity in the developing world. This argument reflects his repeated theme about the rich and the poor, with the latter simply not able to have free and equal access to goods, services, and energy. One thinks here of those countries (for example, Africa and India) where energy access is limited to just a few hours a day.

Given that reality in the developing world, for the developed world the pope's example of energy use of air conditioning is at least a shock in terms of this juxtaposition, if not an outright scandal on its own merits. What is also to be noted is the way energy use is linked to the markets and the issue of purchasing machines (n. 55):

> Some countries are gradually making significant progress, developing more effective controls and working to combat corruption. People may well have a growing ecological sensitivity but it has not succeeded in changing their harmful habits of consumption which, rather than decreasing, appear to be growing all the more. A simple example is the increasing use and power of air-conditioning. The markets, which immediately benefit from sales, stimulate ever greater demand. An outsider looking at our world would be amazed at such behavior, which at times appears self-destructive.

Certainly in today's American culture the example of shopping malls may have a great deal to say about our values in general, consumption of things in particular, and the overuse of energy as collateral damage (but real damage nonetheless). As noted briefly in the previous chapter, I do wonder whether our shopping malls have replaced cathedrals where vast expenditures of money are made for the finest of building materials like marble and wood, which were staples of cathedrals as architectural styles and as testaments of belief in God. I wonder whether fountains, running water, and pools of water in shopping mall atriums have replaced the value we have traditionally placed and should place on baptismal fonts for immersion (as in the baptistery of St. John Lateran in Rome). I wonder whether the financial outlay to hire musicians to play on magnificent pianos and organs in malls has replaced the just compensation that church musicians should receive to play on instruments of equal quality.

What do shopping malls house but temple upon temple to the god of consumption built side by side and on top of each other, floor upon floor, designed to please the consumer? In these temples we are seduced to purchase in order to show our worth and the value we place on things, many of which, if we are completely honest, we do not "need" but simply "want." Generous offerings are regularly sacrificed on the altars dedicated to the god of consumption.[71] These temples are refuges for the terminally bored who drive there (and consume gas in the process) in order to "window shop" and "just look" to see what might entice, not to say tittle the imagination whether one buys anything or not.

That these exist and are so well populated is one thing. That in much of suburban American there are several of them, often containing the very same products, not to say the same stores in very close proximity, is its own scandal. Theologically, the church's magisterium has argued that energy consumption is related to a number of things, such as peace and justice.[72] Once again our faith tradition should be the lens through which we "see, judge, and act." Tragically my sense is that we presume a plethora of shopping malls and do not "see" what these say about our cultural presumptions and decidedly "developed" mores.

Added to this is the concern regarding what kinds of energy we use, for example, coal, oil, gas, or wood, and what damage these do to the environment. The regular use of facemasks in Bangkok, Thailand, is matched with their use in parts of China, even though coal use has declined there. The pope repeatedly refers to the pollution (no fewer than twenty-six times) and offers proposals for how to mitigate its effects, and he links it to the loss of beautiful landscapes (n. 21), the acidification of oceans (n. 24), certain mining, farming, and industrial activities (n. 29), the results of deforestation on bodies of water (n. 41), and the relationship between toxic emissions with visual pollution in urban areas (n. 44). He also indicts those from the developed world who cause pollution in developing countries (n. 49). Americans who live in cities might initially bristle at the pope's comment about pollution linked to fuel consumption and the use of cars (n. 153):

> The quality of life in cities has much to do with systems of transport, which are often a source of much suffering for those who use them. Many cars, used by one or more people, circulate in cities, causing traffic congestion, raising the level of pollution, and consuming enormous quantities of non-renewable energy. This makes it necessary to build more roads and parking areas which spoil the urban landscape. Many specialists agree on the need to give priority to public transportation. Yet some measures needed will not prove easily acceptable to society unless substantial improvements are made in the systems themselves, which in many cities force people to put up with undignified conditions due to crowding, inconvenience, infrequent service and lack of safety.

All of this also raises the question of the adequacy and quality of public transportation within cities. The American dream of owning a car and driving anywhere at will for many has become a nightmare of clogged roads and longer and longer commutes for drivers. (In recent studies the area in and around Washington, DC, is second only to Los Angeles in traffic congestion and average commute times.)

RECYCLING

It may come as a surprise that recycling is treated almost last among the issues raised in this chapter about possibilities for the implementation of *On Care for Our Common Home*. There are two reasons why. The first is that individual responsibility about recycling should be seen in tandem with communal and corporate actions in this regard. The wide-angle lens on the Christian life (based on Judaism) is always communal. The individual is viewed in relation to who we are in relation to a covenanted people. Part of the sense of community and communal belonging should be that we together lobby corporations about what they do or do not do about pollution (more below). The second is that the jury is out on the value of many individual recycling programs in terms of ultimate cost saving and effectiveness.

What is far more important than individuals is recycling on a "macro" level involving the way corporations manufacture products and how they recycle. In addition, the issue of recycling parallels that of pollution. Again here what occurs on the "macro" view matters more than an individual's actions, important as they are. This can be understood as one of the many contexts for why the pope made the following (bold) assertion about climate (n. 23):

The climate is a common good, belonging to all and meant for all. At the global level, it is a complex system linked to many of the essential conditions for human life. A very solid scientific consensus indicates that we are presently witnessing a disturbing warming of the climatic system. In recent decades this warming has been accompanied by a constant rise in the sea level and, it would appear, by an increase of extreme weather events, even if a scientifically determinable cause cannot be assigned to each particular phenomenon. Humanity is called to recognize the need for changes of lifestyle, production and consumption, in order to combat this warming or at least the human causes which produce or aggravate it. It is true that there are other factors (such as volcanic activity, variations in the earth's orbit and axis, the solar cycle), yet a number of scientific studies indicate that most global warming in recent decades is due to the great concentration of greenhouse gases (carbon dioxide, methane, nitrogen oxides and others) released mainly as a result of human activity. As these gases build up in the atmosphere, they hamper the escape of heat produced by sunlight at the earth's surface. The problem is aggravated by a model of development based on the intensive use of fossil fuels, which is at the heart of the worldwide energy system. Another determining factor has been an increase in changed uses of the soil, principally deforestation for agricultural purposes.

A rule of thumb is that if there are two vessels for garbage, one for recycling and the other not, then it is likely that the recycling does no real good. If and when there are several bins available and garbage is sorted into several different vessels, however, then this more specific recycling will be more successful. Having said this, there are clearly egregious examples of what needs not to be used, for example, Styrofoam. The more educational, business, and other institutions deplete their Styrofoam goods and never reorder them again, the better off we are.

Statistics show that 34 percent (more or less) of Americans engage in "curb" recycling, with the west coast states, especially California and Oregon, as much as 50 percent. Among other states, Wisconsin and Massachusetts are also higher than the national average. That progress has been made in recycling is clear. As of summer 2015, the income produced by recycling and selling recyclables has dropped more than 50 percent, making it less lucrative. If a volunteer effort is all that motivates, it is likely that the percentages will stay the same. If and when municipalities (imitating places such as Seattle, Washington) enact laws about recycling (plastics, paper, cardboard, glass, and kitchen waste) and impose penalties on infractions, then real progress might be made. Sadly, two major metropolitan areas on the east coast, New York City and (to a lesser extent) Washington, DC, have minimal requirements in place.

The pope's reliance on the scientific consensus here is very important to show the relationship of a faith-based argument that is scientifically grounded. It is not surprising that the pope would raise the specific issue of paper and, by extension, paper recycling. He says in n. 22: "These problems are closely linked to a throwaway culture which affects the excluded just as it quickly reduces things to rubbish. To cite one example, most of the paper we produce is thrown away and not recycled."

In 1998, the U.S. Congress passed the "Government Paper Elimination Act" which required that by October of 2003 government agencies have in place procedures for severely reducing the amount of paper used for record keeping and communication.[73] At first this initiative from the White House was criticized in some circles, especially "inside the Beltway." Today, it is commonly lauded as having been prophetic.

X. FOOD AND WATER

FOOD

The pope refers to food consumption, the food chain, and how food and water relate to each other, among other things, over a dozen times in the encyclical. None, however, is as poignant and pertinent as n. 50 where he states, "We know that approximately a third of all food produced is discarded, and 'whenever food is thrown out it is as if it were stolen from the table of the poor.'"[74] This stark statistic supports the (scandalous) assessment that the world produces sufficient food for all to eat. Politics gets in the way of its distribution. This makes the assertion that one-fifth of the children on this planet go to bed hungry each day more than a scandal.

If that is true on an international level, it is also true in many parts of the world on an individual community level. In a society where the novels in *The Hunger Games* series and the films they spawned were a huge commercial success, we do need to remind ourselves that hunger is not a game. The existence of food banks in very many communities attests to the charity and goodwill of so many who procure the food and distribute it to those in need. An especially poignant example is when the food is needed by the working poor whose income is simply insufficient to feed themselves and their families. The charity, goodwill, and self-sacrifice on behalf of cadres of volunteers alongside civic and church leaders should never be underestimated, presumed, or unappreciated. Similarly, we can say with great civic and church pride that many people could not even survive without "meals on wheels" (or variations on this service) as well as food delivery services by agencies such as Catholic Charities and the St. Vincent De Paul societies.

However, there is the far more difficult question of a more just and equitable distribution of the world's resources, here specifically food, based on justice, not charity alone. In one of his first audience addresses, John Paul II asserted, "There can be no love without justice."[75] This principle raises the far more complex issue of whom to try to influence to change structures so that food banks and charity based food delivery would not be necessary.[76]

In addition, there are the allied issues of how do we regard food and presume its distribution in myriad forms and ways. Allow me to change genre here a bit and offer two true stories. On commencement eve in May of 2014 at Hampden-Sydney College in rural Virginia, there was a prayer service followed by a reception for the graduates, after which the parents of the graduating class of one of the fraternities laid out a sumptuous buffet for their sons and families in the "frat house." By any estimate the buffet was elegant and the food and drink "first class." Upon returning to the house after the college-sponsored reception, some of the graduates had obviously enjoyed themselves and needed nourishment. Instead they instigated a food fight that resulted in all the food being thrown around the room with not a morsel eaten. One parent observed that it was a way for the lads to "let off some steam." Three miles away there is a food bank and a regional food distribution center. Hunger is not a game in rural Virginia, but that evening food became a weapon.

On the opposite end of the food fight at the college is the fact that the school officials in Washington, DC, are very slow to close schools because of snow. If they do, many students will not eat breakfast, lunch, and the snack which the schools provide for them. Even when schools are closed due to heavy snow, as they did in DC for several days during the "blizzard of 2016," the mayor of DC announced that during the closures the local government would continue to provide the regular school breakfasts and lunches at schools and help centers. One does not live on the word of God alone, but on every food group provided by many schools.

Two dozen years ago when I was a resident in a parish in Silver Spring, Maryland, we hosted a priest from Poland for the summer. One afternoon I brought him to a supermarket and a drugstore. As we made the rounds of the aisles, his eyes got bigger and bigger. He simply could not comprehend the seemingly numberless varieties of foods and brands. He was shocked at the variety and brands for pet foods. He was also surprised to experience that the drugstore was filled with 90 percent products that were not drugs at all.

Once again, on the opposite spectrum is the fact that in many urban areas the poor who have no access to transportation in turn have no access to "green grocers" and to fresh fruit and vegetables. By default, they purchase canned goods whose contents, despite being displayed on labels, go unnoticed. The regular consumption of such foods adds to the obesity epidemic and vitamin deficiencies among the urban poor.

Sometimes seeing things through the eyes and experiences of others helps us envision what might be, not just what is.

WATER

That the crucial issue of water is very much on the Pope's agenda is clear by the number of times he refers to it, half of which are contained in five paragraphs at the beginning of the encyclical under the heading "the issue of water" (nn. 27–31). He places his discussion not surprisingly within the context of present levels of consumption "in developed countries and wealthier sectors of society where the habit of wasting and discarding has reached unprecedented levels" (n. 27). He laments the scarcity of fresh drinking water, the experience of water not being distributed equitably and what occurs as a result of droughts, especially in places like Africa (n. 28). This leads him to catalog the well-known fact that water-related diseases include dysentery and cholera, among others (n. 29). The pope raises the specter of the fact that water is turning into "a commodity subject to the laws of the market" (n. 30). In a particularly poignant and evenhanded text, which includes necessity for change in developing and developed countries, he asserts (n. 30),

> Our world has a grave social debt towards the poor who lack access to drinking water, because they are denied the right to a life consistent with their inalienable dignity. This debt can be paid partly by an increase in funding to provide clean water and sanitary services among the poor. But water continues to be wasted, not only in the developed world but also in developing countries which possess it in abundance. This shows that the problem of water is partly an educational and cultural issue, since there is little awareness of the seriousness of such behavior within a context of great inequality.

Another example of the way the pope sees many ecological issues to be intertwined is the way he relates the scarcity of water to the increased cost of many products. He also warns that "the control of water by large multinational businesses may become a major source of conflict in this century" (n. 31), which warning he first issued to the Second International Conference on Nutrition held at Food and Agricultural Organization of the United Nations.[77]

That access to clean water is a pressing international issue is clear. Remedies are comparatively unclear. The example of water hoarding by residents of gated communities to preserve lawns comes to mind.[78] Here governments need to take initiatives—and prevent—the privatization of water. The example of the Israeli-Palestinian wars over water also comes to mind. That international bodies need to broker water access in this region and other parts of the world is equally clear. That efforts by local, national, and international bodies to change this sorry state of affairs have repeatedly failed appears to be equally clear. In the face of the church's long standing assertion of the right to life in which water is an intrinsic part (n. 30), the lack of effective action is nothing less than a scandal.[79]

XI. THE LONG VIEW

In two places in 1 Corinthians, St. Paul uses the important phrase "for I handed on to you what I myself received" (1 Cor 11:23 and 15:3) about the Lord's Supper and the resurrection. These phrases concretize what the Catholic tradition is and does. We receive the mystery (and mysteries) of faith and pass on what we have received "to the next generation" (Ps 102:18). For me, this can be an important theological framework when reading the pope's question about what kind of world we will pass on to the next generations. He asks this about the environment, but only in the context of a number of other issues he has raised throughout *On Care for Our Common Home.* In n. 160, he asks the following:

> What kind of world do we want to leave to those who come after us, to children who are now growing up? This question not only concerns the environment in isolation; the issue cannot be approached piecemeal. When we ask ourselves what kind of world we want to leave behind, we think in the first place of its general direction, its meaning and its values.

Unless we struggle with these deeper issues, I do not believe that our concern for ecology will produce significant results. But if these issues are courageously faced, we are led inexorably to ask other pointed questions: What is the purpose of our life in this world? Why are we here? What is the goal of our work and all our efforts? What need does the earth have of us? It is no longer enough, then, simply to state that we should be concerned for future generations. We need to see that what is at stake is our own dignity. Leaving an inhabitable planet to future generations is, first and foremost, up to us. The issue is one which dramatically affects us, for it has to do with the ultimate meaning of our earthly sojourn.

With regard to the environment and tangible efforts on behalf of "our common home," he quotes Benedixt XIV's assertion in *Caritas in Veritate* (n. 50) and expands on it when he says (n. 195),

As long as production is increased, little concern is given to whether it is at the cost of future resources or the health of the environment; as long as the clearing of a forest increases production, no one calculates the losses entailed in the desertification of the land, the harm done to biodiversity or the increased pollution. In a word, businesses profit by calculating and paying only a fraction of the costs involved. Yet only when "the economic and social costs of using up shared environmental resources are recognized with transparency and fully borne by those who incur them, not by other peoples or future generations," can those actions be considered ethical. An instrumental way of reasoning, which provides a purely static analysis of realities in the service of present needs, is at work whether resources are allocated by the market or by state central planning.

Modern economics focuses on production, consumption, labor, capital, and profitmaking in the context of competition for scarce resources. Economics in its fuller, classical sense, however, is the science whose concern is gathering, cultivating, and distributing the earth's material resources with a view to the survival and thriving of human communities. Thus understood, economy, *oikonomia*, mediates between ecology on the one hand, and the *oikoumene* (from which the English word "ecumenical" is derived) of human interconnected community on the other. In light of the encyclical, it also means that we need to avoid causing irreversible damage to our common home by what we do to trees, in mountain top coal mining, and in fracking.

The Catholic vision is to "receive and pass on," not only the tradition of the dying and rising of Christ and its celebration in the Eucharist, but the earth itself. For this we all have a responsibility to take the countercultural position that is the long view requiring that we take immediate measures to preserve and protect "our common home" for this and "the next generation," whom the pope cites in his poignant appeal at the beginning of the encyclical that can be viewed as something of an "overture" to the major themes in the document (n. 13):

> The urgent challenge to protect our common home includes a concern to bring the whole human family together to seek a sustainable and integral development, for we know that things can change. The Creator does not abandon us; he never forsakes his loving plan or repents of having created us. Humanity still has the ability to work together in building our common home. Here I want to recognize, encourage and thank all those striving in countless ways to guarantee the protection of the home which we share. Particular appreciation is owed to those who tirelessly seek to resolve the tragic effects of environmental degradation on the lives of the world's poorest. Young people demand change. They wonder how anyone can claim to be building a better future without thinking of the environmental crisis and the sufferings of the excluded.

NOTES

1. Interfaith Summit on Climate Change, "Climate, Faith and Hope: Faith Traditions Together for a Common Future" (September 21, 2014), http://interfaithclimate.org/the-statement.

2.   Francis, *Address to the Joint Session of the United States Congress* (September 24, 2015), http://w2.vatican.va/content/francesco/en/speech es/2015/september/documents/papa-francesco_20150924_usa-us-con gress.html.

3.   Francis, *Address to Members of the General Assembly of the United Nations Organization* (September 25, 2015), http://w2.vatican.va/ content/francesco/en/speeches/2015/september/documents/papa-francesco_20150925_onu-visita.html.

4.   He goes on to say in n. 224,

And yet, when there is a general breakdown in the exercise of a certain virtue in personal and social life, it ends up causing a number of imbalances, including environmental ones. That is why it is no longer enough to speak only of the integrity of ecosystems. We have to dare to speak of the integrity of human life, of the need to promote and unify all the great values. Once we lose our humility, and become enthralled with the possibility of limitless mastery over everything, we inevitably end up harming society and the environment. It is not easy to promote this kind of healthy humility or happy sobriety when we consider ourselves autonomous, when we exclude God from our lives or replace him with our own ego, and think that our subjective feelings can define what is right and what is wrong.

5.   He goes on to say in n. 225,

On the other hand, no one can cultivate a sober and satisfying life without being at peace with him or herself. An adequate understanding of spirituality consists in filling out what we mean by peace, which is much more than the absence of war. Inner peace is closely related to care for ecology and for the common good because, lived out authentically, it is reflected in a balanced lifestyle together with a capacity for wonder which takes us to a deeper understanding of life. Nature is filled with words of love, but how can we listen to them amid constant noise, interminable and nerve-wracking distractions, or the cult of appearances? Many people today sense a profound imbalance which drives them to frenetic activity and makes them feel busy, in a constant hurry which in turn leads them to ride rough-shod over everything around them. This too affects how they treat the environment. An integral ecology includes taking time to recover a serene harmony with creation, reflecting on our lifestyle and our ideals, and contemplating the Creator who lives among us and surrounds us, whose presence "must not be contrived but found, uncovered."

6. One of the much debated issues concerned which regulatory agency—national, state, or local—was responsible to oversee the quality of the water. This raises the larger debate in the United States about "regulations" in general and the way political parties use the shell game of who should be responsible. In the end someone should be responsible and accountable. Empty rhetoric obsesses about who it should be. Another example concerns treating drug addiction in a state like New Hampshire which suffered an outbreak in 2015–16. Only 10 percent of those seeking inpatient treatment at the end of 2015 were able to be admitted immediately. This meant that 90 percent continued to be addicted and did not receive treatment. This is symptomatic of the rhetoric about the value of "small government" and keeping taxes low when fellow citizens are addicted, unable to work, and some face death.

7. Benedict XVI, encyclical letter *Caritas in Veritate* (June 29, 2009), http://w2.vatican.va/content/benedict-xvi/en/encyclicals/documents/hf_ben-xvi_enc_20090629_caritas-in-veritate.html, n. 51.

8. Benedict XVI, *Message for World Day for Peace* (January 1, 2010), http://w2.vatican.va/content/benedict-xvi/en/messages/peace/documents/hf_ben-xvi_mes_20091208_xliii-world-day-peace.html, n. 45.

9. The next sentence reads as follows: "As the bishops of Southern Africa have stated: 'Everyone's talents and involvement are needed to redress the damage caused by human abuse of God's creation'" (n. 14, citing from the Southern African Catholic Bishops' Conference. *Pastoral Statement on the Environmental Crisis* [September 5, 1999]). Francis continues, "All of us can cooperate as instruments of God for the care of creation, each according to his or her own culture, experience, involvements and talents" (n. 14).

10. The full text reads that this feeling is "brought on by densely populated residential areas is countered if close and warm relationships develop, if communities are created, if the limitations of the environment are compensated for in the interior of each person who feels held within a network of solidarity and belonging. In this way, any place can turn from being a hell on earth into the setting for a dignified life" (n. 148).

11. The full paragraph (n. 227) reads as follows:

One expression of this attitude is when we stop and give thanks to God before and after meals. I ask all believers to return to this beautiful and meaningful custom. That moment of blessing, however brief, reminds us of our dependence on God for life; it strengthens our feeling of gratitude for the gifts of creation; it acknowledges those who by their labours provide us with these goods; and it reaffirms our solidarity with those in greatest need.

12. As previously quoted in chapter 1 above, the pope asserts in n. 9 that Christians are called "to accept the world as a sacrament of communion, as a way of sharing with God and our neighbours on a global scale. It is our humble conviction that the divine and the human meet in the slightest detail in the seamless garment of God's creation, in the last speck of dust of our planet."

13. Here, the pope cites the pastoral letter from the bishops of the Patagonia region of Argentina.

14. The paragraph under "weak responses" (n. 54) reads as follows:

It is remarkable how weak international political responses have been. The failure of global summits on the environment make it plain that our politics are subject to technology and finance. There are too many special interests, and economic interests easily end up trumping the common good and manipulating information so that their own plans will not be affected. The *Aparecida Document* urges that "the interests of economic groups which irrationally demolish sources of life should not prevail in dealing with natural resources." The alliance between the economy and technology ends up sidelining anything unrelated to its immediate interests. Consequently the most one can expect is superficial rhetoric, sporadic acts of philanthropy and perfunctory expressions of concern for the environment, whereas any genuine attempt by groups within society to introduce change is viewed as a nuisance based on romantic illusions or an obstacle to be circumvented.

15. The text of n. 57 reads as follows:

Underlying the principle of the common good is respect for the human person as such, endowed with basic and inalienable rights ordered to his or her integral development. It has also to do with the overall welfare of society and the development of a variety of intermediate groups, applying the principle of subsidiarity. Outstanding among those groups is the family, as the basic cell of society. Finally, the common good calls for social peace, the stability and security provided by a certain order which cannot be achieved without particular concern for distributive justice; whenever this is violated, violence always ensues. Society as a whole, and the state in particular, are obliged to defend and promote the common good.

16. The full text reads as follows (n. 196):

What happens with politics? Let us keep in mind the principle of subsidiarity, which grants freedom to develop the capabilities present at every level of society, while also demanding a greater sense of responsibility for the common good from those who wield greater power. Today, it is the case that some economic sectors exercise more power than states themselves. But economics without politics cannot be justified, since this would make it impossible to favour other ways of handling the various aspects of the present crisis. The mindset which leaves no room for sincere concern for the environment is the same mindset which lacks concern for the inclusion of the most vulnerable members of society. For "the current model, with its emphasis on success and self-reliance, does not appear to favour an investment in efforts to help the slow, the weak or the less talented to find opportunities in life." [The quotation comes from the pope's own *Evangelii Gaudium*, n. 209.]

17. Benedict XVI, *Caritas in Veritate*, n. 67.

18. Francis, *Homily*, visit to Lampedusa (July 8, 2013), http://w2.vatican.va/content/francesco/en/homilies/2013/documents/papa-francesco_20130708_omelia-lampedusa.html.

19. Francis, *Address to the Diplomatic Corps* (January 11, 2016), http://w2.vatican.va/content/francesco/en/speeches/2016/january/documents/papa-francesco_20160111_corpo-diplomatico.html.

20. Francis, *Address to the European Parliament* (November 25, 2014), http://w2.vatican.va/content/francesco/en/speeches/2014/november/documents/papa-francesco_20141125_strasburgo-parlamento-europeo.html.

Francis, *Address to the Joint Session of the United States Congress* (September 24, 2015), http://w2.vatican.va/content/francesco/en/speeches/2015/september/documents/papa-francesco_20150924_usa-us-congress.html.

Francis, *Address to Members of the General Assembly of the United Nations Organization* (September 25, 2015), http://w2.vatican.va/content/francesco/en/speeches/2015/september/documents/papa-francesco_20150925_onu-visita.html.

21. In full, the paragraph (n. 49) reads as follows:

It needs to be said that, generally speaking, there is little in the way of clear awareness of problems which especially affect the excluded. Yet they are the majority of the planet's population, billions of people. These days, they are mentioned in international political and economic discussions, but one often has the impression that their problems are brought up as an afterthought, a question which gets added almost out of duty or in a tangential way, if not treated merely as collateral damage. Indeed, when all is said and done, they frequently remain at the bottom of the pile. This is due partly to the fact that many professionals, opinion makers, communications media and centres of power, being located in affluent urban areas, are far removed from the poor, with little direct contact with their problems. They live and reason from the comfortable position of a high level of development and a quality of life well beyond the reach of the majority of the world's population. This lack of physical contact and encounter, encouraged at times by the disintegration of our cities, can lead to a numbing of conscience and to tendentious analyses which neglect parts of reality. At times this attitude exists side by side with a "green" rhetoric. Today, however, we have to realize that a true ecological approach always becomes a social approach; it must integrate questions of justice in debates on the environment, so as to hear both the cry of the earth and the cry of the poor.

22. Francis, *Address to the European Parliament* (November 25, 2014), http://w2.vatican.va/content/francesco/en/speeches/2014/november/documents/papa-francesco_20141125_strasburgo-parlamento-europeo.html.

23. Francis, *Address to the European Parliament.*

24. Francis, *Message for the XLIX World Day of Peace* (January 1, 2016), http://w2.vatican.va/content/francesco/en/messages/peace/documents/papa-francesco_20151208_messaggio-xlix-giornata-mondiale-pace-2016.html.

25. Benedict XVI, *Address to the Clergy of the Diocese of Bolzano-Bressanone* (August 6, 2008), n. 634, cited by Francis in n. 6.

26. Patriarch Bartholomew, "Global Responsibility and Ecological Sustainability," cited by Francis in n. 9:

The balance of Bartholomew's quotation introduces the important notion of "sacrament" to ecological conversations: "As Christians, we are also called 'to accept the world as a sacrament of communion, as a way of sharing with God and our neighbours on a global scale. It is our humble conviction that the divine and the human meet in the slightest detail in the seamless garment of God's creation, in the last speck of dust of our planet.'"

27. John Paul II, encyclical letter *Redemptor Hominis* (March 4, 1979), http://w2.vatican.va/content/john-paul-ii/en/encyclicals/documents/ hf_jp-ii_enc_04031979_redemptor-hominis.html, n. 15.

28. The balance of this section reads as follows: "Authentic human development has a moral character. It presumes full respect for the human person, but it must also be concerned for the world around us and 'take into account the nature of each being and of its mutual connection in an ordered system.' Accordingly, our human ability to transform reality must proceed in line with God's original gift of all that is" (n. 5).

29. The paragraph in full (n. 162) reads as follows:

Our difficulty in taking up this challenge seriously has much to do with an ethical and cultural decline which has accompanied the deterioration of the environment. Men and women of our post-modern world run the risk of rampant individualism, and many problems of society are connected with today's self-centered culture of instant gratification. We see this in the crisis of family and social ties and the difficulties of recognizing the other. Parents can be prone to impulsive and wasteful consumption, which then affects their children who find it increasingly difficult to acquire a home of their own and build a family. Furthermore, our inability to think seriously about future generations is linked to our inability to broaden the scope of our present interests and to give consideration to those who remain excluded from development. Let us not only keep the poor of the future in mind, but also today's poor, whose life on this earth is brief and who cannot keep on waiting. Hence [citing Benedict XVI], he asserts (n. 95), "In addition to a fairer sense of intergenerational solidarity there is also an urgent moral need for a renewed sense of intragenerational solidarity."

30. It is to be admitted that for this statistic exact numbers and percentages vary. That there is a vast imbalance, however, is clearly borne out by all the data.

31. The full text reads as follows (n. 50):

Instead of resolving the problems of the poor and thinking of how the world can be different, some can only propose a reduction in the birth rate. At times, developing countries face forms of international pressure which make economic assistance contingent on certain policies of "reproductive health." Yet "while it is true that an unequal distribution of the population and of available resources creates obstacles to development and a sustainable use of the environment, it must nonetheless be recognized that demographic

growth is fully compatible with an integral and shared development." [Here, he cites the *Compendium of the Social Doctrine of the
Church*, n. 483.] To blame population growth instead of extreme
and selective consumerism on the part of some, is one way of
refusing to face the issues. It is an attempt to legitimize the present model of distribution, where a minority believes that it has the
right to consume in a way which can never be universalized, since
the planet could not even contain the waste products of such consumption. Besides, we know that approximately a third of all food
produced is discarded, and "whenever food is thrown out it is as if
it were stolen from the table of the poor" (citing his own catechesis
from June 5, 2013). Still, attention needs to be paid to imbalances
in population density, on both national and global levels, since a
rise in consumption would lead to complex regional situations, as
a result of the interplay between problems linked to environmental
pollution, transport, waste treatment, loss of resources and quality
of life.

32. It should be noted that Guardini has had and continues to have an
influence on the thought of Pope Francis. As documented in some biographies (for example, Paul Vallely, *Untying the Knots* [London: Bloomsbury,
2013]), the Jesuit Father Bergolio was sent to Germany to earn a doctorate in sacred theology. He chose to focus on the thought of Guardini. By
all accounts the years spent in Germany were accompanied by something
of an extended spiritual crisis. Bergolio returned to Argentina without
the doctorate. Notably, Pope Francis cites Guardini's *Das Ende der Neuzeit*
(ninth edition, 1965) in the encyclical once by name with a quotation
(n. 203) and four other times in footnotes (nn. 83, 87, 92, 154). This text
of Guardini's is available in English as Romano Guardini, *The End of the
Modern World*, trans. Joseph Theman, Helen Burke, and Elinor C. Briefs
(Wilmington: ISI Books, 1998) (the earliest English translation of the
first edition was published by Sheed and Ward in 1956).

33. In both cases it is worth studying the contents of the contexts in
which these assertions are made (n. 22):

These problems are closely linked to a throwaway culture which
affects the excluded just as it quickly reduces things to rubbish. To
cite one example, most of the paper we produce is thrown away
and not recycled. It is hard for us to accept that the way natural
ecosystems work is exemplary: plants synthesize nutrients which
feed herbivores; these in turn become food for carnivores, which
produce significant quantities of organic waste which give rise to
new generations of plants. But our industrial system, at the end of

its cycle of production and consumption, has not developed the capacity to absorb and reuse waste and by-products. We have not yet managed to adopt a circular model of production capable of preserving resources for present and future generations, while limiting as much as possible the use of non-renewable resources, moderating their consumption, maximizing their efficient use, reusing and recycling them. A serious consideration of this issue would be one way of counteracting the throwaway culture which affects the entire planet, but it must be said that only limited progress has been made in this regard.

And in n. 55:

Some countries are gradually making significant progress, developing more effective controls and working to combat corruption. People may well have a growing ecological sensitivity but it has not succeeded in changing their harmful habits of consumption which, rather than decreasing, appear to be growing all the more. A simple example is the increasing use and power of air-conditioning. The markets, which immediately benefit from sales, stimulate ever greater demand. An outsider looking at our world would be amazed at such behaviour, which at times appears self-destructive.

34. In this connection one wonders whether the decline in the number of cars purchased in the United States (especially in urban areas), the greater use of car rentals by the day or hour, and the use of car services offered on the Internet might be steps in the direction the pope is calling for. At the same time, planning for and using alternate means of transportation is asserted by the pope in n. 153, which states the following:

The quality of life in cities has much to do with systems of transport, which are often a source of much suffering for those who use them. Many cars, used by one or more people, circulate in cities, causing traffic congestion, raising the level of pollution, and consuming enormous quantities of non-renewable energy. This makes it necessary to build more roads and parking areas which spoil the urban landscape. Many specialists agree on the need to give priority to public transportation. Yet some measures needed will not prove easily acceptable to society unless substantial improvements are made in the systems themselves, which in many cities force people to put up with undignified conditions due to crowding, inconvenience, infrequent service and lack of safety.

35. In n. 46 he asserts the following:

Implementation

The social dimensions of global change include the effects of technological innovations on employment, social exclusion, an inequitable distribution and consumption of energy and other services, social breakdown, increased violence and a rise in new forms of social aggression, drug trafficking, growing drug use by young people, and the loss of identity. These are signs that the growth of the past two centuries has not always led to an integral development and an improvement in the quality of life. Some of these signs are also symptomatic of real social decline, the silent rupture of the bonds of integration and social cohesion.

36. The text of n. 26 reads as follows:

However, many of these symptoms indicate that such effects will continue to worsen if we continue with current models of production and consumption. There is an urgent need to develop policies so that, in the next few years, the emission of carbon dioxide and other highly polluting gases can be drastically reduced, for example, substituting for fossil fuels and developing sources of renewable energy. Worldwide there is minimal access to clean and renewable energy. There is still a need to develop adequate storage technologies.

37. The text of n. 180 reads as follows:

There are no uniform recipes, because each country or region has its own problems and limitations. It is also true that political realism may call for transitional measures and technologies, so long as these are accompanied by the gradual framing and acceptance of binding commitments. At the same time, on the national and local levels, much still needs to be done, such as promoting ways of conserving energy. These would include favouring forms of industrial production with maximum energy efficiency and diminished use of raw materials, removing from the market products which are less energy efficient or more polluting, improving transport systems, and encouraging the construction and repair of buildings aimed at reducing their energy consumption and levels of pollution. Political activity on the local level could also be directed to modifying consumption, developing an economy of waste disposal and recycling, protecting certain species and planning a diversified agriculture and the rotation of crops. Agriculture in poorer regions can be improved through investment in rural infrastructures, a better organization of local or national markets, systems of irrigation, and the development of techniques of sustainable agriculture. New forms of cooperation and community organization can be encouraged in order to defend the interests of small producers and preserve local ecosystems from destruction. Truly, much can be done!

38. The text of n. 51 reads as follows:

The warming caused by huge consumption on the part of some rich countries has repercussions on the poorest areas of the world, especially Africa, where a rise in temperature, together with drought, has proved devastating for farming. There is also the damage caused by the export of solid waste and toxic liquids to developing countries, and by the pollution produced by companies which operate in less developed countries in ways they could never do at home, in the countries in which they raise their capital: "We note that often the businesses which operate this way are multinationals. They do here what they would never do in developed countries or the so-called first world. Generally, after ceasing their activity and withdrawing, they leave behind great human and environmental liabilities such as unemployment, abandoned towns, the depletion of natural reserves, deforestation, the impoverishment of agriculture and local stock breeding, open pits, riven hills, polluted rivers and a handful of social works which are no longer sustainable" [quoting the Christmas Message (2009), n. 2, from the Bishops of the Patagonia-Comahue Region (Argentina)].

39. The text of n. 172 reads as follows:

For poor countries, the priorities must be to eliminate extreme poverty and to promote the social development of their people. At the same time, they need to acknowledge the scandalous level of consumption in some privileged sectors of their population and to combat corruption more effectively.

40. The text of n. 192 reads as follows:

For example, a path of productive development, which is more creative and better directed, could correct the present disparity between excessive technological investment in consumption and insufficient investment in resolving urgent problems facing the human family. It could generate intelligent and profitable ways of reusing, revamping and recycling, and it could also improve the energy efficiency of cities. Productive diversification offers the fullest possibilities to human ingenuity to create and innovate, while at the same time protecting the environment and creating more sources of employment. Such creativity would be a worthy expression of our most noble human qualities, for we would be striving intelligently, boldly and responsibly to promote a sustainable and equitable development within the context of a broader concept of quality of life. On the other hand, to find ever new ways of despoiling nature, purely for the sake of new consumer items and quick profit, would be, in human terms, less worthy and creative, and more superficial.

Also see n. 109 on the effects of the technocratic paradigm:

The technocratic paradigm also tends to dominate economic and political life. The economy accepts every advance in technology with a view to profit, without concern for its potentially negative impact on human beings. Finance overwhelms the real economy. The lessons of the global financial crisis have not been assimilated, and we are learning all too slowly the lessons of environmental deterioration. Some circles maintain that current economics and technology will solve all environmental problems, and argue, in popular and non-technical terms, that the problems of global hunger and poverty will be resolved simply by market growth. They are less concerned with certain economic theories which today scarcely anybody dares defend, than with their actual operation in the functioning of the economy. They may not affirm such theories with words, but nonetheless support them with their deeds by showing no interest in more balanced levels of production, a better distribution of wealth, concern for the environment and the rights of future generations. Their behaviour shows that for them maximizing profits is enough. Yet by itself the market cannot guarantee integral human development and social inclusion. At the same time, we have "a sort of 'superdevelopment' of a wasteful and consumerist kind which forms an unacceptable contrast with the ongoing situations of dehumanizing deprivation" [Benedict XVI, *Caritas* n. 22, 90], while we are all too slow in developing economic institutions and social initiatives which can give the poor regular access to basic resources. We fail to see the deepest roots of our present failures, which have to do with the direction, goals, meaning and social implications of technological and economic growth.

See n. 112 on liberation from the technocratic paradigm:

Liberation from the dominant technocratic paradigm does in fact happen sometimes, for example, when cooperatives of small producers adopt less polluting means of production, and opt for a non-consumerist model of life, recreation and community.

Finally, see n. 59 on superficial ecology, complacency:

At the same time we can note the rise of a false or superficial ecology which bolsters complacency and a cheerful recklessness. As often occurs in periods of deep crisis which require bold decisions, we are tempted to think that what is happening is not entirely clear. Superficially, apart from a few obvious signs of pollution and deterioration, things do not look that serious, and the planet could continue as it is for some time. Such evasiveness serves as a license to carrying on with our present lifestyles and models of production and consumption. This is the way human beings contrive to feed their self-destructive vices: trying not to see them, trying not to acknowledge them, delaying the important decisions and pretending that nothing will happen.

41. For example, in his address to the Ecclesial Movements on the vigil of his first Pentecost as Bishop of Rome in 2013 (recall that *On Care for Our Common Home* would be dated two years later, Pentecost 2015), Francis called for a "culture of encounter" over and against "a culture of conflict, a culture of fragmentation, a culture in which I throw away whatever is no use to me, a culture of waste." Francis, *Address to the Ecclesial Movements* (May 18, 2013), http://w2.vatican.va/content/francesco/ en/speeches/2013/may/documents/papa-francesco_20130518_veglia-pentecoste.html.

Francis's call for a culture of encounter over a culture of waste has continued to be a consistent feature of his papacy. Among many others, two particularly vivid examples include, on the one hand, his sharp critique of the culture of waste during a papal audience in June of 2013, during which he laments, "Men and women are sacrificed to the idols of profit and consumption: it is the 'culture of waste'. If a computer breaks it is a tragedy, but poverty, the needs and dramas of so many people end up being considered normal." On the other hand, there is his hopeful encouragement to young people on World Youth Day in 2014: "If we are to come through the financial crisis, we must be also ready to change our lifestyle and avoid so much wastefulness. Just as we need the courage to be happy, we also need the courage to live simply." Francis, *Catechesis* (June 5, 2013), http://w2.vatican.va/content/francesco/ en/audiences/2013/documents/papa-francesco_20130605_udienza-generale.html; Francis, *Message for World Youth Day 2014*, (January 21, 2014), http://w2.vatican.va/content/francesco/en/messages/youth/docu ments/papa-francesco_20140121_messaggio-giovani_2014.html).

42. Especially because of its subtlety and nuance, the full text of n. 35 deserves serious reflection:

Implementation

In a climate of mutual trust, the market is the economic institution that permits encounter between persons, inasmuch as they are economic subjects who make use of contracts to regulate their relations as they exchange goods and services of equivalent value between them, in order to satisfy their needs and desires. The market is subject to the principles of so-called commutative justice, which regulates the relations of giving and receiving between parties to a transaction. But the social doctrine of the Church has unceasingly highlighted the importance of distributive justice and social justice for the market economy, not only because it belongs within a broader social and political context, but also because of the wider network of relations within which it operates. In fact, if the market is governed solely by the principle of the equivalence in value of exchanged goods, it cannot produce the social cohesion that it requires in order to function well. Without internal forms of solidarity and mutual trust, the market cannot completely fulfil its proper economic function. And today it is this trust which has ceased to exist, and the loss of trust is a grave loss. It was timely when Paul VI in *Populorum Progressio* insisted that the economic system itself would benefit from the wide-ranging practice of justice, inasmuch as the first to gain from the development of poor countries would be rich ones. According to the Pope, it was not just a matter of correcting dysfunctions through assistance. The poor are not to be considered a "burden," but a resource, even from the purely economic point of view. It is nevertheless erroneous to hold that the market economy has an inbuilt need for a quota of poverty and underdevelopment in order to function at its best. It is in the interests of the market to promote emancipation, but in order to do so effectively, it cannot rely only on itself, because it is not able to produce by itself something that lies outside its competence. It must draw its moral energies from other subjects that are capable of generating them.

43. The full paragraph of n. 109 states the following:

The technocratic paradigm also tends to dominate economic and political life. The economy accepts every advance in technology with a view to profit, without concern for its potentially negative impact on human beings. Finance overwhelms the real economy. The lessons of the global financial crisis have not been assimilated, and we are learning all too slowly the lessons of environmental deterioration. Some circles maintain that current economics and technology will solve all environmental problems, and argue, in popular and non-technical terms, that the problems of global hunger and poverty will be resolved simply by market growth. They are less concerned with certain economic theories which today scarcely anybody dares defend, than with their actual operation in the functioning of the economy. They may not affirm such theories with words, but nonetheless support them with their deeds by showing no interest in more balanced levels of production, a better distribution of wealth, concern for the environment and the rights of future generations. Their behavior shows that for them maximizing profits is enough. Yet by itself the market cannot guarantee integral human development and social inclusion. At the same time, we have "a sort of 'superdevelopment' of a wasteful and consumerist kind which forms an unacceptable contrast with the ongoing situations of dehumanizing deprivation," while we are all too slow in developing economic institutions and social initiatives which can give the poor regular access to basic resources. We fail to see the deepest roots of our present failures, which have to do with the direction, goals, meaning and social implications of technological and economic growth.

44. Bishops of the Patagonia-Comahue Region (Argentina). *Christmas Message* (December 2009), http://www.fides.org/en/news/20516-AMERICA_ARGENTINA_Christmas_Message_from_the_Bishops_of_Patagonia_Christmas_means_saying_no_to_indifference_no_to_only_worrying_about_one_s_own_welfare_without_being_aware_of_the_urgent_needs_of_others_no_to_a_passive_attitude_on_many_urgent_challenges#.VfgAIbRYXww.

45. "Justice" is referred to in nn. 10, 49, 53, 70, 82, 92, 157,159, 200, 207, and 246, some containing more than one reference.

46. Pontifical Council on Justice and Peace, *Vocation of the Business Leader: A Reflection* (Vatican City: Pontifical Council for Justice and Peace, 2012 [see www.justpax.va] / Co-Publisher John A. Ryan Institute for Catholic Social Thought of the Center for Catholic Studies at the University of St. Thomas, Minnesota [see www.stthomas.edu/cathstudies/cst]).

47. In the Roman Catholic lectionary, the covenant with Noah is the first reading for the First Sunday of Lent, Year B, and the whole of the flood and Noahic covenant are recounted over the Tuesday, Wednesday, and Thursday of the sixth week of Ordinary Time, Year I. The Revised Common Lectionary, used by numerous Protestant communities, also provides the covenant with Noah for the First Sunday of Lent, Year B, the reading recounting God's call to Noah and the flood occurs on the Fourth Sunday of Ordinary Time (Year A), and passages from the building of the

ark through to the covenantal promise is read for the Easter Vigil each year.

In addition to the lectionaries, the Roman Catholic Missal provides the following reference, among others, in the Blessing of the Baptismal Water as part of the Easter Vigil:

O God, who by invisible power
accomplish a wondrous effect
through sacramental signs
and who in many ways have prepared water, your creation,
to show forth the grace of Baptism;
O God, whose Spirit
in the first moments of the world's creation
hovered over the waters,
so that the very substance of water
would even then take to itself the power to sanctify;
O God, who by the outpouring of the flood
foreshadowed regeneration,
so that from the mystery of one and the same element of water
would come an end to vice and a beginning of virtue;
O God, who caused the children of Abraham
to pass dry-shod through the Red Sea,
so that the chosen people,
set free from slavery to Pharaoh,
would prefigure the people of the baptized....

48. Abraham Joshua Heschel, *The Sabbath: Its Meaning for Modern Man* (New York: Farrar, Straus and Giroux, 1951; Noonday Press edition, 1975), 10. Precisely because it was so "un-popelike," it is more than notable that John Paul II cited this book in his encyclical *Dies Domini*. John Paul II, encyclical letter *Dies Domini* (May 31, 1998), https://w2.vatican.va/content/john-paul-ii/en/apost_letters/1998/documents/hf_jp-ii_apl_05071998_dies-domini.html, n. 15 fn. 13.

49. The text of n. 237 reads as follows:

On Sunday, our participation in the Eucharist has special importance. Sunday, like the Jewish Sabbath, is meant to be a day which heals our relationships with God, with ourselves, with others and with the world. Sunday is the day of the Resurrection, the "first day" of the new creation, whose first fruits are the Lord's risen humanity, the pledge of the final transfiguration of all created reality. It also proclaims "man's eternal rest in God." In this way, Christian spirituality incorporates the value of relaxation and festivity. We tend to demean contemplative rest as something unproductive and unnecessary, but this is to do away with the very thing which is most important about work: its meaning. We are called to include in our work a dimension of receptivity and gratuity, which is quite different from mere inactivity. Rather, it is another way of working, which forms part of our very essence. It protects human action from becoming empty activism; it also prevents that unfettered greed and sense of isolation which make us seek personal gain to the detriment of all else. The law of weekly rest forbade work on the seventh day, "so that your ox and your donkey may have rest, and the son of your maidservant, and the stranger, may be refreshed" (Ex 23:12). Rest opens our eyes to the larger picture and gives us renewed sensitivity to the rights of others. And so the day of rest, centred on the Eucharist, sheds its light on the whole week, and motivates us to greater concern for nature and the poor.

50. At the same time, this is to admit the variation in interpreting the laws of the Sabbath within Judaism itself and the variety of practices that result.

51. A classic summary of the H. Boone Porter, *The Day of Light: The Biblical and Liturgical Meaning of Sunday* (Greenwich, Conn., Seabury Press, 1960).

52. John Paul II, encyclical letter *Laborem Exercens* (September 14, 1981), http://w2.vatican.va/content/john-paul-ii/en/encyclicals/documents /hf_jp-ii_enc_14091981_laborem-exercens.html.

53. See Vincent Miller, *Consuming Religion: Christian Faith and Practice in a Consumer Culture* (New York: Continuum, 2003), 3. This book is a gem, filled with important insights and challenges.

54. Robert Putnam, *Bowling Alone: The Collapse and Revival of American Community* (New York: Simon and Schuster, 2000).

55. See Vatican II's Constitution on the Sacred Liturgy, n. 26: "Liturgical services are not private functions, but are celebrations of the Church, which is the "sacrament of unity," namely, the holy people united and ordered under their bishops." Vatican II, Constitution on the Sacred Liturgy *Sacrosanctum Concilium* (December 4, 1963), http://www.vatican .va/archive/ hist_councils/ii_vatican_council/documents/vat-ii_const_19631204_ sacrosanctum-concilium_en.html:

Therefore liturgical services pertain to the whole body of the Church; they manifest it and have effects upon it; but they concern the individual members of the Church in different ways, according to their differing rank, office, and actual participation. [The constitution continues in n. 27 below.]

It is to be stressed that whenever rites, according to their specific nature, make provision for communal celebration involving the presence and active participation of the faithful, this way of celebrating them is to be preferred, so far as possible, to a celebration that is individual and quasi-private. This applies with especial force to the celebration of Mass and the administration of the sacraments, even though every Mass has of itself a public and social nature.

56. Timothy Gabrielli, *Confirmation: How a Sacrament of God's Grace Became All about Us* (Collegeville: Liturgical Press, 2013).

57. As of this writing, about a dozen (arch)dioceses have restored or plan to restore this ancient order. This is still obviously a miniscule number of the (arch)dioceses in the United States and will have sporadic impact. A major problem related to the restoration is when a succeeding bishop chooses to "unrestore" the order and return to the former practice of a middle or high school age for confirmation, which leaves its theology hard to pin down, except for the individualism that Gabrielli, among others, rightly critiques.

58. For example, see the following USCCB initiatives: USCCB's pastoral letter *Marriage: Love in the Divine Plan* (November 17, 2009), http://www.usccb.org/issues-and-action/marriage-and-family/marriage/love-and-life/upload/pastoral-letter-marriage-love-and-life-in-the-divine-plan.pdf. Also see the accompanying resources: http://www.usccb.org/issues-and-action/marriage-and-family/marriage/love-and-life/. See also the USCCB's "For Your Marriage" website, http://www.foryourmarriage.org; and the "Marriage: Unique for a Reason" website, http://www.marriageuniqueforareason.org.

Also see the Federation of Diocesan Liturgical Commission's workshops on the Marriage Rite, https://fdlc.org/marriage-rite-workshops.

Finally, see the initiatives of individual dioceses, such as (among many others) the Archdiocese of Washington DC's #visiblesign initiative, http://adw.org/visiblesign/, or the Center for Marriage and Family Life in the Diocese of Richmond, Virginia, http://www.cdrcmfl.org.

59. With regard to the theology of episcopacy now found in the revised rites for ordination, I rely on the insight of James Puglisi who argued that in the second edition of the reformed rite for ordination to the episcopacy, emphasis was placed on the individual candidate for the episcopacy and not his ministry or the ecclesiology of that ministry: the changes were about him. See James Puglisi, *The Process of Admission to Ordained Ministry: Epistemological Principles and Roman Catholic Rites: A Comparative Study*, trans. M. Driscoll and M. Misrahi (Collegeville: Liturgical Press, 1996); Puglisi, "Presider as *Alter Christus*, Head of the Body?" *Liturgical Ministry* 10 (2001): 153–58.

60. See Edward Kilmartin, "The Catholic Tradition and Eucharistic Theology: Towards the Third Millennium," *Theological Studies* 55 (1994): 435; *The Eucharist in the West*, ed. R. Daly (Collegeville: Liturgical Press, 1998), 357. Kilmartin's thinking here is influenced by Heribert Mühlen, *Una Mystica Persona* (München: Schöningh, 1968). See, among others, Wolfgang Vondey, *Heribert Mühlen, His Theology and Praxis: A New Paradigm for the Church* (Lanham: University Press, 2004).

61. See my own "The Arts," in *What We Have Done, What We Have Failed to Do*, 180–96, especially 182–87.

62. Vatican II, Constitution on the Sacred Liturgy *Sacrosanctum Concilium*, n. 123 (see also n. 112 on music in particular).

63. See my own "Sacramentality," in *The Sacraments: Historical Foundations and Liturgical Theology*, 209–30 (Mahwah, NJ: Paulist Press, 2016).

64. While the custom of celebrating the Eucharist on Ash Wednesday at the stational church in Rome at the Church of Santa Sabina with a preceding procession from the Benedictine Ateneo, Sant'Anselmo was revived by John XXII and has been celebrated there since his pontificate, in 1975 Paul VI chose to celebrate the Mass at St. Peter's to accommodate the anticipated Holy Year crowds. Pope Francis celebrated Ash Wednesday at St. Peter's in the Vatican in 2016, during the Year for Mercy, for the same reason.

65. Despite the fact that he acknowledges that he is not a TV watcher!

66. Guardini, *The End of the Modern World*.

67. See the last scene in Alan Bennett's play, *The History Boys*, in which Mrs. Linnott, a fellow teacher, summarizes what has happened to the eight students under the particular tutelage of the main character, the teacher Mr. Hector. When describing the last of them she says, "He lives alone in a cottage he has renovated himself, has an allotment and periodic breakdowns. He haunts the local library and keeps a scrapbook of the achievements of his one-time classmates and has a host of friends… though only on the Internet, and none in his right name."

68. See chapter 1 of the encyclical.

69. Pew Research, "15% of Americans don't use the internet. Who are they?" (July 28, 2015), http://www.pewresearch.org/fact-tank/2015/07/28/15-of-americans-dont-use-the-internet-who-are-they/.

70. See, for example, Executive Office of the President, "Community Based Broadband Solutions: The Benefits of Competition and Choice for Community Development and Highspeed Internet Access" (January 2015), https://www.whitehouse.gov/sites/default/files/docs/community-based_broadband_report_by_executive_office_of_the_president.pdf.

71. For example, a shopping mall was developed in 2015 outside the city of Bristol, Virginia, called "The Falls." Its landmark characteristic was

to be a giant waterfall cascading over enormous boulders. As the mall was being developed, many of the planned stores were erected, some of which (for example, Lowe's) already existed within a few miles of the new store. The waterfall, however, was not constructed because of the problems with construction, including leaks and its location. Did we "need" a new shopping center, especially one that would misuse energy in what is simply a scandalous way?

72. See Pontifical Council of Justice and Peace, *Energia, Giustizia e Pace: Una riflessione sull'energia nel contesto attuale dello sviluppo e della tutela dell'ambiente* (Vatican City: Libreria Editrice Vaticana, 2013).

73. White House Office of Management and Budget, "Implementation of the Government Paperwork Elimination Act," https://www.white house.gov/omb/fedreg_gpea2/.

74. His reference here to stealing from the tables of the poor is from his own audience talk on June, 5, 2013: Francis, *Catechesis* (June 5, 2013), https://w2.vatican.va/content/francesco/en/audiences/2013/documents/ papa-francesco_20130605_udienza-generale.html.

75. John Paul II, *Catechesis* (November 8, 1978), https://w2.vatican. va/content/john-paul-ii/en/audiences/1978/documents/hf_jp-ii_ aud_19781108.html.

76. For decades in the bill that awarded subsidies for farmers also authorized food stamps. The negotiations toward and the final language in the latest "Farm Bill" from the U.S Congress (2014) raised the probability that the U.S. legislators are heading in a different direction. See Ron Nixon's comments from the *New York Times*:

> The new farm bill, which had been mired in partisan gridlock, makes fundamental changes to both nutrition and farm programs. It cuts the food stamp program by $8 billion, and about 850,000 households will lose about $90 in monthly benefits under the change. Anti-hunger groups called the food stamp cuts draconian. Feeding America, a coalition of food banks across the county, said the change would result in 34 lost meals per month for the affected households (Ron Nixon, "House Approves Farm Bill, Ending a 2-Year Impasse" *New York Times* [January 29, 2014], http://www. nytimes.com/2014/01/30/us/politics/house-approves-farm-bill- ending-2-year-impasse.html?_r=1).

77. Francis, *Address to the FAO 2nd International Conference on Nutrition* (November 20, 2014), http://w2.vatican.va/content/francesco/en/ speeches/2014/november/documents/papa-francesco_20141120_visita- fao.html.

78. Water rights in and around the city of Los Angeles is one of the plots in the now classic 1994 film *Chinatown* directed by Roman Polanski, starring Jack Nicholson and Faye Dunaway.

79. See the excellent volume by Christiana Peppard, *Just Water: Theology, Ethics and the Global Water Crisis* (Maryknoll: Orbis, 2014).

CHAPTER FOUR

Beyond

The purpose of this chapter is to raise the questions, "Where do we go from here?" and "How do we move forward?" While these are perennial questions asked (at least rhetorically, if not immediately implemented) after the publication of a church document, from conciliar texts to a pope's daily homily, this is particularly true for an encyclical of this size, scope, breadth, and challenge. The following are meant to be discussion starters for conversations about the nature and scope of papal authority and papal teachings today, and more specifically where we might go and how we might move forward in light of *On Care for Our Common Home*. If it is true that we all "drink from our own wells," then it is important that I acknowledge that I write from the standpoint of an American priest theologian who celebrates the liturgy and preaches regularly. Among my major concerns today is that many cultural assumptions in the U.S. support individualism over a sense of community, except in intergenerational families from other cultures whose sense of "family" and "village" are extraordinary, imitable, and hopefully will be imitated by other Americans. That I have taught at The Catholic University of America for over thirty years will come through, especially in the sections on theology and theological curricula. Of late, I have been concerned to articulate elements that may be said to comprise or be part of what comprises Catholic identity. One major factor is the theology of creation.

I. THEOLOGY AND THEOLOGICAL CURRICULA

THEOLOGY CURRICULUM FOR CATHOLIC COLLEGES AND UNIVERSITIES

One of the contributions of the academic and scientific study of theology and religion has been the quality and depth which has resulted because of the method employed in specialized studies, for example, systematics, moral theology, biblical studies, liturgy and sacraments, church history, religion and culture, and so on. Certainly one advantage of the high degree of specialization required in academic fields today insures quality and that professors are held to the highest professional standards as their careers mature. However, one possible disadvantage may well be that the more specialized one becomes in one field (for example, moral theology), the less one knows about what ought to be allied fields of theological competence, for example, scripture, church history, systematics, liturgy and sacraments, canon law, and so on. For example, in the context of critically rethinking the basic tenets of the Catholic approach to the Bible, Raymond Brown reflects on the need of contemporary theology to assimilate the implications of biblical criticism into Catholic theology, practice, and doctrine.[1] He regrets that theologians have come to appropriate biblical criticism only at a late stage—and later in Catholic scholarship than in Protestant scholarship—such that even highly skilled theologians (for example, Edward Schillebeeckx) have had to come by the methods and skills of biblical criticism independent of their ministerial or academic formations and only late in their careers.

In 2011, the International Theological Commission published a document titled "Theology Today: Perspectives, Principles and Criteria."[2] In the introduction, it cited "a certain fragmentation of theology" (n. 1) and that in theology "the Church clearly needs a common discourse…[and that such discourse] rightly takes a multitude of forms" (n. 2). It then goes on in chapters 1 and 2 to set out in a very helpful manner how theology is based on "Listening to the Word of God," and how the theological enterprise always concerns "Abiding in the Communion of the Church." It makes the not surprising assertion about "the study of scripture as the soul of theology" and then elaborates on this when it says (n. 23):

In saying that the study of sacred Scripture is the "soul" of theology, *Dei Verbum* has in mind all of the theological disciplines. This foundation in the revealed Word of God, as testified by Scripture and Tradition, is essential for theology. Its primary task is to interpret God's truth as saving truth. Urged on by Vatican II, Catholic theology seeks to attend to the Word of God and thereby to the witness of Scripture in all its work.

My own assessment is that this document should be studied, debated, and made part of any ongoing effort at fundamental theology, engaging in the craft of theology today and in establishing a proper university curriculum for the study of theology and religious studies. Not surprisingly, my only quibble with the document is not a critique so much as it is a concern that the liturgy not only be included, but that it be given pride of place in the theological discipline(s) today. This is to ask, if we take "summit and source" language seriously and have a whole new set of revised liturgies with their extraordinary breadth and depth, in what ways should the liturgy be a prominent factor in the entire theological enterprise? This kind of study is explicitly stated in the Liturgy Constitution, nn. 15–17.[3]

The more general point this ITC document makes, however, concerns a certain fragmentation in theology today. My own sense is that part of this could be ameliorated by reflecting on the theme of "interconnectedness" that runs through the encyclical. How might this issue and the breadth of this document help toward a goal of greater integration in the study of theology today?

Along with numerous colleges and universities, Catholic institutions of higher learning sponsor programs in environmental *science*. However, in light of the encyclical might not a truly *Catholic* approach be to offer programs in environmental *studies*. This would mean that a truly interdisciplinary curriculum on the environment include the sciences, politics, economics, law, philosophy, and theology. The reimagining of a curriculum around ecology could be the stimulus for colleagues to work together to craft a curriculum that is of the highest quality academically and yet be both contemporary and interdisciplinary. In addition, each of these individual fields in the university curriculum (for example, sciences, politics, economics, law, philosophy, and theology) should be required to have ecology and the environment as part of their own curriculum. One result, for example, would be that the latest in scientific data about the environment (and the urgency this places on us as citizens of the world) would find its way into theology and philosophy courses, which often are based on classical figures (for example, Plato, Aristotle, St. Thomas Aquinas, St. Bonaventure, and so on), but also on outdated science, causing students to question the value of trusting the wisdom of these seminal figures. This would parallel many theological faculties where, for example, in the 1960s courses were taught on "ecumenism," whereas now it is more common that there be an ecumenical component to all theology courses. On the other hand, there is a growing body of literature which seeks to retrieve themes about creation and the environment that are part and parcel of the Catholic theological tradition but had been neglected or not emphasized.[4] (That other kinds of partnerships between non-Catholic universities and dioceses is exemplified in the "Action Plan" for *Laudato Si'* drafted by the archdiocese with the University of Georgia.)[5]

In addition, on a much broader scale, what would happen if a Catholic approach to ecology derived from *On Care for Our Common Home* were to influence campus ministry service projects and service learning in general? One example of such a holistic approach is found in the preencyclical document *Healing a Broken World* from the (international) Jesuit Social Justice and Ecology Secretariat's Task Force on Ecology as it influences Jesuit theological curricula throughout the world today.[6]

A far bolder approach would be to imitate the example of the CELAM bishops who, when at Puebla (1979), commissioned that the seminary texts and the whole seminary curriculum be contextualized by and emphasize evangelization. In this regard, the text by Antonio Gonzalez Dorado, *Los Sacramentos del Evangelio: Sacramentologia Fundamental y Orgánica,*[7] offers a very comprehensive study of the history, theology, and liturgy of sacraments touching on all the salient issues about sacraments in the Catholic tradition. But the "bookends" in the introduction and epilogue indicate the uniqueness of this particular book—the context of evangelization in Latin America. This "context" also becomes the subtext for the post-Puebla seminary curriculum. In the introduction, Gonzalez

Dorado addresses the intrinsic relationship among "church, liberating evangelization and the sacraments."[8] He carefully parallels the renewal of the liturgy with the renewal of the church and notes specifically the phenomenon of "popular religiosity," the import of "liberation" for the Latin American church, and the ecclesial context of ecumenism and the challenges which secularism offers to the church. The value is that the book is not ideologically narrow and the breadth of the study of sacraments is left intact. Unlike some other modern approaches to sacraments (for example, Karl Rahner and Edward Schillebeeckx), it does not ignore the cultural reality and cultural context in which sacraments are celebrated.[9]

Another example of this bolder approach would be to examine the way Mt. Angel Seminary has redesigned its seminary curriculum around the Eucharist. The rationale for the Mt. Angel curriculum is found in Jeremy Driscoll's *Theology at the Eucharistic Table*.[10] This takes very seriously the mandate of the Liturgy Constitution of Vatican II (n. 16) that:

> The study of sacred liturgy is to be ranked among the compulsory and major courses in seminaries and religious houses of studies; in theological faculties it is to rank among the principal courses. It is to be taught under its theological, historical, spiritual, pastoral, and juridical aspects. Moreover, other professors, while striving to expound the mystery of Christ and the history of salvation from the angle proper to each of their own subjects, must nevertheless do so in a way which will clearly bring out the connection between their subjects and the liturgy, as also the unity which underlies all priestly training. This consideration is especially important for professors of dogmatic, spiritual, and pastoral theology and for those of holy scripture.

The next paragraph (n. 17) is equally important:

> In seminaries and houses of religious, clerics shall be given a liturgical formation in their spiritual life. For this they will need proper direction, so that they may be able to understand the sacred rites and take part in them wholeheartedly; and they will also need personally to celebrate the sacred

mysteries, as well as popular devotions which are imbued with the spirit of the liturgy. In addition they must learn how to observe the liturgical laws, so that life in seminaries and houses of religious may be thoroughly influenced by the spirit of the liturgy.

Such an integral and integrated approach to "liturgical formation" cannot help but also reflect a deep immersion and experience of a theology of creation and of ecology requiring that we "care for our common home."

The latter, however, should not be restricted to seminaries and houses of formation. This kind of liturgical formation should imbue the Catholic university experience through campus ministry programs, liturgies, homilies, and formation sessions.

LITURGY, ESCHATOLOGY, AND JUSTICE

In the Western church, for a variety of reasons, emphasis has been placed on determining how Christ is present in the liturgy, particularly in the eucharistic species.[11] The evolution of the term "transubstantiation" attests to the care and creativity that early scholastic theologians worked toward crafting this term and commenting on its meaning. Trent's teaching that Christ is "really, substantially and truly" present in the eucharistic bread and wine and Pope Pius XII's eucharistic teaching in *Mediator Dei* is expanded on at the Second Vatican Council in the Liturgy Constitution (n. 7):

To accomplish so great a work, Christ is always present in His Church, especially in her liturgical celebrations. He is present in the sacrifice of the Mass, not only in the person of His minister, "the same now offering, through the ministry of priests, who formerly offered himself on the cross," but especially under the Eucharistic species. By His power He is present in the sacraments, so that when a man baptizes it is really Christ Himself who baptizes. He is present in His word, since it is He Himself who speaks when the holy scriptures are read in the Church. He is present, lastly, when the Church prays and sings, for He promised: "Where two or three are gathered together in my name, there am I in the midst of them" (Matt 18:20).[12]

This expansion by the council fathers is a significant restatement of what Catholic believe about his presence in and through the liturgy. Yet at the same time, it is important to recall that the liturgy is inherently eschatological, again as the Liturgy Constitution says (n. 8):

> In the earthly liturgy we take part in a foretaste of that heavenly liturgy which is celebrated in the holy city of Jerusalem toward which we journey as pilgrims, where Christ is sitting at the right hand of God, a minister of the holies and of the true tabernacle; we sing a hymn to the Lord's glory with all the warriors of the heavenly army; venerating the memory of the saints, we hope for some part and fellowship with them; we eagerly await the Saviour, Our Lord Jesus Christ, until He, our life, shall appear and we too will appear with Him in glory.[13]

While this is well attested in the experience and theology of most Eastern liturgies, the council fathers judged it was time that we in the West addressed this issue.

The liturgy is inherently eschatological in that it immerses us into the reality of God and all that is God's kingdom until the kingdom comes in all its fullness. We pray "thy kingdom come" at the liturgy because while the liturgy is an experience of the kingdom of God, it is a promissory experience: it looks and pleads for its fulfillment in eternity. Until we will have no more need for liturgy, one of its major aspects is to allow us to experience even now what we hope to experience in its fullness in eternity. In the meantime, the liturgy is both a promissory and challenging reality. Because "we are not there yet," the liturgy invites us to see and act in the world in such a way that the reality of the kingdom as experienced and expressed in the liturgy can be realized more fully for every creature on this earth. This means that part of the eschatology of the liturgy is to realize the inherent incompleteness of everything and the yearnings of every creature on the earth. Our communion with every other creature is part of the import of this encyclical. It should be a part of our appreciation of how and what we celebrate in the liturgy.

Liturgy is the necessary complement in acting justly in this world, toward all creation, until we meet the Just One face-to-face in heaven. Among other things, this means that we respect those who have manufactured the bread and wine for the Eucharist ("the work of human hands") in particular in terms of just wages and labor practices. It means that we who share the Eucharist as a gift from God through a meal will share our bread with the hungry and care for those who have no food or access to fresh foods. "Do this in memory of me" means service in the ritual action of the liturgy and in the acts of serving others in the rest of life. This is the meaning which Xavier Leon-Dufour has given to the domini- cal command "do this in memory of me."[14] Rather than restrict it to the enactment of the eucharistic sacrifice at the altar, he argues that this command requires that we live lives of self-sacrifice as ritualized at the altar. This is eschatology understood as the "not yet-ness" of what we celebrate. This is also why we have interces- sions in the liturgy: to pray for what is not yet and for what we hope, and to what we commit ourselves to pray for and work for.

That the liturgy is both an experience of the unique and abiding presence of Christ should always be linked with understanding how the liturgy is "an act of the kingdom." That it is always both unique and provisional is why we offer intercessions and pray "thy kingdom come."

THE DIGNITY OF THE HUMAN PERSON / HUMAN COMMUNITY IN OUR COMMON HOME

When Pope Paul VI issued the "Declaration on Religious Free- dom On the Right of the Person and Religious Communities to Social and Civil Freedom" (*Dignitatus Humanae*) in 1965 (dur- ing Vatican II, but not a document from the council itself), it was acclaimed across the political and civic spectrum as a ground- breaking document. Since then it has legitimately been seen as a cornerstone of Catholic theology and social teaching. However, given the intervening fifty years, one could legitimately raise the question whether the phrase "and religious communities" as part of the "Declaration on Religious Freedom" has been sufficiently emphasized, especially in so-called developed countries, like the United States. Some have argued that this is because the American religious culture is heavily influenced by the theology of Calvin and/or Zwingli. Others have argued that this is the result of the influence of Adam Smith and the capitalist ethic. Still others, more recently, have pointed to the oppressive fear that many Americans are feeling about a number of things such as the economy, the rapid changes in society, and the uses of technology, relating to people of different origins, races, and religions, and so on. All of these issues could cause one to withdraw into oneself and to retreat from the wider society.

In addition, one could ask whether the Catholic strong suit of corporate belonging and being essentially a covenanted people has been eclipsed in favor of an individualistic anthropomorphism clearly challenged by the encyclical. Whatever can be said about the dead-ended debate about whether "it takes a family" and/or whether "it takes a village," it, in fact, takes both, and any sense of oneself is always supported and contextualized by the communal reality that is Catholicism, derived from the Jewish sense of belonging to a covenant religion founded by the covenant God of Abraham, Isaac, and Jacob. This particular Catholic attribute could become an important contribution to the hoped for debates about ecology that transcend nation, state, and the individual. Might not the encyclical be one way to retrieve a common sense of purpose and foster what had been the presumed bonds from family, neighborhood, civic clubs, schools, the parish? Certainly the liturgy always presumes a sense of belonging and being part of a larger, wider world than one's own parish or other place of worship. What would happen if we jettisoned "the dignity of the human person" in favor of the phrase "the dignity of the human community?"

Additionally, in light of *On Care for Our Common Home*, we might want to urge that we take seriously the pope's assertion about a "tyrannical anthropocentrism" and always place discussions of anthropology in relation to cosmology, and vice versa.

There are at least two "givens" at work here. The first is the contribution which Paul VI made to international, and not necessarily religious, discourse, by issuing *Dignitatus Humanae* (admittedly nuanced above). The second is Pope Francis's assertions about

221

a misguided or tyrannical anthropomorphism. For example, he asserts that "the Bible has no place for a tyrannical anthropomorphism unconcerned for other creatures" (n. 68), argues that "the *Catechism* clearly and forcefully criticizes a distorted anthropocentrism" (n. 69), and marks the crisis and defects of a modern anthropocentrism with terms such as "excessive," and "inadequate" (nn. 115–23). In n. 118 he asserts that "there can be no ecology without an adequate anthropology." This challenge would certainly be a "work in progress" but a work well worth undertaking.

II. RELATING THE PAPACY WITH EPISCOPACY

I think it is fair to say that the documents of Vatican II—specifically the Dogmatic Constitution on the Church *Lumen Gentium* (1964), the Decree on the Life and Ministry of Presbyters *Presbyterorum Ordinis* (1965), and the Decree on Priestly Formation *Optatum Totius* (1965)— and the documents of the magisterium published since Vatican II have given us a rich theology of the episcopacy (largely influenced by patristic sources), which emphasized, among other things, collegiality over an individual bishop in a diocese and envisioning his working collaboratively with a number of groups of people, including deacons and presbyters.[15] That those same documents leave us a number of unanswered questions and unaddressed issues is equally clear. Among them is the relationship of bishops today with their presbyterates[16] and with the modern papacy.

RELATIONSHIP OF PAPACY TO THE SYNOD OF BISHOPS

The idea that the Catholic church should have a permanent consultative body of bishops was discussed just prior to and during the deliberations at Vatican II. Toward the end of Vatican II, Paul VI established the Synod of Bishops by issuing the *motu proprio Apostolica Solicitudo*.[17] The synod has a permanent general secretariat in the Vatican composed of a General Secretary, an Undersecretary and a fifteen-member council of fifteen bishops, of whom twelve are elected and three of whom are appointed by the pope. There are three kinds of meetings of the synod: ordinary general assemblies (for example, the October 2015 ordinary synod on the family titled "The Vocation and Mission of the Family in the Church and the Contemporary World"), extraordinary general assemblies (for example, the October 2014 extraordinary synod on family titled "The Pastoral Challenges of the Family in the Context of Evangelization"), and special assemblies (for example, on the Middle East, 2010). It is the responsibility of the pope to determine the topic of the synod and to preside personally or through a delegate. It is accepted as fact that Pope John Paul II set the agenda for the synod, set its operating procedures (with little time for discussion), and had a firm sense ahead of time of what should appear in the postsynodal exhortations, with the latter receiving the input of the members of the General Assembly (and others). Pope Benedict XVI followed in John Paul II's footsteps, but he did add time for discussion. In terms of structure, it is noteworthy that Pope Francis created its General Secretary Lorenzo Baldisseri a cardinal. This is "Vatican-speak" meaning that this is a very important person in the church. In terms of the synod topics, the fact that the pope called for two meetings to be held on the topic of the family shows his concern about family life in our day. In terms of synod process, it is significant that at the October 2015 meeting the bishops and other delegates spent much of their time discussing the presynodal document (the *instrumentum laboris*) in small groups (*circuli minores*) assigned by language proficiency. This time dedicated for discussion indicates Francis's strong desire that as many voices be heard as possible. He has repeatedly stressed his desire that the synod fathers debate issues frankly and with charity.[18]

That the pope continues to make changes in the synodal process shows how committed he is to synodality. In his opening address to the synod,[19] Francis emphasized synodality strongly by stating that "the Synod is a journey undertaken together in the spirit of collegiality and synodality, on which participants bravely adopt parrhesia, pastoral zeal and doctrinal wisdom, frankness, always keeping before our eyes the good of the Church, of families and the *suprema lex*, the *Salus animarum* (cf. can. 1752)." However, he continues, such collegiality and synodality is not simply a convention, a parlor, a parliament, or a senate engaged to arrive at a consensus, but he states, "The Synod is rather an ecclesial expression, i.e., the Church that journeys together to understand reality with the eyes of faith and with the heart of God," a process in which the Church's shepherds—her servants—experience and open themselves to the work of the Holy Spirit, and a space for "apostolic courage, evangelical humility and trusting prayer." That some of the bishop delegates to the October 2015 synod found the planned procedures less than clear caused some confusion (not to say rancor; more on this in subsection 3 below). A number of issues are now on the table for discussion about the Catholic church's structures and practices. Some commentators fear that more emphasis on synodality will lessen the universality of the church. Others fear that any move toward imitating the structure of the Anglican Communion could result in the kind of "split" (at least functionally) that occurred when, for example, the gathering of Anglican Primates censured the American Episcopal Church for a three-year period starting in January of 2016. Others point to the leadership of the Orthodox churches and point out the long simmering tensions between the Russian Orthodox and the other Orthodox churches.

At least part of these conversations will necessarily include the various and varied cultures that comprise Catholicism. One characteristic of Paul VI's papacy was his deep regard for the variety of ways that Catholicism is understood and practiced throughout the world.[20] Among the leadership characteristics of both John Paul II and Benedict XVI was a certain centralization of decision-making in the Vatican for the worldwide church, which appears to have been a real concern voiced by members of the college of cardinals at their preconclave meetings in March of 2013.[21] One particularly noticeable example of these centralizing concerns regards "inculturation," the oft-used term to describe the ongoing process of the Catholic church immersing itself all over the world. An emerging consensus among many theologians, missiologists, and liturgists is that, under John Paul II and Benedict XVI, much of the wind was taken out of the sails of the positive assessment of inculturation.[22] One question here concerns how much can or should be adapted to a culture and how much can or should remain the same across cultures. How much should the church seek to influence a culture from within or confront a culture directly? For example, at the October 2015 synod on the family, the issues of polygamy and the pastoral care for divorced people in second marriages were repeatedly brought up by the delegates.

RELATIONSHIP OF THE PAPACY TO EPISCOPAL CONFERENCES

Pope Francis is something of a paradox. He writes, speaks, and acts compellingly about "synodality," the importance of "collegiality" among brother bishops, and being the Bishop of Rome (his preferred self-designation). As previously noted, at the preconclave meetings leading up to his election there was a lot of discussion about the over-centralization of church governance that was fostered by John Paul II and Benedict XVI. At the same time, he exercises important leadership by way of using the "bully pulpit" of the papacy, by issuing (or overseeing the issuing) of a number of decrees that impact the universal church. (While not the meatiest in terms of theology, certainly one that will impact the world wide church and be commented about concerns whose feet can be washed at the Evening Mass of the Lord's Supper on Holy Thursday.)[23] Several issues surface here including papal visibility and papal teachings.

An important example of papal visibility includes papal trips. Papal trips outside of Italy in the modern era began with Pope Paul VI (the last one prior to him was in 1809). He made nine trips from 1964 to 1970. The first was to Jordan and Israel (1964), during which he met Patriarch Athenagoras I on the Mount of Olives. His single-day excursion to the United States was on the Feast of St. Francis of Assisi (1965) when he spoke to the United Nations, urging "war, never again!" His last trip was also his longest (November 25 to December 5, 1970). During it he met the heads of state of Iran, the Philippines, Australia, and Indonesia. It was early on during this trip when the pope was the object of an assassination attack in the Manila International Airport.[24]

Almost immediately after being elected, John Paul II embarked on the first of what eventually numbered 104 trips outside of Italy when he visited the Dominican Republic and Mexico. In Puebla, Mexico (in 1979), he attended and addressed the Third Conference of the Latin American Episcopate (CELAM).[25] The fact that a reigning pope met bishops on their own turf (so to speak) and addressed them is more than notable. That issues surrounding "liberation theology" and the "preferential option for the poor" occupied much of the CELAM (and other) bishops' attention should not be forgotten.[26] Certainly John Paul II established the "playbook" for papal trips, which included numberless (now published) addresses, homilies, prayer services, and greetings. The "photo op" of the pope kissing the ground at the airport of his host country upon his arrival became a signature feature of his papacy. The pope was now cast as a "star" in the constellation of other stars who were the object of media attention and scrutiny. Pope John Paul II visited the United States five times and made two additional "stop over" visits to Alaska during his pontificate.

As another example of increasing papal visibility, John Paul II established the custom of "World Youth Day" in 1985. These were to be celebrated annually in each diocese on Passion (Palm) Sunday and once every two or three years at a designated international location. The highest number of attendees at an international World Youth Day was at Masses in the Philippines celebrated by Pope John Paul II (1995) and later by Pope Francis (2015).

Additional examples of expanding the visibility of the papacy in Rome itself include John Paul II's establishing (in 1983) the celebration of an outdoor Mass in St. Peter's Square annually on the Solemnity of Sts. Peter and Paul in order to distribute the *pallium* to those named archbishops from around the world during the previous twelve months. He also ordained recently named bishops from throughout the world annually on the Solemnity of the Epiphany, and he established a street procession to take place on the Solemnity of Corpus Christi (from the basilica of St. John Lateran to the basilica of St. Mary Major).

While the then Cardinal Ratzinger was understood to be disinclined to favor many papal trips, he himself made twenty-four trips outside of Italy during his eight years as pope. Among the more memorable was his trip to Washington, DC, in 2008, which included meetings with ecumenical and interreligious leaders (as was his custom) along with a visit to the White House and an address to Catholic College presidents at The Catholic University of America.

Pope Benedict continued to issue annual "messages" on World Youth Day on Palm Sunday and attended the international meetings in Cologne (2005), Sydney (2008), and Madrid (2011). Early on in his papacy Benedict XVI asked for research on the tradition of the pallium Mass and whether it was advisable to continue John Paul II's custom. The research confirmed (and the Rite for the Ordination of Bishops attests to) Benedict's understanding that the giving of the pallium is part of the ceremony when archbishops were ordained in metropolitan cathedrals or when already ordained bishops took possession of an archdiocesan cathedral. Benedict took a half measure and moved the "Pallium Mass" inside St. Peter's basilica. He continued the celebration of Corpus Christi and the procession in the streets of Rome.

Like his immediate predecessors, Pope Francis has embarked on an ambitious travel schedule of visits outside of Rome. In the summer after being elected, he attended World Youth Day in Brazil (2013). He made five trips in 2014, including to Israel, Palestine, and Jordan, and five in 2015, including to Cuba and the United States. He began 2016 by returning to North America in February to visit Mexico.[27] Pope Francis celebrates a Mass on the Solemnity of Sts. Peter and Paul in St. Peter's basilica to bless the archbishops' pallia, which are then given to the metropolitan archbishops at a later time in their own cathedrals by the apostolic nuncio of that country.

Certainly these papal trips and additional visibility have been a cause for the papacy's relatively high popularity and lasting impact on the church and the world.

At the same time, Roman Catholicism is a religion led and governed by diocesan bishops in relationship with the pope. What does it mean theologically in terms of what the pope says during these trips and pastorally in terms of what he does on these trips in relation to the leadership in word and deed of the diocesan bishops?

When a bishop is ordained and installed in diocesan cathedrals, one of the most important moments liturgically is when he is escorted to the bishop's chair, the *cathedra*, from which the word "cathedral" comes. From then on no one presides at the sacred liturgy from that *cathedra* because it is reserved for the diocesan bishop. What impact does it have when the pope occupies the *cathedra* in a cathedral as Pope Benedict XVI did when celebrating Mass at St. Patrick's in New York City (April 18, 2008) and Cardinal Edward Egan, the archbishop of New York, took a place with the other concelebrating bishops—or when Pope Francis did the same (September 24, 2015)?

227

As detailed above,[28] one of the initiatives undertaken by John Paul II (with the leadership of the then Cardinal Ratzinger) was to clarify (not to say definitely downplay in a significant way) the teaching authority of an episcopal conference in relation to that of a diocesan bishop or the pope himself. In effect, that "shut down" the USCCB engine that drove the writing of their pastorals on nuclear arms and the economy.[29] The one planned on women in the church never materialized.

However, what does it say that Pope Francis quoted documents from episcopal conferences no fewer than twenty-one times in the encyclical? It is to be granted in terms of the "relative authoritative weight" that an encyclical is above the documents of a bishops' conference or a diocesan bishop. In addition, even (especially) as Pope Francis suggests that "one size does not fit all" in terms of implementing his ecological vision in the encyclical, and presuming that bishops' conferences will follow his lead, the fact remains that he used existing bishops' conference documents as part of his argumentation. This is uncharted territory.

Given the possibilities of transportation, communication, and travel today it would seem highly unlikely that popes will stop traveling and using all effective means possible to spread the church's message. There are theological issues on the table, however, for ample discussion about relating papal authority to episcopal authority and papal ministry to diocesan episcopal ministry.[30]

The publication of *On Care for Our Common Home* was accompanied by several initiatives that Vatican watchers regarded as extraordinary. Even the customary press conference was unusual in that the only Vatican official to make a presentation was Cardinal Peter Turkson of the Pontifical Council for Justice and Peace. There were no fewer than four others (among whom were three laypeople) who made presentations: others included Metropolitan John of Pergamon (John Zizioulas) from the Orthodox church; Professor John Schellnhuber, who is the founding Director of the Potsdam Institute for Climate Change; Dr. Carolyn Woo of the U.S.-based Catholic Relief Services (CRS) and a Rome based teacher; and Ms. Valeria Martano, who spoke about urban ecology, specifically the dangers resulting from pollution.[31] In addition, in the *Memorandum* of June 16, 2015, which accompanied the (then still embargoed) encyclical (recall that the official publication date was May 24, 2015, the Solemnity of Pentecost, but the actual date on which the document was released was June 18, 2015), the Vatican encouraged episcopal conferences to cooperate in the launch of the document by holding press conferences. One example was the press conference held at the National Press Club in Washington, DC, on the day of the announcement of the encyclical cohosted by Archbishop Joseph Kurz, then President of the United States Catholic Conference, and Cardinal Donald Wuerl, archbishop of Washington.[32] The documentation sent to the bishops contained an outline of the encyclical and "talking points" to assist the bishops.

RELATIONSHIP OF PAPACY TO INDIVIDUAL BISHOPS

That there is not unanimity among the bishops themselves on applications of church teachings is a fact of church history and the present reality of the church (for example, the discussions at the October 2015 synod on the family. This is also clear in almost all the debates in which the American bishops engage during their semiannual USCCB meetings). That popes have favored some bishops as collaborators over others is also a fact. (For example, Cardinal Francis Spellman was a very close collaborator of Pope Pius XII, and the day Pius died, Spellman lost that role.) That some bishops have criticized Pope Francis in public and in print is clear and a cause for real scandal.[33] Some bishops who should be overseeing and fostering unity in the church are doing the opposite by word and deed. At the same time, this should not really be a surprise since all the bishops in the church on the day Pope Francis was elected were appointed by either John Paul II (whose papacy was quite long) or Benedict XVI—both men whose vision of church leadership differs in some ways from that of Pope Francis. There is no crystal ball we can look into to find out the number of bishops Pope Francis will name or the number of cardinals he will create and whether a major criterion will be to collaborate fully in fostering Pope Francis's agenda for the church. Sadly, this is not a new problem. Church history is filled with examples. Is it any wonder that each day in the Eucharistic Prayer we pray for the pope, the diocesan bishop, and for the unity of the church?

Some would argue, however, that things are different in a 24/7 news cycle, with almost anything said or done posted on the

Internet, sometimes not for the sake of disclosing information but rather for the sake of fostering the popularity of the "news" outlets that post the information. Sadly, sometimes the voice of the successor to St. Peter is drowned out by the voice of one of his fellow members of the episcopacy. How, then, to build up the body of Christ with some bishops avowed critics of Pope Francis? To use the terminology of Catholic social justice teaching, how does "subsidiarity" work in the day-to-day workings of the church?

Again with regard to the release of the encyclical the documentation, which the world's bishops received on June 16, 2015, contained a handwritten note in Italian by Pope Francis to the world's bishops. It read as follows:

> Dear brother,
>
> In the bond of unity, charity and peace (LG 22) in which we live as Bishops, I send you my letter *Laudato si'* on care for our common home, accompanied by my blessing. United in the Lord, and please do not forget to pray for me. Franciscus.

Many American bishops issued statements about the encyclical on the day of its publication, several within days and many in the weeks following. Some bishops working together in a state (for example, the New York State Bishops Conference is comprised of the Archdiocese of New York and all the other seven dioceses in the state) have issued statements and drew up plans to follow through on the document's implementation, which are clear signs that very many bishops have cooperated with the pope in new and unique ways (for example, the bishops of Ohio who have issued a document on fracking).

III. SPIRITUALITY AND SPIRITUAL TRADITIONS

DEFINITION(S) OF SPIRITUALITY

At the beginning of chapter 6 of the encyclical titled "Ecological Education and Spirituality," the pope writes (n. 202),

Many things have to change course, but it is we human beings above all who need to change. We lack an awareness of our common origin, of our mutual belonging, and of a future to be shared with everyone. This basic awareness would enable the development of new convictions, attitudes and forms of life. A great cultural, spiritual and educational challenge stands before us, and it will demand that we set out on the long path of renewal.

This paragraph introduces a number of important ideas and action steps that derive from the rest of the pope's argument to that point. That one of the goals is change and that the chapter heading concerns "education" and "spirituality" certainly reflect the style and content of Francis's pontificate. That both education and spirituality (leading to change in mind and heart?) are connected is important simply because of the seemingly numberless definitions and descriptions of spirituality that are operative today.

As I have argued elsewhere, a "working definition" of spirituality for me would be the following:

Spirituality is a way of thinking and acting shaped primarily by the church's corporate experience of God, who is imminent and transcendent, revealed yet remains hidden, a triune God who invites us into deep and abiding relationship with Father, Son, and Holy Spirit and through them to the whole church and the wider world. Spirituality enables church members to maintain corporate values and minority positions with confidence in the face of contrary cultural pressures because of the power of God's enlivening Spirit within and among us. Spirituality guides a person's understanding of the world and it provides a basis for discipline in one's life.[34]

What underlies this definition is an appreciation for a Catholic world view and a Catholic way of looking at and reflecting on the spiritual life. "Spirituality" is more than participation in the liturgy, or one's personal prayer, or one's devotional practices. It is a worldview that determines how we look at life and live the life of God. It is a basis for "action," especially in the "think, judge, act" triad. In addition, I understand "spirituality" to have a component that involves theology and the study of theology. This can be of the more strictly "academic" type, and involve or be based on a way of studying (or "doing") theology. For example, in the encyclical the pope relies regularly on his patron, St. Francis of Assisi and, by extension, Franciscan theology through such interlocutors as St. Bonaventure. Other representatives of this kind of scholastic theology include Dominicans such as Thomas Aquinas. Alternatively, authors from the "monastic" theological tradition—for example, Sts. Athanasius, Basil, Augustine, Bernard of Clairvaux, and so on—are equally important in the history and present practice of engaging in Catholic theology. One of the important intersections for both the "scholastics" (Franciscans, Dominicans, Carmelites, Canons Regular, and so on) and the "monastics" (from St. Benedict on) is the important intersection of thought and prayer. This is an important component, not only of the academic study of spirituality; it is imperative for the very identity of Catholicism. We are a thinking and praying church with many academic branches on the tree that comprises the Catholic tradition—theology and spirituality.

Another underlying element of this definition is that Catholicism takes countercultural positions on a range of issues based on the paradoxes at the heart of our faith—obedience leading to peaceful surrender, suffering leading to glory, humiliation leading to exaltation, dying leading to rising, sacrifice leading to absolute fulfillment. Countercultural positions taken in light of the encyclical are many, including seeing the needs of all as our privileged responsibility. All are brothers and sisters to us and we are brothers and sisters to all. This has implications for immigration, pollution, devastation of other's land, misuse of water, and so on. Any focus on immediate economic gains is challenged in light of the Gospel and our belonging to each other—that the long view and long-term gains for all people matter. One concretization of this is in Catholic social teaching's "preferential option for the poor" personified in Pope Francis's continual and repeated appeal that we not forget the poor.[35]

This way of understanding spirituality necessarily leads to discipline in one's life, both communally and personally—from regular participation in liturgy, prayer, devotions, *lectio divina*, study, and ascetical practices (among other things) to corporate witness on behalf of life in all its forms (in the womb, at the end of life, the taking of a human life in imposing the death penalty, workers' rights for a decent wage, caring for our common home, and so on) now helpfully specified in the encyclical. This should, in turn, lead to ever greater trust and confidence in welcoming God's overwhelming mercy and our being merciful toward all creatures who share our common home.

One of the jewels in the crown of Catholicism is that we have many traditional and recognized spiritual traditions, some linked with the great religious communities aimed at different aspects of the Catholic life: monastic, mendicant, apostolic, missionary, and so on. That Pope Francis regularly relies on his Jesuit roots and identity is clear. That he relies on St. Francis and the Franciscan theological tradition in the encyclical is not a surprise. That there are other spiritual traditions to learn from and follow should come as no surprise either.

Under the theme of "Ecological Conversion" and the subtheme of "Joy and Peace" in chapter 6 of the encyclical, the pope applies a Catholic spiritual perspective to consumption (n. 222):[36]

Christian spirituality proposes an alternative understanding of the quality of life, and encourages a prophetic and contemplative lifestyle, one capable of deep enjoyment free of the obsession with consumption. We need to take up an ancient lesson, found in different religious traditions and also in the Bible. It is the conviction that "less is more." A constant flood of new consumer goods can baffle the heart and prevent us from cherishing each thing and each moment. To be serenely present to each reality, however small it may be, opens us to much greater horizons of understanding and personal fulfilment. Christian spirituality proposes a growth marked by moderation and the capacity to be happy with little. It is a return to that simplicity which allows us to stop and appreciate the small things, to be grateful for the opportunities which life affords us, to be spiritually detached from what we possess, and not to succumb to sadness for what we lack. This implies avoiding the dynamic of dominion and the mere accumulation of pleasures.

THE RELEVANCE OF MONASTICISM

While the encyclical is decidedly Franciscan and Bonaventuran in its theological and spiritual outlook, the pope does make reference to "the tradition of monasticism" and the cenobite monastic tradition from St. Benedict (n. 126). The *Rule of St. Benedict* (*RB*) is a sober, direct, and practical document. It binds the monk to stability and a sense of place. Benedictines join a particular community located in a particular set of buildings in a particular geographical location. Because monks are tied to a single place, that is where they must find God. The *Rule* is suffused with the idea of the presence of God, who is everywhere and sees all that happens.[37] Benedict is less inclined to view humanity and other beings as companions than is St. Francis or Pope Francis. Yet he judges human beings to be like other creatures made to praise and glorify God.[38] If human beings give this praise and glory by their prayer and work, they do so in the name of all creation. By their fidelity to the Liturgy of the Hours, they live the fullness of the daily, weekly, and yearly liturgical cycles reflected in the scriptures, especially in the psalms, prayers, hymns, and canticles reflecting praise for and within creation, notably the motif of light and darkness. St. Benedict's emphasis on humility (notably its twelve steps: see *RB*, chapter 7, but even starting in chapter 5 on "obedience"), from the Latin word for "soil" (*humus*), grounds and reflects that human beings were made by God from the dust of the earth, which Pope Francis emphasizes in the encyclical (nn. 2 and 9). St. Benedict's emphasis on humility involves a preference for people over procedures, for service over managerial control. This is clearly enunciated in his description of the monastery cellarer, the one who looks after the temporal needs of the monastery, who is completely subject to the abbot (*RB*, 31). St. Benedict's admonition that the cellarer should "show every concern for the sick, children, guests and the poor" (also see *RB*, 53,1; 7,15; 36,1–3; 37; 41,14–19) is reflected in Pope Francis's repeated reminder to us all that this is constitutive of Catholic belief and practice. St. Benedict also urged moderation and frugality, urging, for example, that monks should wear what is available in the vicinity at a reasonable price (*RB*, 55,7). This admonition fits in well with the pope's critique of "the throwaway culture" (nn. 16, 20, 22). The example St. Benedict gives of finding the sacred in the ordinary refers to the way the cellarer "will regard the utensils and goods of the monastery as sacred vessels of the altar, aware that nothing is to be neglected" (*RB*, 31, 10–11). One interpretation of this text is that St. Benedict is drawing an analogy: just as the vessels which belong to the altar should be carefully cared for, so should the tools which belong to the monastery. Another interpretation is that St. Benedict thinks that tools as such are sacred. Or perhaps he meant both. If so, St. Benedict may be seeing the use of tools as a way to participate in God's ongoing creative care for humanity, to fulfill one's God-given vocation as *homo faber*. Viewed in this way, as instruments by which human necessities are provided, tools are instruments of the kingdom of God. If tools are sacred, then people are more so. This would be a decided contribution to the language Pope Francis uses about "care" and "creatures."

St. Benedict's monks are to be friends of the planet, not its enemies; they are to be looking for Christ where others may be looking for a customer or contributor. St. Benedict's monks are to strive for genuine humility, where others may be seeking for humanly bestowed status and power. St. Benedict's monks are to work to support a frugal and healthy life devoted primarily to prayer and reading, where others may be working in order to consume. While Pope Benedict XVI took the name of the founder of Western monasticism as his own, it may well be that the monastic virtues and values St. Benedict fostered find a very generous welcome in the teachings and example of Pope Francis.[39]

EXPAND THE "SEE, JUDGE, ACT" METHOD TO INCLUDE "LISTEN" AND "CELEBRATE"

Listen

In a particularly moving and contemplative section of the encyclical titled "The Gospel of Creation," Pope Francis cites John Paul II, the bishops of Canada and of Japan, and the philosopher Paul Ricoeur when he writes the following (n. 85):

God has written a precious book, "whose letters are the multitude of created things present in the universe." The

Canadian bishops rightly pointed out that no creature is excluded from this manifestation of God: "From panoramic vistas to the tiniest living form, nature is a constant source of wonder and awe. It is also a continuing revelation of the divine." The bishops of Japan, for their part, made a thought-provoking observation: "To sense each creature singing the hymn of its existence is to live joyfully in God's love and hope." This contemplation of creation allows us to discover in each thing a teaching which God wishes to hand on to us, since "for the believer, to contemplate creation is to hear a message, to listen to a paradoxical and silent voice." We can say that "alongside revelation properly so-called, contained in sacred Scripture, there is a divine manifestation in the blaze of the sun and the fall of night." Paying attention to this manifestation, we learn to see ourselves in relation to all other creatures: "I express myself in expressing the world; in my effort to decipher the sacredness of the world, I explore my own."

John Paul II's turn of phrase "to hear a message [and] to listen to a paradoxical and silent voice" is both compelling and invitational. The issue here is that an attentive listening to the scriptures and a fully attentive celebration of the liturgy (in particular) should accompany any kind of method for prayer which then is followed by action and celebration.

The very first word in the *Rule of St. Benedict* is the Latin *obsculta* (*ausculta*), an imperative form of the verb meaning "to listen attentively." St. Benedict immediately invites his followers to "attend" to the precepts laid down in the *Rule* with "the ear of your heart" (*et inclina aurem cordis tui*).[40] In the Benedictine tradition, this is linked with *obedience*, which derives from the Latin preposition *ob* attached to the verb *audire* also meaning "to hear/listen." (Interestingly, another meaning of the verb *ausculta* is, in fact, "to hear/listen attentively" or "to obey.") This suggests that obedience is a function of listening to the Word of God and putting that Word into practice. The often used verse at the Gospel acclamation at Mass "speak, Lord, your servant is listening" (1 Sam 3:1–10) again emphasizes attentive listening. This phrase is often accompanied with the text from "the bread of life" discourse in the Gospel of John acclaiming, "you have the words of everlasting life" (John 6:68).[41] To "listen attentively to holy reading" (for example, *RB*, 4, 55) is one of the "tools of good works." It is also the kind of attitude which monks should bring to their "reading of holy scripture" where attentive listening can be presumed to underlie this practice (as noted several times in *RB*, 48, on "The Daily Manual Labor" and *RB*, 49, on "The Observance of Lent").[42] It would also be the attitude which anyone should bring to engagement in *lectio divina*.[43] It was St. Bernard of Clairvaux who wrote, "You wish to see; listen. Hearing is a step toward Vision."[44] No wonder that the church's daily prayer begins with Psalm 94(95):7–8:

> Oh, that today you would hear his voice:
> Do not harden your hearts as at Meribah,
>   as on the day of Massah in the desert.

Or as it is frequently used as a refrain in the *Lectionary for Mass*, "If today you hear his voice, harden not your hearts," or another Gospel acclamation: "Open our hearts, O Lord, to listen to the words of your Son."

The pope uses the terms "listen," "think," and "spirituality" in a succinct paragraph about the challenges he lays before us in the encyclical (n. 111):

> Ecological culture cannot be reduced to a series of urgent and partial responses to the immediate problems of pollution, environmental decay and the depletion of natural resources. There needs to be a distinctive way of looking at things, a way of thinking, policies, an educational programme, a lifestyle and a spirituality which together generate resistance to the assault of the technocratic paradigm. Otherwise, even the best ecological initiatives can find themselves caught up in the same globalized logic. To seek only a technical remedy to each environmental problem which comes up is to separate what is in reality interconnected and to mask the true and deepest problems of the global system.

In a sense, one could well assert and argue that to discern (again, a very important word in Jesuit spirituality) the "signs of the times" (as recent popes have led us to do) requires seeing with depth perception for insight (not "just" sight) and listening (not passive hearing) with an obedient heart.

Celebrate

As previously noted, Pope Francis speaks directly about the relationship of the Eucharist and the spirituality of the Christian life. He asserts the following (n. 236):

> It is in the Eucharist that all that has been created finds its greatest exaltation. Grace, which tends to manifest itself tangibly, found unsurpassable expression when God himself became man and gave himself as food for his creatures. The Lord, in the culmination of the mystery of the Incarnation, chose to reach our intimate depths through a fragment of matter. He comes not from above, but from within, he comes that we might find him in this world of ours. In the Eucharist, fullness is already achieved; it is the living center of the universe, the overflowing core of love and of inexhaustible life. Joined to the incarnate Son, present in the Eucharist, the whole cosmos gives thanks to God. Indeed the Eucharist is itself an act of cosmic love: "Yes, cosmic! Because even when it is celebrated on the humble altar of a country church, the Eucharist is always in some way celebrated on the altar of the world [quoting John Paul II]." The Eucharist joins heaven and earth; it embraces and penetrates all creation. The world which came forth from God's hands returns to him in blessed and undivided adoration: in the bread of the Eucharist, "creation is projected towards divinization, towards the holy wedding feast, towards unification with the Creator himself [quoting Benedict XVI]" Thus, the Eucharist is also a source of light and motivation for our concerns for the environment, directing us to be stewards of all creation.

At the very heart of the Christian life is the celebration of the liturgy, especially the Eucharist, where all of liturgy helps us to put our lives in proper order and the world in proper perspective as revelatory of our creator God.

The Eucharist commemorates Christ's paschal victory through his death and resurrection among and for us. This combination of life and death, positive and negative puts the world into proper perspective as both grace filled and flawed and in need of complete redemption. Our eucharistic liturgy prevents us from becoming too optimistic about the world.

Yet sacramental liturgy also combats pessimism about the world and world events. By its very shape and structure, sacramental liturgy is a ritual experience that reflects an optimistic approach to human life. In the end, "all will be well." In the meantime, we need sacramental liturgy to put the world into focus and perspective. Opportunities for experiences of hope abound in the celebration of sacraments—hope in the act of liturgy and hope derived from the act of liturgy that enables us to deal with life.

The celebration of sacramental liturgy grounds and expresses the contemporary emphasis on the theology of creation and places it on a truly theological ground by emphasizing that God's goodness is the source of the things of this earth used in liturgy. The water is a natural symbol from God's providence; bread and wine result from human manufacture of what the earth has produced.

Sacramental liturgy also enacts our belief that we worship God by using the things of this world. This means that sacramental liturgy is always both anthropological and cosmic; it articulates what we believe about the human person and the cosmos. Even better, through sacramental liturgy, human persons put their lives and the world itself into proper perspective. We use "daily and domestic things" in liturgy, specifically in the Eucharist, food and dining, and they remind us of the goodness, generosity, and largesse of the God we worship.

Among the things that the enactment of the Eucharist accomplishes is that bread and wine, taken and shared, are the regular ritual reminders of what it means to share in God's very life and grace throughout our lives. It is the liturgical taking of food and drink, the liturgical act of blessing food and drink, the liturgical act of sharing the Eucharist as food and drink that puts human dining into perspective and gives it its depth. The three steps of manufacture, proclamation, and sharing of food apply not just to the eucharistic liturgy. They happen in daily life too and echo the sacramentality of human life, because sacramentality means that we experience God in and through the world and all that dwell on it, and because we use words and actions to communicate with each other and to sustain life. The sacrament of the Eucharist articulates and specifies for believers that here and now God is operative in all of their lives. Thus, sacramental liturgy provides the lens we need in order to view all of reality, which is always integrative of the sacred and secular and of what is both fully divine and fully human.

The task then is to make sure we view liturgy as a deep and strong ritual expression of the fact that God lives among us prior to, in a unique way within, and following upon sacramental engagement. The function of sacramental liturgy in its uniqueness is about bringing to the world what we have experienced in the liturgy. Even more important is to underscore how what we do in liturgy derives from the world and everyday life. Its liturgical ritualization helps us order our lives and our world once more in God's image and likeness. From the perspective of sacramentality, one can say that sacraments are less doors to the sacred than they are the experience of the sacred in and through human life, which experience is shaped by the liturgical action of the Eucharist.

Every time we take bread and wine in the act of doing the Eucharist we articulate the theology of the goodness of creation and our need for food to sustain us as the "pilgrim church on earth" until we are fed at the "Supper of the Lamb." In the meantime, the very taking, blessing, and sharing of the bread and wine make the central theological statement about our place in the cosmos. All sacramental liturgy makes sense in the first place because the use of goods from the earth remind us of our place in this world.

Having a wide-angle lens on as much of life as possible is true to the Catholic principle of sacramentality. Part of the challenge which celebrating sacramental liturgy can offer is to help us reflect back on the world in which we live and to ponder our care for it as well as our concern for those who dwell on it. This means taking seriously our obligation of being in communion with and caring for our common home. We are never to presume that we are its masters or its lords. We are fellow companions, responsible to succeeding generations for our care of it.

IV. CHALLENGES TO DISSEMINATING PAPAL TEACHINGS

DEBATABLE VALUE OF USING FEMININE IMAGES FOR THE EARTH

The encyclical opens with the following text (n. 1):

"Laudato si, mi' Signore"—*"Praise be to you, my Lord"*. In the words of this beautiful canticle, Saint Francis of Assisi reminds us that our common home is like a sister with whom we share our life and a beautiful mother who opens her arms to embrace us. "Praise be to you, my Lord, through our Sister, Mother Earth, who sustains and governs us, and who produces various fruit with colored flowers and herbs. [followed by a footnote reference to St. Francis's canticle]

The next paragraph goes on to say, with searing and provocative rhetoric (n. 2),

This sister now cries out to us because of the harm we have inflicted on her by our irresponsible use and abuse of the goods with which God has endowed her. We have come to see ourselves as her lords and masters, entitled to plunder her at will. The violence present in our hearts, wounded by sin, is also reflected in the symptoms of sickness evident in the soil, in the water, in the air and in all forms of life. This is why the earth herself, burdened and laid waste, is among the most abandoned and maltreated of our poor; she "groans in travail" (*Rom* 8:22). We have forgotten that we ourselves are dust of the earth (cf. *Gen* 2:7); our very bodies are made up of her elements, we breathe her air and we receive life and refreshment from her waters.

However, a female colleague in the national American theological community commented about this rhetoric, asking whether a few feminist theologians could have advised Pope Francis to displace the gender-infused rape of the earth that opens this encyclical. She asks whether reintroducing this gender language, which rests on

241

male dominance over women, is the only way to wake humanity up from our destruction of the earth. From her perspective, the rhetorical opening seems to say, we are outraged because humanity is raping our mother and our sister. What an awful way to invite the reader into St. Francis's canticle (quoted later in n. 87 and n. 92), which speaks of brother sun, brother wind, brother fire, and brother river. Are we not raping and plundering our brother as well? Could we not find rhetorical poetics that might invite us into care for the earth in a different way altogether?

She continues that in Romans 8:22 (cited in the opening) the earth groans in *labor pains* (because labor is painful), but Pope Francis's gender scenario seems to suggest that the biblical text has the earth groaning because "she's" been raped, plundered, and maltreated. She opines that it will be difficult for her to read this document and to teach it in the years to come, without harboring a sense of disappointment at the opening.

The contribution of ecofeminists to theological aspects of ecology is clearly enormous and should be assessed as would any other scholarly contribution to the dialogue. Certainly my colleague's strong reaction needs to be taken into consideration in any ongoing dialogue about our common home. For some who share my colleague's reaction, such a use of feminine images may limit their willingness to endorse and teach the encyclical.

MORE THAN ONE DAY OF PRAYER FOR CREATION

As previously noted,[45] the establishment of a feast for the environment by Patriarch Dimitrios in 1989 provides an annual opportunity in the Orthodox church for patriarchs and others to speak and raise consciousness about ecology. Pope Francis followed suit and in 2015 established September 1 as a "World Day of Prayer for Creation." Inaugurating such a feast publicizes the Roman church's concern for the environment and that in doing so it solidifies ecumenical ties with the Orthodox.

At the same time, the evidence points to the fact that the Roman liturgy is filled with references to creation and that in almost all sacramental liturgies (with the exception of penance and marriage when celebrated outside of Mass) we revere the goods of creation (for example, water) and from creation (for example, bread and wine) to worship God.[46] (Recall the argument about "the sacramental principle" above in chapter 2, section 9, subsection 6.) The celebration of Morning and Evening Prayer from the Liturgy of the Hours always incorporates references to light and darkness at dawn and sunset. Several of the psalms during the Hours refer to creation, for example, Psalms 8, 103, 121, and so on. At Evening Prayer for the weekdays of Ordinary Time, the Latin version assigned the traditional hymns praising God for the days of creation. As previously noted,[47] in the American *Liturgy of the Hours* these hymns were not used and other hymns were added as substitutes. It is anticipated that in a revised edition of the American *Liturgy of the Hours* (and perhaps for all English-speaking Catholics) these hymns will be reinstated.

In addition, two practices that were not continued after the Vatican II liturgical reforms were Ember Days and the "greater litanies" on April 25. Among other meanings, the Ember Days marked the four seasons of the year and concerned prayer and fasting for the benefit of good crops during all phases of the preparation, planting, harvesting, and thanksgiving process. While some European countries have continued this practice (with some in an accommodated form), the U.S. bishops judged that this would not be our practice. The celebration of the "greater litanies" on April 25 (also the Feast of St. Mark) involved a procession where the fields were blessed and over which invocations for a good harvest were sung. Could either or both of these practices be revived, especially in agricultural areas?

Also given the prevalence of the general intercessions in the liturgy, might it be a "sign of the times" if an occasional petition concerned "for the preservation of our common home, this good earth, and for the conversion of mind and heart for those who do it harm?"[48]

DECLINING INFLUENCE OF CHURCH TEACHINGS AND LITURGICAL PRACTICE

For many American Catholics, the research of Robert Putnam is well attested in our experience—we are increasingly a nation of "believers, not belongers," who are "spiritual, not religious." This is from the data of sociology today, yet it does reflect the tension that Catholics in America have experienced between the founding of the Republic based on a prideful "rugged individualism" and belonging to a church that defines itself as a community.

How do we connect in an American culture that is increasingly mobile and whose citizens are increasingly busy? The evolution in two parent families with both parents working reflects increasing numbers of the population. Childcare is an institution, not a luxury. Membership in civic societies like scouts, PTAs, and the like are shrinking simply because of the business of life today.

One of the challenges is how to connect church communities in addition to Sunday liturgy, which cannot sustain all that church membership means. Base communities? A revival of the small groups in RENEW? As far back as 1985 the priest sociologist Philip Murnion argued for Benedictine-like communities.[49]

The pope speaks of social media, sometimes not in a complimentary way. Yet this phenomenon may well be a way to "stay connected" even when physical proximity is impossible. Among the challenges for this is how to connect with the diversity of the Roman Catholic Church community in a social media age. Will it become like-minded people whose backgrounds are the same, talking to each other? Diversity under the umbrella of Catholicism is one of our strong suits. Another would be the requirement that the dialogue carried on would be "authentic," to borrow a word the pope often uses.

In survey after survey, the PEW organization has documented the declining influence of churches in American society today. The PEW poll taken in May of 2015[50] led to a *New York Times* headline that read, "A Survey Says: Big Drop in Share of Americans Calling Themselves Christian." The GALLUP poll taken in June of 2015[51] was about confidence in our U.S. institutions. The chief finding here is that compared with the "historical average" of 55 percent, the percentage of Americans with confidence in organized religion has fallen 13 percent to 42 percent.

The categories of those who practice or do not practice their faith in a church now include the word "nones," meaning those who are not affiliated with any religion—none. Another category lists those who sometimes practice their faith in an organized religious body as the "somes." In a world when some would optimistically say about aging that "sixty is the new forty," when it comes to regular religious practice in worship the phrase is "monthly is the new weekly," despite Sabbath rules in the Old Testament and church precepts about the Lord's Day. Put succinctly, if Catholics do not celebrate the liturgy regularly, will or can they ever assimilate the ethos of Catholicism, including the value of all creatures on this good earth in the worship of God? In addition, if they do not hear homilies regularly, whence comes Catholic literacy at a time when Catholic schools are fewer and fewer, and many faith formation programs are on life support?

Another category that is less studied sociologically regards those who self-define as "dones." They were once committed to a religion, but now they are "done" with listening to sermonizing and being lectured to.

This is to suggest that, given the erosion of confidence in organized religion, the pope's document may well be rejected or ignored out of hand as one more teaching from what they judge to be an irrelevant institution and structure that has nothing to do with their real lives.

On the other hand, lest all seem to be "gloom and doom," is there not something in the pope's personal style that makes him stand somewhat outside of those studies and categories? The personal charisma and magnetic character of the pope make for a very broad appeal, both inside organized religion and outside it. Addressing the encyclical to all people on the earth may well be a careful way of sidestepping these criticisms of organized religion and adopting an invitational posture for all who look for leadership on the environment.

NOTES

1. Raymond Brown, "'And the Lord Said'? Biblical Reflections on Scripture as the Word of God," *Theological Studies* 42 (1981): 3–18. See especially footnote 3, in which he admires Schillebeeckx for his dedication in setting aside several years to attempt to incorporate biblical criticism into his Christology.

2. International Theological Commission, *Theology Today: Perspectives, Principles and Criteria* (November 29, 2011), http://www.vatican.va/roman_curia/congregations/cfaith/cti_documents/rc_cti_doc_20111129_teologia-oggi_en.html.

3. The Catholic theological tradition has always had many types of theology, with a variety of authors and perspectives. Because the liturgy is a theological action and an act of theology, how can this reality be reflected in approaches to theology and in theological schools today? My own reflection on the theological scene today is that theological faculties rightly prize specialization and precision within one's specialization. But what happens to theology as presenting a way to claim and sustain one's bearings on this earth as we ceaselessly search for God and search for ever less inadequate ways of describing God, especially in our search for and experience of God within the Roman Catholic church? Certainly that is what the liturgy does–draws us into an ever richer and deeper experience of God in rites and prayers of inestimable theological value. Clearly the liturgy had a privileged place in what we might (loosely?) call patristic and monastic theology. It also played a role in scholastic theology (for example, St. Bonaventure and St. Thomas Aquinas, for whom the mendicant context of the daily celebration of the Eucharist and the Hours is important to bear in mind when interpreting them), but it was diminished. Post-Tridentine theology was understandably preoccupied with apologetics and defending the Canons of the Council of Trent so that the liturgy had little place in it.

It should be noted that if and where the celebration of the liturgy is reintegrated into the entire scheme and sweep of Catholic theology, its rites and prayers are inherently multivalent, and its language is rich in metaphor and imagery. Liturgical sources need to be treated as they are, more like biblical interpretation when differing versions of the same event or occurrence appear in different books of the Bible. Such liturgical sources are abundant, among which are sacramentaries, pontificals, lectionaries, evangeliaries, antiphonals, ordines, and rituals. They should not be gleaned for "proof texts" to already predetermined theological assertions. They should, however, find themselves in an important place along with all the other sources for theological study, where, admittedly, the scriptures have pride of place. When the study of and from the liturgy is removed from its roots in such traditional sources and contemporary rituals, then we risk the danger of developing a theology about the liturgy and about several other things without reliance on the *theologia prima* of the liturgy itself. My own suspicion would be a revitalization of what is often termed "monastic" theology, in which the search for God and understandings about God are much less scholastic, distinction-filled, and influenced by Aristotelian philosophy. The example of Cipriano Vagaggini might be helpful here. Long after *Il sense teologico* (*The Theological Dimensions of Liturgy*) was in its fourth edition, he was still writing about a new kind of theology that would accommodate and be influenced by the celebration of the liturgy.

Beyond

In some places he called it "sapiential" (after his study of and use of Augustine's distinction between *sapientia* and *scientia*) or "gnoseological" (again upholding the notion of "wisdom"). What we now distinguish as a theology of creation, Christian anthropology, Trinity, Christology, ecclesiology, eschatology, and then the theologies of individual liturgies and sacraments could be collapsed, or at least telescoped. One minor example would be to collapse the separate courses in our theological curricula in ecclesiology, Christology, and the sacraments of initiation and orders into a single unified unit of theological study.

4. See, for example, Jame Schaefer, *Theological Foundations for Environmental Ethics: Reconstructing Patristic and Medieval Concepts* (Washington, DC: Georgetown University Press, 2009).

5. See http://www.archatl.com/wpdm-package/laudato-si-action-plan-university-georgia/?wpdmdl=9131.

6. Jesuit Social Justice and Ecology Secretariat, Task Force on Ecology, *Healing a Broken World* (2011), http://issuu.com/sjssj/docs/healing_a_broken_world.

7. Antonio Gonzalez Dorado, *Los Sacramentos del Evangelio: Sacramentologia Fundamental y Orgánica*, vol. IX-1, Colección de Textos Básicos para Seminarios Latinoamericanos (Santa Fe de Bogota: CELAM, 1991), 13–30, 575–85.

8. *Ibid.*, 18–30.

9. The point here is by no means to ignore the contributions that Rahner and Schillebeeckx have made to the study of sacraments; it is simply to note that neither addressed the post–World War II context in which they were writing about sacraments.

10. Jeremy Driscoll, *Theology at the Eucharistic Table* (Rome: Centro di Studi Sant'Anselmo, 2003/Herefordshire: Gracewing, 2003).

11. See Nathan Mitchell, *Cult and Controversy: The Worship of the Eucharist Outside of Mass*, Studies in the Reformed Rites of the Catholic Church 4 (New York: Pueblo, 1982); Alexander Gerken, "Historical Background of the New Direction in Eucharistic Doctrine," *Theology Digest* 21 (1973): 46–53; Miri Rubin, *Corpus Christi: The Eucharist in Late Medieval Culture* (Cambridge: Cambridge University Press, 1991); Gary Macy, *The Banquet's Wisdom: A Short History of the Theologies of the Lord's Supper* (New York: Paulist Press, 1992); Edward Kilmartin, *Eucharist in the West: History and Theology*, ed. Robert Daly (Collegeville: Liturgical Press, 1998).

12. Vatican II, Constitution on the Sacred Liturgy *Sacrosanctum Concilium* (December 4, 1963), http://www.vatican.va/archive/hist_councils/ii_vatican_council/documents/vat-ii_const_19631204_sacrosanctum-concilium_en.html.

13. Vatican II, Constitution on the Sacred Liturgy *Sacrosanctum Concilium*.

14. See Xavier Leon Dufour, *Sharing the Eucharistic Bread*, trans. Matthew O'Connell (New York/Mahwah, NJ: Paulist Press, 1987), 109–16.

15. See my own *Serving the Body of Christ* (New York/Mahwah, NJ: Paulist Press, 2014), 77–100.

16. *Ibid.*, 101–06. That diocesan bishops have come to pay greater attention to seminarians and (especially more recently ordained) priests is clear, through personal contacts and vicars for seminarians and clergy. The other side of the coin is that many "veterans of the campaign" and "Vatican II" priests judge that they are out of the loop.

17. Paul VI, apostolic letter *motu proprio Apostolica Sollicitudo* (September 15, 1965), http://w2.vatican.va/content/paul-vi/en/motu_proprio/documents/hf_p-vi_motu-proprio_19650915_apostolica-sollicitudo.html.

18. In his address at the opening of the synod, Francis encouraged participants to "bravely adopt parrhesia, pastoral zeal and doctrinal wisdom, frankness, always keeping before our eyes the good of the Church, of families and the *suprema lex*, the *Salus animarum.*" Francis, *Introductory Remarks at the First General Congregation of the 14th Ordinary General Assembly of the Synod of Bishops* (October 5, 2015), http://w2.vatican.va/content/francesco/en/speeches/2015/october/documents/papa-francesco_20151005_padri-sinodali.html.
At the end of the same synod, he reflected on its work:

[The synod] was about listening to and making heard the voices of the families and the Church's pastors, who came to Rome bearing on their shoulders the burdens and the hopes, the riches and the challenges of families throughout the world. It was about showing the vitality of the Catholic Church, which is not afraid to stir dulled consciences or to soil her hands with lively and frank discussions about the family. It was about trying to view and interpret realities, today's realities, through God's eyes, so as to kindle the flame of faith and enlighten people's hearts in times marked by discouragement, social, economic and moral crisis, and growing pessimism. It was about bearing witness to everyone that, for the Church, the Gospel continues to be a vital source of eternal newness, against all those who would "indoctrinate" it in dead stones to be hurled at others. It was also about laying closed hearts, which bare the closed hearts which frequently hide even behind the Church's teachings or good intentions, in order to sit in the chair of Moses and judge, sometimes with superiority and superficiality, difficult cases and wounded families. It was about making clear that the Church is a Church of the poor in spirit and of sinners seeking forgiveness, not simply of the righteous and the holy, but rather of those who are righteous and holy precisely when they feel themselves poor sinners. It was about trying to open up broader horizons, rising above conspiracy theories and blinkered viewpoints, so as to defend and spread the freedom of the children of God, and to transmit the beauty of Christian Newness, at times encrusted in a language which is archaic or simply incomprehensible (Francis, *Address at the Conclusion of the 14th Ordinary General Assembly of the Synod of Bishops* [October 24, 2015], http://w2.vatican.va/content/francesco/en/speeches/2015/october/documents/papa-francesco_20151024_sinodo-conclusione-lavori.html).

19. Francis, *Introductory Remarks at the First General Congregation of the 14th Ordinary General Assembly of the Synod of Bishops.*

20. In his address of January 29, 2016, to the participants in the *plenarium* of the Congregation for the Doctrine of the Faith, Pope Francis reiterated his insistence that "synodality" be even more apparent in the life of the church, even in matters dealing with doctrine. See http://en.radiovaticana.va/news/2016/01/29/pope_meets_with_congregation_for_the_doctrine_of_the_faith/1204600.

21. Among many others, see John R. Quinn, *The Reform of the Papacy: The Costly Call to Christian Unity* (New York: Herder and Herder, 1999); Quinn, *Ever Ancient, Ever New: Structures of Communion in the Church* (New York/Mahwah, NJ: Paulist Press, 2013).

22. See, for example, the positive assessment of inculturation found in chapter 9 of the *General Instruction of the Roman Missal* ("Adaptations within the Competence of Bishops and Bishops' Conferences") and Congregation for Divine Worship and the Discipline of the Sacraments, Fourth Instruction on the Liturgy Constitution *Varietates Legitimae* (March 29, 1994), http://www.ewtn.com/library/curia/cdwinclt.htm.

In comparison, see the relatively restrained approach toward inculturation found in the Congregation for Divine Worship and the Discipline of the Sacraments, Fifth Instruction on the Liturgy Constitution *Liturgiam Authenticam* (March 28, 2001), http://www.vatican.va/roman_curia/congregations/ccdds/documents/rc_con_ccdds_doc_20010507_liturgiam-authenticam_en.html.

23. Clearly inspired by the example and at his direction, the Congregation for Divine Worship issued the decree. See http://www.vatican.va/roman_curia/congregations/ccdds/documents/rc_con_ccdds_doc_20160106_decreto-lavanda-piedi_en.html.

24. In the middle of the 1970s, two stories circulated around Rome as to why Paul VI stopped traveling. One was that he learned of their costs and was shocked at the financial outlay. The other was that the assassination attempt left a deep impression and he did not want to make any host country bear the irreparable burden of having a pope killed on their soil.

25. *John Paul II Address to the Third General Conference of the Latin American Episcopate* (January 28, 1979), https://w2.vatican.va/content/john-paul-ii/en/speeches/1979/january/documents/hf_jp-ii_spe_19790128_messico-puebla-episc-latam.html.

26. Recall the importance of the Aparecida meeting of CELAM in 2007 (see chapter 1, section 4, subsection 1). Pope Benedict XVI addressed the opening session of this CELAM meeting as well.

27. As of this writing, he has four more trips scheduled for 2016, three (so far) in 2017, two (so far) in 2018, and then as yet unscheduled trips to fourteen other countries.

28. Chapter 1, section 3, subsection 3.

29. U.S. National Conference of Catholic Bishops, "The Challenge of Peace: God's Promise and Our Response: A Pastoral Letter on War and Peace" (May 3, 1983), http://www.usccb.org/upload/challenge-peace-gods-promise-our-response-1983.pdf.

U.S. National Conference of Catholic Bishops, "Economic Justice for All: Pastoral Letter on Catholic Social Teaching and the US Economy" (1986), http://www.usccb.org/upload/economic_justice_for_all.pdf.

30. In addition, as I argued in *Serving the Body of Christ* there is the present phenomenon of bishops being transferred from diocese to (arch)diocese and being required to submit their letters of retirement at age seventy-five. This in itself can weaken the sense of episcopal authority and ministry, especially as described in the documents of Vatican II. See "What the Magisterium Says about the Ordained Priesthood," in *Serving the Body of Christ*, 70–100, especially pp. 78–83 on Vatican II's Dogmatic Constitution on the Church *Lumen Gentium* (1964) and pages 86–89 on the implications of the transfer and retirement of bishops.

31. See the comments on the encyclical's authorship by Cardinal Turkson (discussed above in chapter 2): Vatican Press, "Conferenza Stampa per la presentazione della Lettera Enciclica *Laudato si* del Santo Padre Francesco sulla cura della casa commune" [Press Conference for the Presentation of the encyclical letter *Laudato Si'* of the Holy Father Francis on the Care for Our Common Home]," *Bulletin* (18 June 2015), http://press.vatican.va/content/salastampa/en/bollettino/pubblico/2015/06/18/0480/01050.html#eng.

32. Donald Wuerl, "Remarks at the National Press Club" (June 18, 2015), on *Seek First the Kingdom: A Blog by Cardinal Donald Wuerl*, http://cardinalsblog.adw.org/2015/06/remarks-at-the-national-press-club/.

33. See the report on Cardinal Wuerl's remarks on the critiques of his fellow bishops against the pope. Amid more specific responses to the critique of many bishops against the synodal process outlined by Francis for the Ordinary Synod on Family and Marriage in October of 2015, Cardinal Wuerl stated more generally, "There are always people who are unhappy with something that is going on in the church, but the touchstone of authentic Catholicism is adherence to the teaching of the pope." Gerard O'Connell, "Cardinal Wuerl Calls Out Pope's Opponents," *America* (October 18, 2015), http://americamagazine.org/content/dispatches/cardinal-wuerl-calls-out-popes-opponents.

This issue is also evident among ordained priests and deacons in relation to the pope. Anecdotally many argue that those ordained during the pontificates of John Paul II and Benedict XVI also have their struggles with Pope Francis's leadership. Many of the "veterans of the campaign" ordained just prior to, during, and immediately after Vatican II have found Pope Francis's leadership most welcome.

34. Kevin W. Irwin, *What We Have Done, What We Have Failed to Do: Assessing the Liturgical Reforms of Vatican II* (New York/Mahwah, NJ: Paulist Press, 2014), 225.

35. One example is his letter to world leaders gathered at the 2016 World Economic Forum in Davos, Switzerland. Francis, *Message to the 2016 World Economic Forum Annual Meeting in Davos* (January 2016), http://en.radiovaticana.va/news/2016/01/20/pope_to_world_economic_forum_do_not_forget_the_poor!/1202385.

36. See the discussion of consumerism in chapter 3, section 5.

37. See the thematic index to *RB80: The Rule of St. Benedict*, ed. Timothy Fry (Collegeville: Liturgical Press, 1981), 565.

38. See the brief but insightful article by Terrence Kardong, "Ecological Resources in the Benedictine Rule," in *Embracing the Earth: Catholic Approaches to Ecology*, ed., Albert J. LaChance and John E. Carroll, 163–73 (Maryknoll: Orbis Press, 1994); also published in *Assumption Abbey Newsletter* 23/1 (January 1995) 1–8.

39. That the "work" of the monastery can include energy production is exemplified in the German monastery where the energy produced by the abbey is sold back to the energy grid of their government. See http://www.abtei-muensterschwarzach.de/.

40. See the very important work by Aquinata Bockmann, *A Listening Community: A Commentary on the Prologue and Chapters 1–3 of Benedict's Rule,*

trans. Matilda Handl and Marianne Burkhard, ed. Marianne Burkhard (Collegeville: Liturgical Press, 2015).

41. It is to be noted that sometimes translations differ, and the word "hear" is used where attentive listening is meant. In modern theology, the classic example is the title of Karl Rahner's *Hearers of the Word.* Karl Rahner, *Hörer des Wortes: Zur Grundlegung einer Religionsphilosophie* (Munich: Kösel, 1963); English translation Karl Rahner, *Hearers of the Word,* trans. A. Tallon and J.F. Donceel (Milwaukee: Marquette University Press, 1988).

42. In the *Rule of Saint Benedict* (48, 23), St. Benedict states for "anyone [who] is so remiss and indolent that he is unwilling or unable to study or to read, he is to be given some work in order that he may not be idle." Interestingly, the Latin for "to study or to read" is *meditare aut legere.*

43. Among others, see Duncan Robertson, *Lectio Divina: The Medieval Experience of Reading,* Cistercian Studies 238 (Collegeville: Liturgical Press, 2011); Raymond Studzinski, *Reading to Live: The Evolving Practice of Lectio Divina,* Cistercian Studies 231 (Collegeville: Liturgical Press, 2009).

44. See http://blog.gaiam.com/quotes/authors/saint-bernard-clairvaux.

45. See chapter 1, section 5, subsection 1.

46. Among others, see my own "The Sacramental Principle," in *What We Have Done, What We Have Failed to Do,* 89–113; idem., *Sacraments: Historical Precedents and Liturgical Theology* (New York/Mahwah, NJ: Paulist Press, 2016), 209–30.

47. In chapter 1, fn. 75 above.

48. See my own "The Sacramentality of Creation and the Role of Creation in Liturgy and Sacraments," in *Preserving the Creation: Environmental Theology and Ethics,* ed. Edmund J. Pellegrino and Kevin W. Irwin, 67–111 (Washington, DC: Georgetown University Press, 1994).

49. See the still very insightful essay by Philip J. Murnion, "A Sacramental Church in the Modern World," *Origins* 14 (June 21, 1984): 81–90.

50. See Pew Research, "A Closer Look at America's Rapidly Growing Religious Nones" (May 13, 2015), http://www.pewresearch.org/fact-tank/2015/05/13/a-closer-look-at-americas-rapidly-growing-religious-nones/.

Also, Pew Research, "Key Findings About the Changing U.S. Religious Landscape" (May 12, 2015), http://www.pewresearch.org/fact-tank/2015/05/12/5-key-findings-u-s-religious-landscape/.

51. From, Gallup Poll, "Confidence in US Institutions Still Below Historical Norms" (June 15, 2015), http://www.gallup.com/poll/183593/confidence-institutions-below-historical-norms.aspx?utm_source=Politics&utm_medium=newsfeed&utm_campaign=tiles.

Conclusion

PRAY THIS DOCUMENT

This enormously rich and often penetrating document deserves to be prayed over and not just simply "read" or "understood." The opportunity to see things differently is offered on every page. The interconnectedness of many things often judged to be separate is reflected on every page. The breadth of the Catholic theological and spiritual tradition is apparent on every page.

This is a document for the ages even as it faces into the environmental crises of our day. While its sections on spirituality specifically are nothing less than contemplative in style, content, and intention, the entire document is a gem in the way that it exemplifies how the Catholic tradition is ever ancient and ever new. It is filled with erudite learning. It is filled with the wisdom that comes from being a Catholic.

Nothing can substitute for praying over this document.

CONVERSION

There are many ways to understand what conversion means. Among them is to allow one's mind and heart to be changed. That, of course, is easier said than done. One needs to come to this document (as to almost all of Pope Francis's documents) with an open mind and heart, ready to receive and be imbued with its depth, insight, and wisdom. Preconceived ideas about "environmentalism," the business of business, individual responsibility, and what

253

spirituality mean (among other things) are likely to be shaken up by reflecting on what the pope says here. This is evidence that conversion can and does take place, but it can only take place when one comes to this document with as open a mind as we can have and as open a heart as we ask God to grant us. Then we have to decide to "listen" well and allow conversion to take place in whatever ways and on whatever levels God desires of us.

THE FRANCIS EFFECT

From as early as a few months into Francis's papacy, people were asking, "What is the Francis effect?" This was largely due to the fact that it was clear that his papacy was going to be a game changer, both in style (living quarters) and content (daily homilies and interviews online). Initially in Italy (where I was in the spring of 2013), there was a documented "uptick" in the numbers of people celebrating sacraments (notably penance) and in attendance at papal events in Rome. That there has been a marginal "uptick" in sacramental participation in the United States has been commented on by some church leaders.

In the end, however, is counting the number of people who participate in sacraments or increase their weekly church offerings the real measure of "the Francis effect"? What would happen if we welcomed and capitalized on the enormous goodwill that this pope is spreading? This can only redound to the credibility of the Catholic church, which, in our age, has had more than its share of scandals. Increased credibility can only lead us forward, hopefully with increased liturgical practice.

In light of this encyclical, this would mean appreciating the way that Pope Francis welcomes dialogue with all peoples from all parts of the world. It would mean taking stock of the way he has weighed into controversial issues with pastoral sense and sensitivity. These include, but are not limited to, marriage and the family, ecumenism, and ecology viewed from a number of "interconnected" perspectives and including a number of issues like migration, economics, politics, spirituality, and so on. While none of these are measurable the way that counting the number of communicants can be measured, all of these—and more—cannot help but put a new face on the Catholic church in our day.

If "we all drink from our own wells," then Pope Francis offers us a deep well to drink from in order to gain insight, knowledge, and wisdom.

Pray this document.

Index

Index

Index

Index

Index

Index

Index